Sapphic Primitivism

Sapphic Primitivism

Productions of Race, Class, and Sexuality in Key Works of Modern Fiction

Robin Hackett

Rutgers University Press

New Brunswick, New Jersey, and London

Library of Congress Cataloging-in-Publication Data

Hackett, Robin, 1963–
    Sapphic primitivism : productions of race, class, and sexuality in key works
of modern fiction / Robin Hackett.
        p. cm.
    ISBN 0–8135–3346–5 (hardcover : alk. paper)—ISBN 0–8135–3347–3
(pbk. : alk. paper)
    1. English fiction—20th century—History and criticism. 2. Lesbians in
literature. 3. English fiction—Women authors—History and criticism.
4. Schreiner Olive, 1855–1920—Characters—Women. 5. Warner, Sylvia
Townsend, 1893–1978—Summer will show. 6. Cather, Willa, 1873–1947—
Characters—Women. 7. Woolf, Virginia, 1882–1941. Waves. 8. Homosexuality
and literature. 9. Social classes in literature. 10. Primitivism in literature. 11.
Modernism (Literature) 12. Race in literature. 13. Sex in literature. I. Title.

PR888.L46H33 2004
823'.91099287—dc21

                                                                        2003005944

British Cataloging-in-Publication information for this book is available from
the British Library.

The publication program of Rutgers University Press is supported by the
Board of Governors of Rutgers, The State University of New Jersey.

Manufactured in the United States of America

For Patti Palen
In loving memory of Jason Bench

Contents

Acknowledgments

This book would not have been written without the help of many people who generously offered me material and emotional support as I wrote. Most importantly, I offer my boundless gratitude to Jane Marcus for her own scholarship, which has been tremendously influential and helpful to me, as well as for her expert advice, her warmth, her encouragement, and her willingness to read and comment on countless drafts. She has been my most consistently enthusiastic and demanding reader. Michele Wallace and Wayne Koestenbaum guided me through the early phases of writing this book; Michele Wallace's admonishment to "write beautifully" has been ringing in my ears since I was first her student, and Wayne Koestenbaum's comments on numerous drafts encouraged me to both take risks and be precise. The women's studies program and the English department at the City University of New York graduate center provided financial support as well as a congenial atmosphere in which to work, and faculty and colleagues in writing groups offered invaluable suggestions and encouragement. Thank you especially to Jackie DiSalvo, Joan Richardson, William Kelly, Jason Tougaw, Shaun Carey, Pati Cockram, Kimberly Engber, Gloria Fisk, Matthew Goldie, Kathryn Coad Narramore, and Leo Parascondola. Linda Camarasana has been an especially attentive and gracious reader of many drafts and a source of invaluable information and encouragement.

I am indebted to Carolyn Ferrell for her wise suggestions on drafts and regular doses of sanity. Not least, she suggested I read Toni Morrison's *Playing in the Dark,* which has given shape to this book and influenced my thinking about literature more than any other single book I have read. A tremendous thank-you goes to Gay Wachman, who is great fun to work with, and whose collaboration has been essential to the development of my ideas about Virginia Woolf and Sylvia Townsend Warner as well as lesbian modernism. I am grateful to Diane Harriford, Colleen Cohen, Ann Imbrie, and Gretchen Gerzina at Vassar College for their encouragement and for giving me the opportunity to develop my ideas through teaching seminars in women's studies and English. Helen Dunn, J. J. Wilson, Kristen Montgomery, and Julia Allen at Sonoma State University have read drafts and been continuously encouraging. I would especially like to thank Julia Allen for being constantly enthusiastic, reading drafts, and helping me develop my ideas in many delightful conversations over the last ten years. I am grateful to my colleagues at the University of New Hampshire for their material support and for providing a collegial atmosphere in which to work. Petar Ramadanovic, Catherine Peebles, and Jennifer Selwyn have provided many valuable suggestions and wonderful meals. I am especially grateful to my colleagues Monica Chiu and Siobhan Senier, as well as Eve Raimon, Lisa Botshon, Melinda Plastas, and Rebecca Herzig, who all welcomed me into their writing group and have generously read drafts, offered suggestions, and provided constant reminders to write something we can all use as antiracist and feminist teachers. Members of a graduate seminar in literary modernisms at the University of New Hampshire, including Freda Hauser, Edith Butler, Greg Guthrie, Joelle Ryan, Sharon Kehl Califano, Zoe Wettach, T. J. Moretti, Emily Hinnov, and Peter Walsh, provided valuable feedback about how Olive Schreiner's work contributed to Sapphic primitivism. Tremendous thanks go to my parents and siblings, Myra, Richard, and Jeremy Hackett, and Andrea and Pat Quinn, as well as to the Bench and Russell families, Molly Freeman, Joseph Matosian, and Judith Zaborowski for their encouragement and for constantly believing in me. Finally, I would like to thank Patti Palen, my partner and ideal reader, for her love, her inspiration, her many editorial suggestions, and her insistence that I write something she wanted to read.

Sapphic Primitivism

One

Sapphic Primitivism, an Introduction

The most substantial innovation of late twentieth-century sexuality studies is, arguably, the idea that "homosexuality" and "heterosexuality" are historically rather than naturally produced. This means, among other things, that "the homosexual" and "the lesbian" exist in civil-rights era medical, legal, political, and social discourse,[1] but, as human types, they have not existed in all times and places and will not necessarily continue to exist into future interpretations of sexual behavior. *Sapphic Primitivism* is built upon the work of scholars who have provoked skepticism about naturalized sexual identity categories.[2] My focus is not on material that further challenges civil-rights era categories of identity, however. Instead, I begin with the assumption that such categories have been constructed as natural, and I explore the period of transition during which these effects were produced. More precisely, I focus on literature of the late nineteenth and early twentieth centuries, literature that reflects what I argue is one characteristic of this transition—the overlap between markers of race, class, and sexuality in representations of female homoerotics. I often use the term "lesbian," although it sometimes feels impossible to do so in light of discursive theories of homosexuality. "Erotics between women" may be more precise, but is too clunky to be practical for consistent use; it also points to the fluidity of categories of sexuality at the cost of solidifying the term "woman," which is itself unstable, as scholars and artists including Simone de Beauvoir, Monique Wittig, Leslie Feinberg, and David Henry Hwang, to name a few, have repeatedly shown. I sometimes use "female sexual autonomy," but using this phrase consistently would compromise my ability to refer specifically to homosexual relations. Throughout this study, I keep in mind the contradictory truths that, for many people, embracing identity categories including gay and lesbian have offered a great deal of comfort, joy, and political agency, and that, for other people, recognizing such identities as products of a naturalization process has similarly offered joy, comfort, and agency. Both ways of thinking can and have been deployed to further aims of social justice; both can be and have been used to reiterate injustices of the status quo.

The works of fiction I bring together in this analysis of the transition toward naturalized identity categories make an unlikely collection of texts. Olive Schreiner's *The Story of an African Farm,* Virginia Woolf's *The Waves,* Sylvia Townsend Warner's *Summer Will Show,* and Willa Cather's *Sapphira and the Slave Girl* are authored and set in three different continents over a span of fifty-seven years. They differ in form and content, ranging from proto-modernist exploration of New Womanhood,[3] to high-modernist "play-poem,"[4] to historical realism, to nostalgic southern pastoral. Their reputations in mainstream literary history also vary tremendously. *The Story of an African Farm* was widely praised when it first came out in 1883, but is now mostly ignored. Alternately, neither *Summer Will Show* (1936) nor *Sapphira* (1940) were especially well received when they first appeared, especially compared to the wide acclaim of some others of Warner's and Cather's works. In the last two decades, though, both have risen to nearly cult status among scholars seeking to expose what Terry Castle would name in 1993 the "apparitional lesbian" of pre-Stonewall literature. Of the four novels I discuss, *The Waves* (1931) is by far the most consistently and widely celebrated. Some readers praise its formal complexity while others explore its involvement in the political issues of Woolf's era. *The Waves* only rarely figures in accounts of lesbian modernism, though, while some of Woolf's other works head the list.

Despite these differences in form, context, and reputation, important similarities draw these novels together. Three of the four feature erotics between women, and all four explore autonomous female sexuality. In addition, each has its aesthetic foundations in modernist primitivism, the twentieth-century Euro-American self-representational mode in which images of people and cultures projected as other than the self or outside time and history are used as symbols of violence, energy, sensuality, regeneration, *degeneration*, and freedom. This combination of female erotics and modernist primitivism is my focus. I discuss texts by Schreiner, Woolf, Warner, and Cather as examples of a literary phenomenon I am calling Sapphic primitivism, a mode of writing in which figurations of blackness and working-class culture appear as constitutive elements of white-authored fictional representations of female sexual autonomy including homoerotics. Key to my understanding of Sapphic primitivism is that it is characteristic of a transitional time in the understanding of homosexuality. It is part of—simultaneously contributing to and the result of—the production of homosexuality as a naturalized category of identity. This identity is familiar to readers in a post–civil rights era, but it is an identity that, for all its familiarity, is nonetheless a product of a specific set of discursive maneuvers that can be identified in history.[5] Also key to my understanding of Sapphic primitivism is that it is not a means of disguising lesbian content; rather it is an aesthetic mechanism of displacement that exposes lesbianism at the same time that it exploits primitivist modes of self-representation.

My goals in identifying and analyzing Sapphic primitivism are multiple and reflect my multiple perspectives as an academic working simultaneously in literary studies, women's studies, and lesbian-gay-queer studies. I discuss Sapphic primitivism in order to provide a new focus of analysis for a wide variety of twentieth-century literature. I also discuss Sapphic primitivism specifically because, as a literary structure of transition, Sapphic primitivism exposes the mechanics by which constructions of race, class, and sexuality came to overlap in the development of homosexual identities. The pragmatic significance of this study is that exposing the fictional manipulations of late nineteenth- and early twentieth-century constructions of race, class, and sexuality can facilitate coalition-building among twenty-first-century feminists doing antiracist and queer work. I take it as a given that Schreiner, Woolf, Warner, Cather, and their texts sometimes reflect the racism and/or homophobia of many people of their eras and locations. Nevertheless, assumptions and insights revealed in their efforts to represent female homoerotics can be used to further current antiracist and antihomophobic political agendas.

My analysis of Sapphic primitivism relies, in part, on Toni Morrison's theory of American Africanism. In *Playing in the Dark: Whiteness and the Literary Imagination,* Morrison argues that in white-authored American literature, ubiquitous figurations of blackness—of black people and dark expanses, of slaves and slavery—operate as shorthand expressions of a "not-free," "not-me," of what is both feared and benevolent, voluptuous and sinful (38). Major themes of American literature, such as individuality, ruggedness, newness and difference, autonomy, and absolute power, are made possible by the awareness and use of this presence—a literary phenomenon Morrison calls American Africanism. Morrison's book has dramatically changed the way I read figurations of blackness in white-authored works of Sapphic modernism.[6] Before I read *Playing in the Dark,* for instance, I barely noticed a "coloured man" who appears driving a carriage and exists for only half a sentence in Gertrude Stein's "The Good Anna." In the context of Morrison's argument, however, the man becomes central to my reading of the story, as does the fact that Mrs. Lehntman's loss of status and increasing submission to the good Anna are described as "blackening." Attention to figurations of blackness in the story exposes "The Good Anna" as a parody of hierarchies, a hyperbolization of the intricate system of control-over-others into which the immigrant, Anna, fits herself in the process of becoming American.

Following Morrison, I demonstrate that Olive Schreiner creates the late-Victorian New European Women of her fiction and nonfiction by comparing her New Women to South African people she thinks of as belonging to old races. This sexually autonomous European New Woman is not a lesbian as Schreiner imagines her, but readers and writers who subsequently participated in late-Victorian discussions of New Womanhood conflated her with the invert. *The Story of an African Farm* is thus an important forerunner of the other three novels I discuss. As an early feminist text, it helps build the structure of imagination through which Woolf, Warner, and Cather, among others, developed their reliance on figurations of blackness. Subsequently, in *The Waves* Woolf relies on figurations of blackness and colonial space as place-holders for lesbianism. Early drafts of the novel show that the character Rhoda came into being in Woolf's imagination as a girl who loved other girls. In the final version of the novel, Woolf suppresses lesbian references, but when other characters talk about sex, Rhoda talks about Africa, India, Turks, dark pools, tigers, or ships that cross oceans. In *Summer Will Show,* Warner uses racialized Jewishness, working-class sexuality, and mixed-race and Caribbean origins as tropes that explain her central character's transformation from "frigid" and arrogant landowner to sexually awakened lesbian communist. In *Sapphira and the Slave Girl,* Cather presents Sapphira's homoerotic obsession with the bodies of two women she holds as slaves as a mirror image of cannibalism and mythological African savagery. Reading *The Story of an African Farm, The Waves, Summer Will Show,* and *Sapphira and the Slave Girl* together exposes Sapphic primitivism as a primary structure in all four of these diverse works.

My focus on writers who are women is not the result of a lack of homoerotic writing by men that might be called queer primitivism. E. M. Forster, for instance, is known for having eroticized class differences and for having developed homoerotic texts involving white people in colonial settings. It might be worthwhile to examine Forster's work by identifying it as queer primitivism and analyzing it in the context of sexological generalizations about working-class sexuality, or orientalist notions that hot lands and dark-skinned people encourage whites to adventure into the realm of various taboo sexualities. But the Sapphic primitivism I discuss here has specificity, with regard to lesbianism and whiteness, that sets it apart from the larger body of work that might be called queer primitivism. Widespread assumptions about sexlessness among middle-class white women—assumptions that pervade Euro-American legal, religious, and medical discourse—mean that writers seeking to represent lesbian sexuality in characters who are white, female, and middle class have challenges and develop artistic strategies specific to these assumptions. If Forster seeks to texture the erotic charge of his work by putting white characters in colonial settings, this is not because anyone would have assumed, by virtue of their whiteness or their maleness, that Forster or his white male characters had no sexuality. Conversely, in seeking to represent lesbian desire as a motivating force in a middle-class white female character, Virginia Woolf, among others, has to both create the possibility that she can author such a text and develop a character in whom desire, femaleness, middle-class status, and whiteness can co-exist.

Similarly, my focus on white-authored texts is not the result of an absence of literature in English by women of color, particularly African American women, who struggle to represent lesbian desire or other kinds of sexual autonomy for women in the context of late nineteenth- and early twentieth-century sciences of race and sexuality. Nella Larsen, Pauline Hopkins, Zora Neale Hurston, and Harriet Jacobs, for instance, have received critical attention for the ways in which each addresses issues of lesbian desire and/or autonomous female sexuality, in some cases also working with primitivist tropes.[7] The stakes are particularly high for black women writers discussing female sexuality. Harriet Jacobs, in asserting the rights of her narrator to determine her own sexual and reproductive life, challenges the ideological foundations of the U.S. slave system in which rape is a primary tool of oppression and assertion of white supremacy. In *Contending Forces* Pauline Hopkins challenges ideological products of race-sex sciences that many white people used as justifications for post-emancipation lynching. At the same time, she hints at homoerotic bonds between her characters Dora and the suggestively named Sappho. Nella Larsen speaks directly against a wide range of institutional and individual efforts to discipline and police bodily autonomy among black women. Larsen's *Quicksand* (1928) and *Passing* (1929) were written in the context of what Hazel Carby describes as a "moral panic" over the large-scale migration of black people into urban areas and northern states in the early twentieth century. Social and political problems of migration were discussed largely in terms of the sexual behavior of working-class black women, which was characterized as degenerate. Individual and institutional efforts to restore a moral social order centered around policing the bodily autonomy of black women. Discussion about black female sexuality in this era, argues Carby, "registers the emergence of what would rapidly become a widely shared discourse of what was wrong with black urban life" ("Policing the Black Woman's Body" 117). *Passing* might also be discussed in terms of Sapphic primitivism. In that novel, middle-class status forecloses homoerotic possibility for the character Irene Redfield, while Clare Kendry's cross-class alliances threaten erotic normativity. Careful analysis of the literary strategies employed by African American writers exploring questions of sexual autonomy contributes much to the history of lesbian-erotic writing and offers important insights into the workings of historical and contemporary sex-gender-race systems.

In this book, though, I also argue that one important and potentially antiracist function of discussions of modernist primitivism is to expose the processes and the racist effects of primitivist art that is involved in constructing and de-racializing whiteness. Toni Morrison makes this clear in subtitling her theoretical exploration of figurations of blackness *"Whiteness" and the Literary Imagination* [quotation marks added]. White-authored primitivism such as that in the novels I discuss is often an aggressive construction of a raced other in order to identify a powerful and benevolent un-raced white self. *Sapphic* primitivism in white-authored novels is a similarly aggressive construction of whiteness by writers seeking to build a white womanhood that can also be desirous, assertive, and sexually autonomous. Understanding how and why blackness was available as a metaphor for early twentieth-century white artists trying to represent female homoerotics can help create a cultural context where neither blackness nor whiteness, whether or not they are identities around which people sometimes choose to cohere, work as facile metaphors. I focus on Sapphic primitivism as it is employed by white middle-class women who write female homoerotics because dealing with white-authored Sapphic primitivism as a distinct phenomenon can help illuminate some of the ways in which racial and sexual boundary markers are mutual constructions, and because insights and historical information about this mutuality can help us produce antiracist effects in the academic departments, classrooms, and political organizations in which we work. I confine my discussion to only a few texts, but there are many other novels that might be productively read in terms of Sapphic primitivism.[8] I hope that others will take from my discussion a commitment to reading a wide variety of twentieth-century texts with attention to the overlap between racial and sexual boundary markers and to the phenomenon Sapphic primitivism.

I examine Sapphic primitivism in the novels I discuss in their historical contexts, attentive to the specific manifestations of ideologies of race, class, and sexuality in the times and places in which the novels I discuss were produced. Paradoxically, however, this book taken as a whole—the simple fact of discussing such diverse works together—also emphasizes the similarities in ideologies about race, class, and sexuality across several decades and national boundaries. Some of the reasons for these similarities are the broad influence and broad scope of late nineteenth- and early twentieth-century Euro-American scientific discourses of sexology, anthropology, and psychology. I take this science, more fully discussed in chapter 2, as my starting point. Bonnie Kime Scott points out that European and American writers of the late 1920s and 1930s "were working with lesbian identifications and expressive forms at a time when the 'sexology' of Havelock Ellis and Edward Carpenter and the developmental theories of Freud were just becoming known."[9] In this racial-sexual science, figurations of blackness are used to construct and make claims about homo- and heterosexuality; conversely, discussions of homo- and bisexuality are used to construct and make claims about racial boundaries. If, as Michel Foucault argues, the modern concept of the homosexual is discursively constructed through scientific discourse about sexuality, the specific language through which "homosexual" is constructed is that of race and class.[10] In a discussion of lesbian writing, Julie Abraham argues that "literary conventions are one method through which 'the age' determines where we look and what we see as 'homosexual content'" (xiv). I argue that Schreiner, Woolf, Warner, and Cather all appropriated literary conventions of turning to comparative ethnography in scientific writing about homosexuality in their efforts to see and represent autonomous female sexuality and lesbian-erotic content in their fiction.[11] This is not the same as saying that figurations of blackness or markers of working-class status are effective analogies or metaphors for lesbianism in fiction or anywhere else. Rather, in scientific writing about sexuality, markers of race, class, and sexuality significantly overlap; I discuss this overlap as it is reflected in fiction by Schreiner, Woolf, Warner, and Cather.

In making this analysis, I keep in mind the censorious legal atmosphere in which these novelists wrote. Three of the four novels I discuss were written in the immediate aftermath of the 1928 obscenity trial involving Radclyffe Hall's *The Well of Loneliness*. Bonnie Kime Scott calls 1928 a "watershed" date in cultural history because "the literary world . . . focused on the trial," which in turn "opened to discussion aspects of sexuality of central importance to feminism" (*Refiguring Modernism* 242). In the history of the lesbian novel, the 1930s and 1940s are a "second phase . . . dominated by responses to *The Well*" (Abraham 5). During this period, novelists wrote with the knowledge that "identifiably lesbian texts might be banned" and that "female writers of lesbian novels faced being publicly identified by their texts" (Abraham 26). But since only formulaic realist lesbian novels might be identified as lesbian, "this left a great deal of space for the development of a wide range of other lesbian writings" as, for example, Virginia Woolf's fantasy, *Orlando,* which was not censored.[12] Among the possibilities for lesbian representation that flourished in this "second phase" following the trial—given the ethnographic conventions of sexology, anthropology, and psychology—is the mode of lesbian representation I am calling Sapphic primitivism.

The novels I discuss are also written in the contexts of intense debates about imperialism and the rise of fascism in Europe. Woolf and Warner are critical of European imperialism and fascism in the 1930s, and Warner in particular uses contemporary sexualized and racialized discourse with an explicitly antiracist intent if not effect. Cather's work reflects engagement with issues of empire building, European and American, as well as American abolitionist and anti-abolitionist discussions of race. Schreiner's critique of imperialism is at once the most explicit and the most ambivalent. But her analyses of English colonial rule and patriarchal rule over women are consistently intertwined. The simultaneous interest in questions of empire, race, gender, and sexuality on the parts of all four of these authors gives rise to the Sapphic primitivism of the novels I discuss. Morrison's theory of American Africanism, combined with the histories of the overlap between late nineteenth- and early twentieth-century sciences of race and sexuality, enables me to discuss the overlap between markers of race and sexuality in works by Schreiner, Woolf, Warner, and Cather. As Morrison's concept "American Africanism" enables critics to focus on the ways in which white authors in the United States have used an Africanist presence to make the themes of individuality, freedom, and autonomy visible, a discussion of Sapphic primitivism enables readers to perceive the uses middle-class white women writers have made—both intentionally and unwittingly—of the (homo)sexual subtext of stereotyped dark and working-class bodies.

Primitivism and Modernism

Primitivism is not an invention of the twentieth century. Pablo Picasso's masks, Igor Stravinsky's drums, and Joseph Conrad's *Heart of Darkness* are indebted to travel writings by early-modern explorers who described what they saw as exotic or savage.[13] T. S. Eliot's *The Waste Land* and Paul Gauguin's Tahitians descend from discourses on the noble savage, discourses such as Aphra Behn's *Oroonoko* and Jean Jacques Rousseau's *Discours sur l'origine de l'inégualité,* which idealize an imagined superior naturalness of so-called primitive man and enable a critique of his civilized but corrupt counterpart.[14] But the widespread European preoccupation with so-called primitive people and places begins in the 1890s when British imperialists looted bronze and ivory artwork from Benin, and when, as a result, European scholars and museum curators began to try to classify this and other art from West Africa.[15] These efforts to classify, along with a gradually increasing appreciation for the Benin art as a result of such efforts, provided "a whole new aesthetic category for European connoisseurs" and "a new idiom for Western art" (Barkan and Bush 1). In dance, literature, painting, and music as well as anthropology, psychology, and sexology, Western Europeans repeatedly sought to define their own humanity in opposition to a monolithic usually dark-skinned being who was imagined to be supremely savage, barbaric, natural, *un*natural, exotic, or some contradictory combination of these. Picasso and others embraced the primitive of their imaginations—including constructions of people, arts, cultures, and landscapes—for that primitive's violence, energy, and natural sensuality. Barbarism and savagery were to provide antidotes to corrupting, over-civilized, effete modern Euro-American societies as well as, paradoxically, to explain the violence unleashed in world wars. Poor and working-class Europeans, especially those who organize to agitate for social reform, are among those who flesh out the imagined and infinitely productive category "primitive." Robert Nye discusses this primitivized status of the working class in his "Savage Crowds, Modernism, and Modern Politics," arguing that "the 'modernity' of fin-de-siècle crowds resided in their status as atavisms, savage phenomena in an overrefined and exhausted urban civilization" (43).

Cultural critics have been discussing primitivism as a problematic set of assumptions underlying modern art and art criticism at least since 1984 when William Rubin published his catalog of the New York Museum of Modern Art exhibit "'Primitivism' in Twentieth-Century Art: Affinity of the Tribal and the Modern." Rubin's catalog reflects the widespread assumption that African art is a raw material, the importance of which is its power to inspire

Euro-American artistic genius. In response to Rubin and to this assumption, critics have analyzed systems of thought underlying Euro-American discussions about African art, about the creators and subjects of that art, and about the continuously shifting categories of people who are the subjects of primitivizing discourses.[16] In *Gone Primitive,* for instance, Marianna Torgovnick describes the phenomenon of primitivism and critiques its contemporary manifestations. She argues that modern and post-modern primitivizing tropes, which are infinitely flexible and contradictory, form a discourse about the Euro-American sense of self. In this discourse, "primitive" fills the positions of both the Euro-American past and the Euro-American opposite. Torgovnick shows, through examination of several modernist texts, the ways in which "for Euro-Americans the primitive as an inexact expressive whole—often with little correspondence to any specific or documented societies—has been an influential and powerful concept, capable of referring both to societies 'out there' and to subordinate groups within the West."[17]

Philosopher of race David Theo Goldberg criticizes Torgovnick for perpetuating us–them thinking by her use of "we" to mean Euro-Americans. Goldberg is principally interested in explaining the logic of contemporary racism, and in explaining how simply calling it illogical is part of the problem, by tracing the origins of that logic back to the Enlightenment. Primitivism, he shows, is part of the logic of racism—a belief among colonizers that those they colonize have neither history nor culture. This belief has been used to sanction violence, paternalism, and ghettoization as well as the erasure and appropriation of cultures. Though their approaches are different, Torgovnick and Goldberg both insist on historical, geographical, and political specificity in reference to people and places that have been used as examples of a monolithic primitive. Specificity, they both argue, is a useful corrective to some of the violent contemporary effects of primitivism. Paradoxically—a word that comes up constantly in any discussion of primitivism—both Torgovnick and Goldberg would agree that *primitives* don't exist; rather, *primitivism* "denotes an Occidental construction, a set of representations whose 'reality' is purely Western" (Barkan and Bush 2).

Toni Morrison doesn't use the term primitivism in *Playing in the Dark,* a choice that makes a sharp critique of "primitivism" as a conceptual category and as a term of literary and art history. Her approach suggests that the focus of what some critics call primitivist art is the white self despite explicit and inexplicit claims to the contrary. Representations and discussion about an other serve, above all, to produce a self whose superiority is confirmed by the position of that self as white and as at the center of knowledge. Morrison's critique of white-authored uses of figurations of blackness has been picked up by later critics who continue to try to use the term "primitivism" for antiracist purposes. Such scholars analyze the ways in which African, African American, and Euro-American arts and cultures are "mutually constituted" and have all been informed by primitivizing discourse.[18] Sieglind Lemke, for instance, recognizes the racist origins and functions of the concept of the primitive as it was used by colonizers. But she argues that in the sphere of the arts, primitivist modernism was usefully appropriated by black intellectuals and artists of the New Negro movement (146). "Primitivist modernism," she writes, "opened up a space comparable to what Homi K. Bhabha called the third space of enunciation, an ambiguous space that undermined the opposition that the colonialist enterprise was predicated upon" (149). Lemke shows that many artists, writers, and critics of the African diaspora in the United States and Europe, including Claude McKay, Alain Locke, Nella Larsen, and Zora Neale Hurston, appropriated and re-formed primitivist styles of representation. This art and literature helped to create powerful ethnic identities and otherwise contributed to the fight against racism. I opt here to use the terms "primitive" and "primitivism" cautiously, while also foregrounding the idea that white-authored aesthetic strategies based on primitivisms are exactly this: anxious efforts to define a superior, unraced self.

Sapphic Modernism

I am also engaged with literary discussions of Sapphic modernism as a genre of its own. Susan Gubar, Shari Benstock, Jane Marcus, Karla Jay, Cassandra Laity, Ruth Vanita, Erin Carlston, and Yopie Prins have worked to carve out boundaries for this genre.[19] Susan Gubar uses the term "Sapphistries" to denote twentieth-century writers' rediscovery and reinvention of Sappho as literary foremother and as representative of all the lost women of genius in literary history, especially all the lesbian artists whose work has been destroyed, sanitized, or heterosexualized (46). Shari Benstock includes as Sapphic modernists those women writers who "fused 'asexual poetics' and 'sexual politics' in the continuation of a female poetic tradition that extended back to Sappho and forward to H.D.'s rewriting of the classical tradition" (452). Benstock focuses particularly on the women who created a literary circle within the Paris of the expatriate—a Paris that was often seen by others as a female muse seductive to men. More recently, Yopie Prins argues that Sapphic modernists such as H.D., as well as contemporary feminist critics who use Sappho to evoke lost female literary traditions, are responding to Victorian renderings of Sappho as essentially fragmentary and lost. Importantly, Erin Carlston suggests that in characterizations of writers and their work, Sapphism should be "taken to express itself not as an organized identity or as a *mise-en-texte* of biography, but as a hypersensitivity to sexuality in, and as, the aesthetic and the political" (6). The works of Siobhan Somerville on Pauline Hopkins, Deborah McDowell on Nella Larsen, Carla Kaplan on Zora Neale Hurston, and Angela Davis on blues singers including Gertrude "Ma" Rainey make it clear that many black writers who have not been discussed as Sapphic modernists must also be included in this genre for their hypersensitivity to sexual autonomy for women as, in Carlston's words, both aesthetic and political issues.

Sapphic modernism is not a lesser subset of literary modernism. Rather, it is central to the birth of modernism as a movement, and hence needs to be central to our understanding of modernism. This becomes clear by bringing together two claims made by Michael North in *The Dialect of Modernism*. North argues that in 1906 "Stein and Picasso take the first steps into Cubism and literary modernism by performing uncannily similar transformations on the figure of Gertrude Stein herself" (61). Picasso finishes a portrait of Stein by covering a realistic rendering of her face with a mask modeled after ancient Iberian reliefs he had seen at the Louvre. Similarly, Stein, perhaps even motivating Picasso's use of the mask, rewrites an autobiographical story, *Q.E.D.*, into a new story, "Melanctha," by giving her characters, including the authorial figure Dr. Jeff Campbell, African American masks. For Picasso and for Stein, North says, "the step away from conventional verisimilitude into abstraction is accomplished by a figurative change of race" (61). With this Picasso-Stein collaboration, North argues, modernism coheres as a movement. By pushing to extremes colonialist contradictions about Africans and African art—contradictory beliefs that the people and the artifacts are the most naked of representations and at the same time the most opaque and obviously artificial—modernists explored contradictions about gender, nationality, and genre. This exploration was enabled by the use of the African mask in particular because of the mask's susceptibility to contradictory interpretations, and because those contradictions exposed the similarity of visual arts to writing—both are signs.

But North also describes another important set of circumstances surrounding the use of masks over Stein's face. Picasso's use of the mask has to do with his feelings about what North calls Stein's "unconventional sexuality." North writes, "the mask she wears is a sign of . . . sexual ambiguity, the impersonal immobility of it associated in Picasso's work of the time with a physical bulk and power not at all conventionally feminine" (69). Also significantly, Picasso uses the same mask to express sexual ambiguity in a series of studies leading up to the final version of *Les Demoiselles*. In one study, a male figure appears; in the following study, the same Iberian mask with which Picasso had covered Stein's face covers the male figure's face, the mask accompanying a change of gender (North 69). Stein's use of masking in "Melanctha" is also about gender, sexuality, and race combined. In the original *Q.E.D,* Stein records her unhappy lesbian love affair with fellow Johns Hopkins student May Bookstaver (Katz iii). "Melanctha" includes lines of dialogue from *Q.E.D.,* but Stein peoples the story with black characters. In addition, she flips conventions of masculinity and femininity by making it a man—Dr. Jeff—who worries at home, and a woman who wanders. North argues that Stein's use of black masks presents race as a role; it is "an open invitation to consider it as culturally constituted and perhaps to consider gender as a role as well" (70). Ambiguity created by Stein's racial masquerade, as well as by her insertion of ambiguity and doubt into words of distinctness such as "certainly," "makes gender and, finally, the body itself seem a mask" (70). Most importantly, North says, as with Picasso's use of the mask, Stein's masking "is not a cover for an unconventional sexuality but a revelation of it, even a means of achieving it" (70).

My project begins by bringing together two parts of North's analysis of Picasso's and Stein's use of African and African American masks. North says that this moment of masking is "one of the most important episodes in the birth of [modernism]" (61). And, he says, for Picasso and Stein, this masking is about revealing "unconventional sexuality." It follows, then, that exposing unconventional sexuality by the use of African and African American masks is the "episode" that signals the birth of modernism. More specifically, as Stein's unconventional sexuality is lesbian sexuality, North's essay suggests, without saying it directly, that this important episode is about exposing lesbian sexuality with the use of African and African American masks. In the pages that follow, I explore this aspect of modernism by looking at the ways in which Olive Schreiner, Virginia Woolf, Sylvia Townsend Warner, and Willa Cather have done exactly that: exposed lesbianism and female sexual autonomy, to varying degrees, by manipulating figurations of blackness—by metaphorically giving female sexual autonomy, including lesbianism, African and African American masks.

Race Studies, Queer Studies

Finally, I participate in a larger discussion about a complex, unstable network of socially constructed and interdependent identity categories; in particular, I participate in the part of this discussion that is focused on the intersecting constructions of race and of sexuality. "Race," writes Peter Sanjek, is a "framework of ranked categories segmenting the human population that was developed by western Europeans following their global expansion beginning in the 1400s" (1). While "race" is very real in its effects, "its roots and growth lie in nothing more 'real' than the conquest, dispossession, enforced transportation, and economic exploitation of human beings over five centuries that racial categorization and racist social ordering have served to expedite and justify." Nevertheless, "millions of people today continue to accept inherited racial categories as fixed in nature, and to interpret the systemic inequalities of racist social orders as based on 'real' differences among 'real' races" (Sanjek 2). This is what it means to live, as we do, in a racialized world.[20]

Similarly, critics working against homophobia and heterosexism have argued that sexual identity categories including "homosexual" and "heterosexual" are very real in their effects, but that one of those effects is the very idea that homosexual and heterosexual exist as natural and fixed kinds of humanity. Instead, these categories themselves are culturally produced and reproduced.[21] In casual and formal discourse, people employ "homosexual," "heterosexual," "gay," and "lesbian" as if each were definable and knowable. But, as Eve Sedgwick points out, arrangements of same-sex relations vary so tremendously over time and place, and are so profoundly and integrally rooted in other cultural differences, "that there may be no continuous defining essence of 'homosexuality' to *be* known [emphasis in the original]" (44).

Moreover, these racial and sexual identity categories are constituted and thus have meaning through one another in mutually dependent ways. There is a long history of ideological work, done in service to imperialism and other economic systems based in exploitation, through which whiteness and middle-class status have come to define, and be defined by, sexual normalcy, while darkness and working-class status define, and are defined by, sexual deviance.[22] European race scientists of the eighteenth and nineteenth centuries sought to delineate racial categories by making reference to physical traits including head and hip size, but very often also by genitalia and/or imagined sexual behavior.[23] The most commonly cited example of this is the treatment of Saartjie Baartman, a !Kung woman from South Africa who was taken to England in 1810 and shown in England and France as an ethnographic exhibit of the Hottentot racial type. The focus of public and scientific attention on Baartman was her genitalia and buttocks, by which the so-called racial difference between Hottentot and European was defined.[24] A great deal of scholarship exposes the ways in which racial and sexual identity categories have meaning through one another. Charles Stember argues that "in the early history of the American colonies" assertions of black hypersexuality were "concretized in myth into specific anatomical and physiological details—his penis was larger, his sexual capacity greater, his desire harder to satisfy" (57). Angela Davis provides a corrective to Stember's androcentric view by pointing out that there is an "inseparable companion" to the male rapist image: "the image of the Black woman as chronically promiscuous."[25] In *Disfigured Images,* Patricia Morton charts the ways in which, in American historiography, African American women are constructed as the most nurturing, the most sensual, and/or the most castrating of all women. And Anne McClintock writes that "by the nineteenth century," European popular lore had firmly established Africa as the quintessential zone of sexual aberration and anomaly."[26] As a corollary to this hypersexualization of dark-skinned bodies, bodies that appear white, middle-class, and female are very unlikely to be taken as representations of female sexual desire.[27] This is because the combined identity of white, middle-class, and woman has been delimited by the qualities of purity, piety, submissiveness, and domesticity. As Hazel Carby puts it, according to the nineteenth-century cult of true womanhood, these qualities are attributable only to white women, and, together with whiteness, are "the parameters within which women were measured and declared to be, or not to be, women" (*Reconstructing Womanhood* 23).

One characteristic of the interdependence between constructions of racial and sexual identity is that images of black and white together are likely to represent illicit and/or dangerous female sexuality, including lesbianism. Historians of colonialism and of the presence of black people in England discuss the often specifically sexual meaning of black and white together. About the association between taboo sexuality and the image of black and white together in the 1600s, for instance, Peter Fryer writes that the "status of London's black population in the second half of the seventeenth century is best conveyed in a little book published in 1675, called 'the Character of a Town Misse.' 'Town miss' was a euphemism for the fashionable high-class whore of the period, who the book says 'hath always two necessary Implements about her, a Blackamoor, and a little Dog; for without these, she would be neither Fair nor Sweet'" (31–32). Eugenicists of the early 1900s combined ideas about black hypersexuality with assumptions about white working-class female hypersexuality in order to drive their racial "hygiene" campaigns. And in their pro-slavery arguments, West Indian planters characterized sexual relations between black men and the "lower orders" of white women as both common and "unnatural" (P. Fryer 160–164). Accounts of riots in England in the 1920s also "manipulated fears of miscegenation by conflating dark skin with moral corruption" (Hovey 394). In these examples, working-class sexuality, black sexuality, and autonomous sexuality among white females of every class are imbricated and defined persistently in terms of their potential to disrupt the social order.

Sander Gilman explains the iconography of dark-skinned and white-skinned bodies together in eighteenth- and nineteenth-century European paintings including Edouard Manet's *Olympia* and Franz von Bayros's *The Servant*. In *Olympia,* Gilman writes, "the central white female figure is associated with a black female in such a way as to imply a similarity between the sexuality of the two" (81). In *The Servant,* a nearly naked black girl touches the back of an also naked, but much less revealed, white woman.

The detail of the black girl's genitalia as well as her open-mouthed smile and elaborate adornments make up what Gilman calls the "hypersexuality of the black child," which, he also says, "signals the hidden sexuality of the white woman."[28] As a result of the association between black and white figures in both paintings, the sexuality that adheres to the white women is pathological and specifically lesbian. In representational systems of the other in general, Gilman says, overt connections link sexuality and race with pathology as well: "sexual anatomy is so important a part of self-image that 'sexually different' is tantamount to pathological—the Other is 'impaired,' 'sick,' 'diseased.' Similarly, physiognomy or skin color that is perceived as different is immediately associated with 'pathology' and 'sexuality'" (25). Specifically lesbian sexuality is evoked in the paintings through a series of analogies in which "the black female comes to serve as an icon for black sexuality in general" and in which, through associations with pathology and prostitution, "the concupiscence of the black is . . . associated with the sexuality of the lesbian."[29]

As images of black and white bodies together can "elicit a presumption of lesbianism," Siobhan Somerville argues that the figure of the mulatto and the concept of racial hybridity are also conceptually linked to the figure of the homosexual in sexological writing. Late nineteenth-century sexologists used the figure of the mulatto as an analogy in their efforts to either defend or condemn the "invert," whom they believed was characterized by a sexual hybridity similar to racial hybridity. Later, twentieth-century psychological models of desire began to replace medical models of inversion, but the mulatto and the homosexual continued to be conceptually linked. Somerville writes, "Whereas previously two bodies, the mulatto and the invert, had been linked together in a visual economy, now two tabooed types of desire—interracial and homosexual—became linked in sexological and psychological discourse through the model of abnormal sexual object choice" (*Queering* 34). None of these histories or analyses assert that white and black together is the same as or analogous to lesbianism. But they show that unnaturalness, taint, and moral and racial corruption characterize discussions of homosexuality as consistently as they characterize discussions of blackness. The fact of this overlap warrants reading practices and analytical frameworks, such as Sapphic primitivism, that emphasize the simultaneity and multiplicity of sexual and racial characterizations.

Such reading practices are all the more urgent given the fact that historically produced overlapping constructions of sexual and racial identity categories have negative contemporary effects. Jewelle Gomez provides a contemporary U.S. example of the ways in which a black woman and a white woman together elicit a presumption of lesbianism where two women of color, like two white women, do not. Even despite the history of hypersexualization of black people, she writes, "almost without exception it has been when I've been with white women that I've been harassed, in public, as a lesbian. It seems that two women of color walking down a city street together are invisible or inconsequential, but a Black woman walking with a white woman sets off alarms in the minds of bigots" (160). In this book, I am not writing about contemporary examples of Sapphic primitivism or directly about experiences such as Jewelle Gomez describes. But Gomez's experience points to the perseverance of the structures of imagination that I am attributing to Schreiner, Woolf, Warner, and Cather as well as to the importance of unraveling the legacy these writers have passed down to us. In understanding this legacy, we prepare ourselves to manipulate the overlap between constructions of race and sexuality for antiracist and antihomophobic purposes.

One way in which people involved in struggles for justice might manipulate this overlap to advantage is to cull from the historical interdependence of constructions of identity the basis for a politics of empathy. In her essay "American Kabuki," Patricia Williams points to the possibility of this kind of empathic thinking by outlining a *failure* of empathy in her discussion of responses to the trial of O. J. Simpson. She argues that many black women had difficulty seeing Nicole Brown Simpson as a casualty of racist, sexist culture because of her blond-beauty standard good looks. This was despite the fact that had Simpson left her husband and his money at the first sign of violence, she was unlikely to have had anything but welfare, if that, between herself and her children and homelessness. Many white women had difficulty imagining that the sympathy generated by pictures of Nicole Brown Simpson's battered face, as well as the abuse she suffered, were the product of racist, sexist culture in which ravishing white fragility is idealized femininity. The sympathy generated by Simpson's face is in sharp contrast to the "de-aesthetizing masculinization of black women" iterated constantly in the media and in public policy debates about welfare (Williams

285). Williams writes: "If we have difficulty imagining the beautiful Nicole Brown Simpson as a putative welfare mother, then surely this is as much a problem of race as it is of feminism. By the same token, if we have difficulty imagining Emma Mae Martin as the beaut[y] . . . to whom our hearts rush out in all her ravishing fragility, then we must understand this as a problem of sexism as much as it is of race. The failure to see one in the embodied distress of the other is a cultural blindness that afflicts every segment of our culture."[30] Similarly, the Human Rights Campaign's 1998 endorsement of New York Republican senator Alfonse D'Amato for reelection despite his antiabortion and antiwelfare voting records suggests that many individuals and groups organizing under the single-issue banner of gay rights cannot see their own plight in the embodied distress of people of color, women, and the poor. Human Rights Campaign (HRC) and other organizations that embrace single-issue politics might succeed in procuring the "rights" of heteronormative white and male supremacist culture for a few more people—might enable some gay and lesbian assimilation into white and male supremacy. But such politics do nothing to disrupt the racist, sexist, and class-biased violences perpetrated to maintain those supremacies.[31]

The failures described by Williams and the failures of HRC, however, point to an alternative politics of empathy in which individuals can see their own plight in the particular embodied distresses of others. Such a politics relies not on people liking one another, but rather on an understanding of the many ways in which categories of race, sex, class, and sexuality are mutually constructed. The following discussion contributes historical detail about the production of this mutuality that can be used in building an argument for politics based on empathy in organizations such as the Human Rights Campaign. Where people of color, poor and working-class people, and some kinds of queers have, at best, been "invited" to bring their concerns to the table as sideshows, a politics of empathy for HRC would involve combating racism, class bias, and sexism as central, constitutive concerns of the organization.

Two

The Homosexual Primitivism
of Modernism

Victorian sexologists whose work helped construct the boundaries of modern homosexuality and heterosexuality laid the groundwork for the structure of imagination I am calling Sapphic primitivism by borrowing the methodology of nineteenth-century race science—comparative ethnography—in their studies of sexuality. As race scientists built a concept of racial difference by making reference to sexuality and genitalia, sex scientists built their concepts of sexual difference by making reference to notions of racial difference they inherited from race scientists (Somerville, *Queering* 25). Hence, literature about human sexual behavior both reflected and helped to construct symbolic linkages between lesbianism and male homosexuality, blackness, disease, criminality, working-class status, degeneracy, taint, pollution, and prostitution. As Margaret Gibson puts it in a discussion of the language used by American doctors discussing lesbianism in the late nineteenth century, "the use of body metaphors such as the hypertrophied clitoris banded together a motley collection of prostitutes, nymphomaniacs, masturbators, insane women, women of nonwhite races, poor women, criminals, and finally, the female invert" (110). Reading *The Story of an African Farm, The Waves, Summer Will Show,* and *Sapphira and the Slave Girl* through these social-science discourses illuminates the ways in which

Schreiner, Woolf, Warner, and Cather use overdetermined markers of race and class in their representations of female sexual autonomy and lesbianism.

Marianna Torgovnick argues that in their respective fields, Sigmund Freud, James Frazer, Bronislaw Malinowski, and Havelock Ellis shared similar goals: to define universal truths about human nature by using what they thought of as primitive societies as testing grounds, as keys to those universal truths (7). These goals often have particularly to do with establishing universal truths as well as moral guidelines about human sexuality. This use of "the primitive" as a trope upon which to build a sexual comparison reinforced the widespread perception that whatever and whoever filled out the category "primitive" existed, as Torgovnick says, in a highly sexualized field (3). And, in a circular way, the always already-sexualized character of the imaginary primitive encouraged social scientists to rely on comparisons between Europeans and a monolithic primitive in discourses of sexuality.

This didactic, comparative, scientific structure is used abundantly by researchers who discuss homosexuality. Whether they write to condemn homosexuality as degenerate and dangerous to the Empire (Malinowski) or to soften legal and social censure of the congenitally inverted (Ellis, Krafft-Ebing, Freud) or to celebrate morally elevated homogenic love (Symonds, Carpenter) or some combination of these, researchers of homosexuality all sought to establish the measure of European middle-class white homosexuality by means of writing comparative ethnography. Lynda Hart writes that "a composite of Ellis's 'typical' invert . . . might well appear as a working-class woman of color who was either a criminal or a lunatic" (4). This is a little bit misleading, as the vast majority of sexological writing on homosexuality consists of case studies about middle- and upper-class white men. If any composite were drawn from Ellis's case studies, it would be of an upper-middle-class white Englishman with a family history of neuroses who had been exposed to homoerotic behavior in early life. But Hart's claim is somewhat justified and very revealing: sexologists including Ellis repeatedly made their arguments about middle-class white homosexuality by making reference to people of color and to places outside of Western Europe, and to what Richard Burton defined in 1886 as the "Sotadic Zone." This is an area characterized, Burton claimed, by homosexuality. It includes "Meridional France, the Iberian Peninsula, Italy and Greece, with the coast regions of Africa from Morocco to Egypt" also "Asia Minor, Mesopotamia and Chaldea, Afghanistan, Sind the Punjab and Kashmir" as well as "China, Japan . . . Turkistan" and "the South Sea Islands and the New World where, at the time of its discovery, Sotadic love was . . . an established racial institution" (Cory 208). Each sexologist paints specifics about white middle-class European homosexuality against a backdrop of remarks about generalized, uncivilized peoples, lower races, lower classes, savages, and primitives as well as reference to places frequently outside of Western Europe. Additionally, many sexologists suggested that social approval of homosexuality would prove fertile soil for its development in individuals with a predisposition but who might not become homosexuals in a socially disapproving context. Examples of approving cultures are invariably those of working-class people, criminals, prostitutes, or specific sites outside of contemporary Western Europe. Such examples make the indirect argument that people of color, the working classes, and non-Western cultures can produce homosexuality where it might not be otherwise.

It bears emphasizing that sexologists made diverse arguments about homosexuality and that some changed their minds over time.[1] While some understand homosexuality to be characteristic of one race or another, others insist that homosexuality is a genetic trait distributed across race and nation. Still others believe homosexuality to be an evolutionary throwback to a sexually undifferentiated phase of human development. Hence it is part of the evolutionary past of all people, and evidence, in the present, of atavism or evolutionary primitivism such as is common, they argue, among criminals, prostitutes, and the working class, as well as people of the Sotadic Zone.[2] The following examples represent some of the variety in sexological writings; more significantly, the examples below show that despite major differences among sexologists and changes in thinking over time, "cultural and historical fascinations, anxieties and desires . . . produced race and sexuality as inextricable" and that sexology is "thoroughly imbricated in the discourse of race" (Somerville, Introduction 203) and, I would add, class.

Sexology

The bulk of Richard von Krafft-Ebing's *Psychopathia Sexualis* (1882) is case studies describing homosexuality and other "perversions" among the population the book is written for—educated middle- and upper-class white men. However, comparative ethnography and reference to dark-skinned people are central to Krafft-Ebing's characterization of homosexuality. His goal is to differentiate between kinds of homosexuals in order to give medico-juridical professionals a way to decide whom to punish for homosexuality. He describes pathological homosexuality—unpunishable—as a congenital and degenerate condition of good and talented citizens produced by some hereditary taint in combination with external influences, such as the seduction of a boy or girl by a confirmed homosexual. Individuals thus afflicted are diseased or insane rather than responsible. Alternately, Krafft-Ebing describes nonpathological homosexuality as acquired and punishable. It usually starts, he posits, with masturbation which, if unchecked, leads to a life of sensual indulgence and a refusal to be governed by morality. Moreover, sensual men are the ones who indulge in the vice of sodomy, a practice that, according to Krafft-Ebing, most congenital homosexuals abhor.

The case studies that make up the bulk of Krafft-Ebing's book assert no particular relationship between race and homosexuality, though one could surmise from the cases alone that homosexuality is a condition seen exclusively among the white middle-class men he discusses as individuals. The introductory and concluding remarks that frame those case studies, however, suggest that homosexuality is an interesting condition in the populations that concern him specifically because it is unusual. Among civilized men, he explains, sexual morality inhibits the development of sensuality, which, through the whole volume, is nearly synonymous with acquired perversion, masturbation, and sodomy. By contrast, among "uncivilized races" and "lower classes" homosexuality is less strongly abhorred, and thus more prevalent (Krafft-Ebing 2). "The savage races, e.g., Australasians, Polynesians, Malays of the Philippines," he writes, are "still in the uncivilized, sensual stage" and "southern races," it is "well known" have a "greater sensuality" than "the sexual needs of those of the north" (2, 25). Moreover, since Christianity is singularly responsible for sexual morality, Europeans "are certainly far beyond [the] sodomitic idolatry... of ancient Greece" and less likely to acquire perversions than "the polygamic races, and especially... Islam" (6, 5). When the Christian "drags pure and chaste love from its sublime pedestal and wallows in the quagmire of sensual enjoyment and lust," it is the result of a failure of willpower—of his having lost track of the moral guides Christianity offers him (5). When others slip into sensuality, which is more likely, it is the result of their existence in a less-civilized phase of human development. In other words, when a Christian errs, he is being like a Mohammedan. Krafft-Ebing abandons such comparisons while he makes his way through the cases that form the focus of his book, but he circles back to them to conclude. "Ethnological data," he writes, provide "interesting confirmation" of the foregoing facts concerning acquired antipathic sexual instinct (homosexuality) and effeminization (302). These ethnological data include remarks about the Scythians, the Tartars, the Apaches, the Navajos, the Pueblo Indians of New Mexico, and the Aztecs.

Havelock Ellis's multi-volume *Studies in the Psychology of Sex,* an attempt to catalog human variety in sexual behavior, is much less condemnatory of "inversion" than is Krafft-Ebing's study, but Ellis relies no less heavily on comparative ethnography to make his claim than does Krafft-Ebing. In volume two, *Sexual Inversion* (1897), Ellis argues that homosexuality is a naturally occurring human phenomenon, and, because of this, people who are congenitally inverted ought not be punished. As proof that homosexuality exists naturally, he argues that it is no more prevalent in one nation than it is in another (4, 8, 9, 264). However, the catalogs of people and places he uses as evidence contradict his point. They include some European examples: homosexuality is, for instance, strongly represented among Europeans who are either of particular ability or who are criminals or lunatics. But the European examples are amidst a great abundance of examples from places in Burton's Sotadic Zone.[3] A recent example of modern European pederasty is the Albanians, especially the Moslems, possibly because they belong to the same stock that produced the Dorian Greeks (Ellis 11). Other examples are from China, India, Afghanistan, the New World from Alaska to Brazil, Tahiti, Madagascar, the Negro population of Zanzibar (with a frequency due to Arab influence), various people and places of Africa including the Unyamweze, Uganda, the Bangala of the Upper Congo, as well as Papuans of New Guinea, primitive Australians, and the working masses of England and Scotland (who are not averse to prostituting themselves to upper-class men), Russians, Emperors in Rome, American Negroes, among whom homosexuality is much more prevalent than it is among American whites (Ellis 19n). Homosexuality is evident in the Rigo district of British New Guinea among people who "belong to a primitive race, uncontaminated by contact with white races, and practically still in the stone age" (20).

The discrepancy between Ellis's claim that homosexuality is present everywhere and the examples he chooses to prove his point has largely to do with the fact that he differentiates between congenital and acquired homosexuality. *Congenital* homosexuality may be spread evenly around the globe and from era to era. *Acquired* homosexuality cannot be evenly spread around the globe, though he doesn't say this directly, because acquired homosexuality is a direct result of social acceptance of homosexuality, which varies from place to place. Such acceptance, and by implication an abundance of acquired homosexuality, is prevalent in the "lower races" among whom "homosexual practices are regarded with considerable indifference" and among "the lower classes"; with regard to acquired homosexuality, he continues, "the uncultured man of civilization is linked to the savage" (21).

In "The Psychomorphology of the Clitoris," Valerie Traub argues that even before sexologists developed this comparative ethnographic language for discussing homosexuality—by which they mostly meant male homosexuality—early-modern travel narratives had produced the terms through which erotics between women could be represented.[4] She argues that early-modern anatomy texts and travel narratives "generated at the same historical moment" are a discursive pair: where anatomies dissect a corpse to fashion a normative, abstract body, "travel accounts create an exoticized body that reveals the antithesis of normativity" (85). Narrators who described the New World, Africa, or the East "obsessively remark upon those cultural practices that differentiate native inhabitants from Europeans," including inexplicit but clear descriptions of women pleasuring one another (Traub 88). Such descriptions are almost always accompanied by accounts of exceedingly large clitorises. Although this same-gender female eroticism is mentioned only rarely (and nowhere as often as male sodomy), its presence is routinely associated with certain locales: Turkey and North Africa. "In the absence of narratives about similar practices among Englishwomen," Traub argues, "tales such as these imply that African and Muslim women are uniquely (if amorphously) amoral in their erotic desires and practices"

(89). Hence "notwithstanding assumptions about the nonexistence or invisibility of 'lesbians' a vocabulary was available to Western writers with which to describe women's erotic desire for and contact with one another."[5]

In *Three Essays on the Theory of Sexuality* (1910),[6] Sigmund Freud condenses the correlation between homosexuality and "primitive races" presented by sexologists including Ellis and Krafft-Ebing and facilitates the process by which this correlation is passed down to his readers as scientific fact. His analysis of homosexuality in the essay entitled "The Sexual Aberations" is based on sexological writings, including those which assert that homosexuality is equally present in all populations.[7] But Freud collapses sexologists' various claims about homosexuality and race into the assertion that homosexuality is "remarkably widespread among many savage and primitive races . . . and, even among the civilized peoples of Europe, climate and race exercise the most powerful influence on the prevalence of inversion and upon the attitude adopted towards it."[8] He also proposes that there is a similarity between the sexuality of children, primitives, and inverts. He claims that all human beings have, at some point, made at least an unconscious homosexual object-choice. This "freedom to range equally over male and female objects" characterizes "childhood," "primitive states of society," and "early periods of history" (11–12n). Freud suggests here not only that what we might call bisexuality is common in "primitive states," but also that primitives and children are more similar to each other in their bisexuality than either are to adult Europeans. Finally, inverted types are like children and primitives as well. He writes, "In inverted types, a predominance of archaic constitutions and primitive psychical mechanisms is regularly to be found. Their most essential characteristics seem to be a coming into operation of narcissistic object-choice and a retention of the erotic significance of the anal zone" (12n). In these various reiterations of the idea that homosexuality is a characteristic of so-called primitive people in particular, Freud takes up the claim of sexologists who argue outright that homosexuality is a racial characteristic and ignores contradictory ideas. This suggests, I would argue, that the sexologists' rhetorical use of comparative ethnography has much greater meaning-making power than their direct arguments that homosexuality is evenly distributed throughout human populations.

Bronislaw Malinowski's *The Sexual Lives of Savages* (1929) reverses the claim that homosexuality is more prevalent among "savages" than among "the civilized" with his assertion that homosexuality in the Trobriand Islands is a product of European taint. But as in the work of the previous generation of sexologists, Malinowski's use of comparative ethnography to discuss homosexuality speaks more loudly than his actual argument. While Ellis, Krafft-Ebing, and Freud did fieldwork at home and built ethnographic comparisons between dark-skinned and working-class people and homosexuality using the writings of explorers and historians, Malinowski did fieldwork in the Trobriand Islands. He used ideas about English sexuality developed by Ellis and others to assess Trobriand sexuality and, simultaneously, to define normalcy and perversion for Europeans. Malinowski's book describes Trobriand sexuality as pure human sexuality untainted by civilization (though missionaries threaten), outside time (except for a bemoaned future of European intrusion), and characterized by egalitarian relations between the sexes. The Trobrianders as Malinowski describes them are at once supremely and constantly potent as well as healthfully calm, almost to the point of indifference, about sexual matters. Malinowski says he doesn't mean to make a comparison, but he uses detailed descriptions of Trobriand sexual and social behavior to weave a corrective to what he presents as its opposite—overly excitable and degenerate European sexuality. The Trobriand jungle is "virgin." Bathing and water constantly "rejuvenate," give a "suggestive gloss of freshness," or "present the human body in a fresh and stimulating light" (10). "Scrupulous cleanliness is an essential in the ideal of personal attraction" (448). Most significantly for my purposes, Malinowski describes Trobriand sexuality as normatively heterosexual in order to define European homosexuality as a product of degeneracy, over-civilization, and over-excitability. Trobriand Islanders' sexual habits, if promiscuous, produce stable, loving marriages; "morality" is a constant; sexual habits are characterized by "decency," "decorum" and "modesty." Among Trobrianders, he asserts, oral sex, masturbation, and homosexuality are virtually unknown. Nor do Trobrianders, unlike Europeans, need the discouragement of laws and penalties to avoid homosexuality since "orgasm, in man or woman, requires more bodily contact, erotic preliminaries, and, above all, direct friction of the mucous membranes for its production" (439, see also 448, 453, 469, 472). As a result, "preparatory erotic approaches . . . have less tendency to . . . develop into perversions, than is the case among nervously more excitable races" such as Europeans (477). He does admit there is some homosexual behavior, citing the "existence of such expressions as . . . 'he copulates excrement' . . . 'he penetrates rectum' and the well-defined moral attitude towards [homosexuality]" as evidence "that sporadic cases have always occurred" (473). But it exists among Trobrianders, he argues, only as the result of "unnatural" conditions imposed by whites: "Many natives are, under the present rule of whites, cooped up in gaol, on mission stations, and in plantation barracks. Sexes are separated and normal intercourse made impossible; yet an impulse trained to function regularly cannot be thwarted. The white man's influence and his morality, stupidly misapplied where there is no place for it, creates a setting favorable to homosexuality. The natives are perfectly well aware that venereal disease and homosexuality are among the benefits bestowed on them by Western culture" (472–473). Malinowski's argument about homosexuality among Trobrianders, taken literally, contradicts the characterization of homosexuality as more prevalent in Burton's Sotadic Zone. His argument, like many others, however, relies on a comparative ethnographic mode for both titillation and to admonish Europeans against homosexuality.[9]

John Addington Symonds and Edward Carpenter use a similar trope of racial comparison in works that, unlike Malinowski's, make concerted efforts to soften social disapproval of homosexuality. In *Sexual Inversion: A Classic Study of Homosexuality* (1928), Symonds argues that ancient Greek homosexuality—Greek love—can be a model for ennobled masculine love among his contemporaries. In contrast, Symonds uses what he calls an Oriental addiction to sensuality to provide a negative model for masculine love. Greek love itself, he argues, is modeled on the friendship between Achilles and Patroclus—a powerful and masculine emotion "in which effeminacy had no part" (12). There is nothing "which indicates the passionate relation of the lover and the beloved" in Homer's *Iliad,* but neither did it "exclud[e] the ordinary sexual feelings" (11, 12). Hence, ancient Greek students of Homer "selected the friendship of Achilles for their ideal of manly love" and added to it "a sensuality unknown to Homer" (11, 17). They thus developed "that mixed form of paiderastia upon which the Greeks prided themselves": a military, romantic love that inspired great achievement (17, 18–23). It was "not free from sensuality" but neither did it "degenerate into mere licentiousness" (17). The Dorian Greeks, in particular, turned this mixed paiderastia into a noble custom.

The source of the sensuality that the Greeks added to the ideal masculine love, on the other hand, is according to Symonds, "an Oriental importation" and an "Asiatic form of luxury"; the Greeks distinguished "whatever [they] received from adjacent nations . . . with the qualities of their own personality," but "paiderastia in its crudest form was transmitted to the Greeks from the East" (14). Herodotus may assert, Symonds argues, "that the Persians learned the habit, in its vicious form, from the Greeks," but he knows "from the Jewish records and from Assyrian inscriptions that the Oriental nations were addicted to this as well as other species of sensuality" (13). Given this information, he says, it is not reasonable to presume that Greeks were the source of crude paiderastia among all "the barbarians who were [their] neighbours" (13).

As he takes it as a matter of fact that "Oriental nations" are addicted to "crude" forms of sensuality, Symonds also presents it as a matter of fact that homosexuality is common among "savages." This kind of paiderastia, Symonds reiterates constantly, is the model to avoid: accounts of "paiderastia as it exists in various savage tribes" do not "illustrate the Doric phase of Greek love," which is "almost unique in the history of the human race" (30, 17). Rather, the "unisexual vices of barbarians" involve effeminacy such as is found among "the Scythian impotent effeminates, the North American Bardashes, the Tsecats of Madagascar, the Cordaches of the Canadian Indians, and similar classes among Californian Indians, natives of Venezuela, and so forth." His "and so forth" suggests that the groups he mentions are in a class with others the reader will have no problem recalling: they have in common the European-conferred status "primitive." Similarly, nothing about Dorian love resembles "what we know about the prevalence of sodomy among the primitive peoples of Mexico, Peru and Yucatan, and *almost all half-savage nations* [emphasis mine]" or "the semi-religious practices of Japanese Bonzes or Egyptian priests" (30–31).

Edward Carpenter was exceptional in late Victorian England for his frank assertions that he was a homosexual, and his book *The Intermediate Sex: A Study of Some Transitional Types of Men and Women* (1908) differs significantly in tone from all the writings discussed above. But a primitivizing, comparative ethnographic mode is still central to his argument. Carpenter celebrates contemporary British homosexuality as the sexuality of an "intermediate race" that has a special affectional temperament. This love ranks as a great human passion with great attendant social value, such as the advantages to boys nurtured by older boys and men. Like all love, the homogenic attachment is "the foundation of human society" with "social uses and functions which will become clearer to us the more we study it" (200).[10] Accordingly, Carpenter's use of cross-racial evidence serves not to define a lesser kind of homosexuality, but rather to show that people "occupying an intermediate position between the two sexes ... have always, and among all peoples, been more or less known and recognized" and that they have been a positive social force (185–186). In order to make this point, he chronicles great achievements among homosexuals, mostly citing European examples which he arranges chronologically from antiquity to the present. But he begins his chronicle with examples from Polynesia as if they are chronologically first and thus more original and pure examples of human behavior. "Polynesian Islanders," he writes, are "a very gentle and affectionate people" among whom "the most romantic male friendships are (or were) in vogue" (202). He quotes Herman Melville as saying that "in the annals of the island (Tahiti) are examples of extravagant friendships, unsurpassed by the story of Damon and Pythias" (202). So strong are these friendships that "if two men of hostile tribes or islands became thus pledged to each other, then each could pass through the enemy's territory without fear of molestation or injury" (202).

Carpenter's second example is African, and given as if evidence of homosexuality in Africa is especially useful for proving that homosexuality has been known among all people. Romantic love among Polynesians, he writes, is probably evidence that they have "inherit[ed] the traditions of a higher culture than they now possess"; but "*even* among savage races lower down than [Polynesians] in the scale of evolution," such as "the Balonda and other African tribes," there is "a genuine sentiment of comradeship beginning to assert itself [emphasis mine]" (202). Footnotes refer readers to the Africa volume of the *Natural History of Man* and to Livingstone's *Expedition to the Zambesi* (302n). If, Carpenter's logic goes, homosexuality is even in Africa, and if, as he says later, homogenic customs "have prevailed among many semi-barbaric races on the threshold of civilisation," it must be everywhere (225).

Later in *The Intermediate Sex,* Carpenter cites the development of homogenic love among the "Dorian Greeks or the Polynesian Islanders or the Albanian Mountaineers, or any of the other notably hardy races among whom this affection has been developed" as disproof of Krafft-Ebing's opinion that "there is generally some neurosis or degeneration of a nerve-centre, or inherited tendency in that direction, associated with the instinct (60). It is instead, he argues, an original human trait—a universal truth—a fact that is, following racist science that says Africans are an older and thus more primary race than Europeans, best shown by African and Polynesian examples.

Carpenter's *Intermediate Sex* also has a companion piece: *Intermediate Types among Primitive Folk* (1914). In this later work, as in the former, Carpenter seeks to show that European homosexuals "might possibly fulfil a positive and useful function" (247). Again Carpenter uses what he calls "primitive" examples as sources of human truth about homosexuality. He cites evidence that among primitive groups, homosexuals have often held positions of high social regard because they were believed to have highly developed spiritual, artistic, and magical powers. And he argues that these primitive examples are valuable for contemporary British society because "the germ" of "late and high developments" in the "slow evolution of society" has often been "indicated . . . in primitive stages" (*Intermediate Types* 276). His examples of this "germ" of truth for contemporary society, based largely on travel writings of the sixteenth, seventeenth, and eighteenth centuries, include tribes "in the neighborhood of the Behring's Straits—the Kamchadales, the Chukchi, Aleuts, Inoits, Kadiak islanders, and so forth" (250), other North American Indians including the Illinois, Sioux, Sacs, Fox, Modoc, Louisiana, Florida, Yucatan, and Pueblo Indians (253–255), Pacific Islanders (255), the Syrians (256–258), the Negroes of the Slave Coast of West Africa (258), people throughout China, Japan, and much of Malaysia (259), the priestly castes from Mesopotamia to Peru (200), ancient Scandinavians, and the Konyagas in Alaska (261), Morocco (262), Pelew islanders, the Sea Dyaks of Borneo, the Bugis of South Celebes, the Patagonians of South America, people of Madagascar and Congo, more American Indians including Sauks, Foxes, Mandans, Crows, Blackfeet, Dakotas, Assiniboins, and Grenada (263–264), the Tsecats of Madagascar (274), and the Areoi of Polynesia (275).

On the very first page of the introduction to *Intermediate Types,* Carpenter asserts that people who are congenitally between man and woman—intermediate types—exist "in considerable abundance in all ages and among all races of the world" (247). But again the logic that underlies his work is that this ubiquity, as well as the possibility that homosexuality is correlated with highly developed spiritual and artistic capacities, is best shown by cross-racial comparisons and examples from groups he categorizes as primitive. The point I want to emphasize here is that each sexologist, despite significant differences in the argument each makes about homosexuality, makes his argument about white middle-class European homosexuality against a backdrop of reference to uncivilized peoples, lower races, lower classes, savages, and geographies outside of Western Europe. The sexual gauge against which European homosexuality is held is an imagined, and naturally superior and/or naturally inferior, primitive being.

Degeneracy

This discourse linking figurations of blackness and homosexuality is embedded in a much larger network of discourses about degeneracy and contamination. In his discussion of modern and postmodern cultures, Andreas Huyssen argues that the defining characteristic of modernism is "an anxiety of contamination" by mass culture (vii). Also discussing modern culture, David Theo Goldberg claims that degeneration is the binding principle in a set of allied terms such as corruption, pollution, purity, gentrification, and cleanliness—terms which are common to historical and present-day racist expression. It is not, he argues, that "these terms bear the same connotation whenever and wherever they have occurred" (*Racist Culture* 200). (And he speaks variously about situations specific to the United States and British, European, and African locations.) But because the terms are conceptually general, malleable, and parasitic, they can "reflect prevailing social discourse at a specific time and place" but also influence the character of variously located discourses (Goldberg, *Racist Culture* 200).

According to Goldberg, in the nineteenth century, degeneracy was a central concept to discourses defining sex, nation, and race. A "Native" or "Negro" displaced from his or her "proper or normal class, national, or ethnic positions" would generate pathologies—slums, criminality, poverty, alcoholism, prostitution, disease, insanity. These pathologies, "if allowed to transgress the social norms would pollute the (white) body politic and at the extreme bring about racial extinction" (*Racist Culture* 200). Although Goldberg fails to include a discussion of lesbianism or male homosexuality in his analysis, it is important to note that the criminality and prostitution that he discusses as imagined products of the displacement of the "Native" or" Negro" out of his or her "proper . . . positions" were often cloaked references to lesbianism. While it is an often-repeated truism that lesbianism has been mostly ignored by criminal justice systems even when male homosexuality brings convictions and harsh sentencing, Ruthann Robson argues that working-class women and women of color were prosecuted for lesbianism in the 1920s and 1930s in England. However, officials maintained a legal fiction that lesbianism did not exist by naming the charges, ambiguously, "crimes against chastity," "lewd and lascivious behavior," or prostitution (Robson 31–32).

Also, if not explicitly about lesbianism, the late Victorian debate about feminism and New Woman fiction also formed part of the wider discourse on degeneracy. Ann Heilmann writes that hysteria, the quintessentially female disorder of the nineteenth century, "was at once a 'normal' correlative of the female body with its strange fluids and cycles, and yet a symptom of an 'abnormal' development, manifesting itself as a sexual and/or mental disorder: lack of compliance *or* lack of restraint" (46). This included women who refused or were too enthusiastic about marital sex, were "addicted" to masturbation, or insisted on having male educations and political rights. Heilmann writes that "in their consummate challenge to social and sexual norms, the feminist and the gay man, the New Woman writer and the decadent artist seem perfectly complementary representations of the subversive politics of the *fin de siècle*" (46–47).

Annie Coombes discusses a similar, specifically imperialist, use of the concept of degeneracy in art history. Degeneracy, as a theme, she argues, was central to British Empire Exhibitions such as the one Virginia Woolf attended at Wembley in 1924.[11] Ethnographic exhibits were designed, Coombes argues, to reconcile the contradiction between the idea that the

Benin bronzes, for instance, had high aesthetic value and the idea that African societies were basically savage and in need of civilizing intervention. The cultures of the artists who produced the bronzes were characterized as once-great societies that had degenerated. This discourse on degeneracy circulated with particular persistency in Britain because it was also simultaneously being used "as the basis of a critique of European colonisation in West Africa by West Africans" (Coombes 38). Degeneracy results, critics of colonization argued, when Africans take up the "vices rather than the virtues of civilization"; coastal races who had had more prolonged contact with Europeans were said to have suffered the most serious deteriorations (39).

Lucy Bland and Jeffrey Weeks both discuss degeneracy as a central term in the late nineteenth- and early twentieth-century debate about sexuality. Middle-class women were said to be causing race degeneracy and inviting the decay of the imperial race when they did not have children. Poor women, weak women, unfit women—from alcoholics to prostitutes and criminals—were said to cause degeneracy of the imperial race when they did reproduce (Bland). Racial degeneracy was key to nineteenth- and twentieth-century discussions specifically about homosexuality, as well. While sexologists such as Havelock Ellis aimed to soften legal and social attitudes toward male homosexuality, environmentalist notions of corruption or degeneration such as Krafft-Ebing's flourished alongside less condemnatory congenital theories. The corruption of youth in terms of the decay of empire was a central theme. In the 1880s, for instance, the Reverend J. M. Wilson, headmaster of Clifton College, wrote, "Rome fell; other nations have fallen; and if England falls it will be this sin, and her unbelief in God, that will have been her ruin" (Weeks, *Coming Out* 107). "Sin" here referred to masturbation, but masturbation, Weeks argues, especially in the context of the public school, was intimately linked to male homosexuality. Weeks argues that such moralisms were also commonplaces of early twentieth-century culture. In the early 1900s, for instance, Sidney and Beatrice Webb made connections between homosexuality and national decay. The open practice of homosexuality in China "was proof, for them, of the degeneracy of the Chinese. Beatrice Webb visited numerous 'boys' homes' for male prostitutes while in China in 1911, and commented in her diary in typical fashion: 'it is the rottenness of physical and moral character that makes one despair of China—their constitution seems devastated by drugs and abnormal sexual indulgence. They are essentially an unclean race'" (Weeks, *Coming Out* 19).

With regard to lesbianism in particular, Linda Hart shows that lesbianism among white women enters historical discourse as the product of taint and intrusion in a 1921 juridical decision. Based on the idea, suggested by sexological writings, that homosexuality, including lesbianism (though lesbianism is much less directly discussed than male homosexuality) was common among dark-skinned and working-class women, British legislators in 1921 opposed the institution of legal sanctions against lesbian sexuality. They reasoned as follows: lesbianism was better left unmentioned since 999 of 1,000 "women" had probably never heard of such behaviors, but would be tainted by exposure to them if lesbianism were explicitly prohibited (Hart 4). The legislators were afraid, specifically, of "taint" and "suspicion" being "imparted" into "the homes of this country" (Hart 4). Embedded in the logic of this decision is an identity for "woman" as simultaneously distinct from both lesbianism and dark-skinned or working-class women. In addition, lesbianism is constructed as that which, if not secreted, is liable to spread and contaminate others: contact with the displaced—the black, the criminal, the working-class—makes lesbians out of women (white, middle-class, feminine-looking non-lesbians by definition).[12]

The combination of these histories does not add up to a simple equation between figurations of blackness or degeneracy and lesbianism in either the United States or England in any specific historical period. None of the theorists and historians I discuss above make that claim; nor do I want to make that claim about late nineteenth- and early twentieth-century British or U.S. cultures or about the authors I am studying. And I must emphasize that by the 1930s, Woolf and Warner were strongly resisting prohibitions and censorship of homosexuality and lesbianism, including censorship based on rhetorical linkages between homosexuality and decay. However, lesbianism and male homosexuality, blackness, disease, criminality, working-class status, taint, pollution, and prostitution coexist as multiple features of the trope of degeneracy in the imbricated discourses of sex, race, and nation in the nineteenth and twentieth centuries in both England and the United States. They are linked as locations for the "displacement of deviant sexuality" away from "the worlds where [white legislators of turn-of-the-century England] wished to keep their wives and daughters" (Hart 4). And they are linked, as well, in writings that aimed to soften attitudes toward male homosexuality and/or lesbianism by showing that homosexuality was prevalent in the Sotadic Zone. In brief, race science was also sex science, and visa versa. Because of these linkages, when a dark or working-class body is figured as the embodiment of sexuality, and when such figures show up alongside white middle-class female bodies, it is useful to wonder if and how lesbianism is also being figured.

Three

Olive Schreiner and the Late Victorian New Woman

Olive Schreiner (1855–1920) was an English South African[1] whose novels, political tracts, short stories, dreams, allegories, and letters are all principled, passionate, and also contradictory efforts to advance the cause of human freedom. Her early novels, including *The Story of an African Farm* (1883), written while she was in her teens and twenties working as a governess,[2] develop themes about women's emancipation, a cause for which she never stopped writing thoughtful, analytic, and influential prose. Later writings promote the cause of an integrated South African society based on racial and sexual equality and freedom. Her allegorical novel *Trooper Peter Halket* (1897), for instance, criticizes European immigrants who seek to extract wealth from South Africa by using Africans as an expendable labor force. The villain of the novel is a character modeled after Cecil Rhodes, who Schreiner condemns for waging wars of expansion against the Boers and for antiblack violence. Schreiner was interested in Rhodes when she first met him, but she became an outspoken critic of his politics as he continuously advocated aggression against the Boers, sought to justify such violence in the name of protecting black Africans, but also backed antiblack policies such as the Strop Bill of 1891, which made it legal for European diggers to beat African laborers.

By the end of her life, Schreiner had begun to address her own racism as part of her effort to combat racism in white South African society. In *Thoughts on South Africa* (1923) she writes, "I started in life with as much insular prejudice and racial pride as it is given to any citizen who has never left the little Northern Island to possess. . . . I cannot remember a time when I was not profoundly convinced of the superiority of the English, their government and their manners, over all other peoples." To illustrate the degree to which she disliked blacks as a child, she describes a girlhood fantasy in which she is Queen Victoria and orders "all black people in South Africa to be collected and put into the desert of Sahara, and a wall built across Africa shutting it off" (*Thoughts* 15–16). Her feeling was so strong, she says, that as queen in her fantasy she would have cut off the heads of any who tried to return across the wall. As an adult working against racism, however, she builds the pervasiveness of such feeling among white South Africans into her program for creating a just South Africa. She argues that the best an English South African can do is "treat [the black man] as if we love him: and in time the love may come" (361). She acted on her own resolution in 1908 when she resigned from the Women's Enfranchisement League, of which she was vice president, because they published an announcement that their "object" was women's enfranchisement "on the same terms as men" which would deny black women and men the vote (First and Scott 261–264).

As passionately as Schreiner advocated for a more just South African society, however, her social analyses remained firmly grounded in Victorian assumptions that humanity was divided into more- and less-developed races, with development equaling superior knowledge as well as superior capacity for knowledge. *From Man to Man, or Perhaps Only,* a novel she worked on all her life, envisioned alliance between black and white women based on equal rights and equal humanity. But her vision of this alliance, as described in both *From Man to Man* and *Thoughts on South Africa,* is based on presumptions of English racial superiority. The "doctrine of equal rights" and a fierce determination to defend freedom, she argues, are particularly English racial characteristics (*Thoughts* 360). Hence, racially advanced, intellectually superior, English women have a responsibility to help less-developed others rise to the highest capacity of their race. She writes, "We are here to endeavour to raise them as far as it is possible; we are determined to make them a seed-ground in which to sow all that is greatest and best in ourselves" (361). She is writing here specifically to persuade an English audience not to back violent and racist policies, such as Rhodes's, that would eventually lead to the Anglo-Boer war, which she worked hard to prevent. But she is also reflecting Victorian notions about human racial divisions that were an entrenched if contradictory part of her vision of the world.

Contradictions and paradoxes such as those that characterize Schreiner's beliefs about race figure largely and variously in her contributions to late Victorian discourse about freedom in sexuality. Schreiner was a lifelong friend and correspondent of two of the sexologists discussed earlier. In 1884,[3] Havelock Ellis began the correspondence with Schreiner by writing to Ralph Iron, the pseudonym under which Schreiner had recently published *The Story of an African Farm,* saying how much he had enjoyed the novel. A few months later, Schreiner and Ellis met Edward Carpenter at a meeting of the Fellowship of the New Life, a social renovation organization founded on communal principles out of which the Fabian Society grew.[4] Schreiner corresponded with both men for nearly forty years about questions central to the intellectual lives of all three—questions related to sex, gender, women's emancipation, and modernity.[5] She was also friends with and had high regard for two women—Betty Molteno and Alice Greene—who lived together as "partners," in Schreiner's own words. Despite these friendships, however, and despite her friendships with Ellis and Carpenter, arguably the two most outspoken scholars of homosexuality of their generation in England (Schreiner could not have known Carpenter, in particular, without having known that he was a proud and outspoken lover of men), Schreiner leaves very little direct reference to homosexuality in any of her extant writings, either public or private.[6] Joyce Berkman explains that as a woman without scientific credentials Schreiner would have risked a great deal of social censure had she spoken in detail about sexual behavior of any kind, or made reference to homosexuality (153–154). A 1914 letter to Ellis supports the claim that Schreiner would have avoided reference to homosexuality over concern for her reputation, and suggests that she worried about Ellis's reputation, too, despite his scientific credentials. While Ellis was working on revisions to *Sexual Inversions,* Schreiner wrote, "Dear, I hope you won't get mixed up with any of these inverted peoples['] affairs. People may not understand you are studying these things merely scientifically" (Draznin 486–487). Berkman may be right that Schreiner avoided mentioning homosexuality to avoid censure. My impression from Schreiner's writing, however, including fiction, letters, and nonfiction, is that she simply wasn't very interested in discussing homosexuality, and certainly not interested enough to do so at the risk of undermining her authority to speak on her more constant and passionate concerns, which were ensuring women's freedom in work, education, and sexual relations with men. She wrote vehemently against prostitution and equally vehemently in favor of freely chosen, fulfilling, sexual relations for women in the context of monogamous marriage.[7]

Nonetheless, to add to the layers of contradiction that characterize Schreiner's work, I argue that, no less than Ellis and Carpenter, Schreiner made significant if indirect contributions to public discourse about homosexuality as well as to discourse about autonomous, freely chosen heterosexuality for women. Lyndall, from *The Story of an African Farm,* is hailed as one of the earliest New Women to appear in fiction; late Victorian and subsequent public discussion of the New Woman—feminist and antifeminist alike—often conflated the New Woman with the lesbian and paired her with the New Man—variously effeminate, inverted, and/or degenerate. As feminists of the early 1900s became increasingly vocal about education, suffrage, and the sexual double standard, Havelock Ellis and Edward Carpenter, among other English sexologists, increasingly believed that the women's movement was encouraging acquired female inversion (Bland 264). Carroll Smith-Rosenberg writes that by 1900, medical men, sex reformers, and educators had labeled the New Woman as a "secretly and dangerously sexualized figure. Her social liminality was rooted in sexual inversion. She belonged to an 'intermediate sex.' She embodied the unnatural and the monstrous. She was a 'Mannish Lesbian.'"[8] The New Woman delineated by Schreiner—a woman who passionately sought education, economic independence, and sexual autonomy—may have been heterosexual as Schreiner imagined her, but she passed into public discourse as a lesbian in the years immediately following the publication of *The Story of an African Farm.*

Moreover, contradictions at the center of Schreiner's beliefs about race also shape her contributions to late Victorian discourse about freedom in sexuality. The ideal, sexually autonomous New Woman figure of Schreiner's prose is built on her contradictory beliefs about freedom and human racial divisions. As Ellis and Carpenter, among others, wrote to delineate the boundaries of the homosexual against a backdrop of references to uncivilized peoples, lower races, lower classes, savages, and geographies outside of Western Europe, Schreiner defined her European New Women and Men against a backdrop of southern African people whom she thought of as old—including, in her terms, the "races" Bushmen, Hottentot, Bantu, and Boer. This reliance on black and Boer figures to do metaphorical work in arguments about gender relations among Europeans is one expression of Schreiner's consistent belief in European—particularly English—racial superiority. My argument in this chapter is that Schreiner uses African figures to define an ideal modernity for European women and men. In her nonfiction works *Woman and Labor* and *Thoughts on South Africa,* European women, including Schreiner herself, become modern New Women by taking the role of scientific observer in relationships with African women. In the novel *The Story of an African Farm,* African figures are essential to the delineation of Waldo's and Lyndall's European newness. New Women and Men are not African themselves—indeed, in making New Women *like* Africans, they are, syntactically at least, *not* African; but Schreiner's representations of New Women and Men are dependent on proximity to Africans. Despite her efforts to address her own racism and to promote freedom for all elements of South African society, Schreiner, in all her work, uses African people and the southern African landscape rhetorically, as the raw material with which to construct a misbehaving, forward-thinking, sexually autonomous, intellectually advanced race of New European Women and Men capable of leading humanity into the modern age.

Both Schreiner and this figure of the New Woman strongly influenced the feminism of the early twentieth century and would have informed Virginia Woolf's, Willa Cather's, and Sylvia Townsend Warner's thinking about gender, sexuality, and women's roles and work. *The Story of an African Farm* was a best seller in the 1880s when it was newly published, and it meant a great deal to feminist readers (Lerner 67). Yaffa Claire Draznin calls it "the first British novel whose protagonist was openly and unabashedly feminist in the 20th century mode" (3). Virginia Woolf admired *The Story of an African Farm* and claimed that Schreiner "won fame and popularity enough to gratify the most ambitious" with that first novel ("Olive

Schreiner" 181). *Woman and Labor* was also celebrated by several generations of feminists. Vera Brittain writes that to her mother's generation, the
suffragists of 1911, the emancipation tract "sounded as insistent and inspir-
ing as a trumpet call summoning the faithful to an urgent crusade"; it was
known as "the Bible of the Women's Movement" to Brittain's own generation.[9] Partly because of this influence on feminists, who were interested in
exploring possibilities for sexual autonomy for women in particular, including homoerotic possibilities, Schreiner's arguments about New Womanhood
supplement sexological delineations of the homosexual (usually a man) in
terms of figurations of blackness. Built as they are upon claims of affiliation between so-called Old and New Women, Schreiner's works, together
with sexological literature, help produce the structure of imagination on
which writers such as Woolf, Warner, and Cather, among others, developed
Sapphic primitivism as one of their metaphoric and aesthetic tools for representing female homoerotics in their narratives. I emphasize that this version of women's freedom is contrary to many versions of feminism, built as
it is on the perpetual existence of black women and men as static, natural,
emblems of freedom. One of the dangers of this structure of imagination is
that it denies real racist violence perpetrated against people of color. I discuss it here neither to resuscitate nor to critique Schreiner, but in order to
understand her work as part of the history of the production of overlap between the figures of the black and of the homosexual.

Women "Old" and "New"

Schreiner's use of African figures to define European New Womanhood is most explicit in *Woman and Labor* (1911) and the posthumously
published *Thoughts on South Africa* (1927). Although both were written
later than *The Story of an African Farm,* I discuss them first because looking at Schreiner's explicit delineations of New Womanhood makes her use
of figurations of blackness in the less explicit, fictional representations of
New Womanhood stand out more clearly. In both *Woman and Labor* and
Thoughts on South Africa, Schreiner's arguments rely on "inventions" described in retrospect by Ann McClintock as panoptical time, anachronistic space, and the family of man—ideological, regulatory "technologies"
central to late Victorian discourse about empire. McClintock describes panoptical time, well established by the end of the eighteenth century, as

"progress consumed at a glance" (39). Panoptical time makes scientific racism visual in images that enable European observers to imagine that they "see" the progress of global history in single images that fuse culture with nature. These images are of an evolutionary family tree of man with branches representing racial stages in the progress toward Aryan, the most advanced human type. In late Victorian discourse about empire, this family tree was accompanied by other visual assertions of panoptical time—graphics in which racially-inscribed, single male heads represent sequential epochs in the progress of human development, the culminating racial type always being the European *Homo sapiens.* These graphics marshal "the world's discontinuous cultures" into "a single, European Ur-narrative" (McClintock 37). In addition, McClintock points out, evolutionary time presented in images of all male heads is a "time without women" (39). This paradox of all-male evolution is addressed by the additional invention of anachronistic space, "an administrative and regulatory technology" that "reached full authority in the late Victorian era" and "projects the colonized, women and the working class onto anachronistic space: prehistoric, atavistic, and irrational" (40). Women, the colonized, and the working class do not inhabit history; instead, they exist in a permanently anterior time within the geography of the modern empire as anachronistic humans, the living embodiment of the archaic "primitive." Hence, anthropologists and travelers can imagine that by moving across the globe they can see across time to prior stages of human development. For Schreiner and many others of her era, including Freud and the sexologists discussed earlier, the European past is evident in the African present. Furthermore, the authority to thus interpret anachronistic space is restricted to those at the most progressive edge of time. These ideas pervaded Victorian sciences and discourse to the degree that critics of the abuses of imperialism grounded their arguments in such progress narratives as consistently as did proponents of imperial expansion.

In both *Woman and Labor* and *Thoughts on South Africa,* Schreiner relies on the technologies of anachronistic space and the family of man in her efforts to advance the cause of women's freedom. Establishing new and egalitarian relations between men and women based on freedom, she argues, is the only route to healthy development of the "race," by which she means, in this case, all of humanity.[10] Both *Woman and Labor* and

Thoughts on South Africa tell progress narratives in which the most developmentally advanced, eugenically sound New Woman is a modern European who is somehow similar to a contemporary African woman, or to a European woman of the historical past. Schreiner pairs these progress narratives with threats about racial degeneracy. The most advanced point of human progress is characterized by freedom for women; alternately, she threatens, denying women's freedom is a sure route to degeneracy. Most significantly, the New Woman is not an African herself; she is a European with a special capacity to take the gender equality Schreiner thinks is characteristic of so-called old races and work it into the modern, technologically advanced social order. Similarly, in both *Woman and Labor* and *Thoughts on South Africa,* Schreiner seeks to establish her authority to speak about contemporary European women by positioning herself as an expert who observes and analyzes African women.

Woman and Labor is a short volume—more pamphlet than book—that challenges women to fight for an equal share in the meaningful labor of society, as well as education that suits them for such labor, and wages in exchange for their work. New Women of today, Schreiner cries, "claim . . . all labor for our province! Those large fields in which it would appear sex plays no part, and equally those in which it plays a part" (203). Only under conditions of equality in labor, she argues, can society progress securely and healthfully into the modern age. Furthermore, in modern society in which so much of the work is intellectual, nothing except backward thinking bars women from participating fully in the work of society. The crux of Schreiner's argument for equality in labor in this pamphlet is a cautionary anti-progress, or degeneracy, narrative about the ways labor and gender relations have changed over time. She begins with "first man," a "savage" in whose society women and men labored free together and "were contented!"[11] Technological advances in agriculture, industry, and warfare, however, have left more and more men increasingly free from the need to make war and hunt, and thus also freed them to take over more of what previously had been women's work. As a result, Schreiner argues, the role of women has become increasingly limited: more and more often, women can live parasitically off of men in exchange for women's sexual function. Such sex parasitism has reached a crisis point in modern society, she warns, and threatens the virility of men and women alike.

While Schreiner's obvious focus and concern in *Woman and Labor* is the progress, degeneracy, and parasitism of European societies, African figures are key to her argument. Just as many of the sexologists had done, Schreiner authorizes her study of European gender relations by beginning, in her introduction, with references to contemporary African geography and people. Following the assumptions of anachronistic space and panoptical time, these references are designed to assert the originality, legitimacy, and purity of her knowledge about sexual matters because they are the earliest examples of relations between the sexes. She doesn't give any detailed material about African societies; rather she refers to such material by describing another book she started as a youth, but which was destroyed during the Anglo-Boer war. The destroyed book included several chapters about the "differences of sex function" from their "earliest appearances in plants and animals," material she gathered as "child" when she "wandered alone in the African bush and watched cock-o-veets singing their inter-knit love-songs, and small singing birds building their nests together, and caring for and watching over, not only their young, but each other" (*Woman and Labor* 4). Other chapters she describes from the destroyed book are on human behavior in "the most primitive, the savage and semi-savage states" of the "native African women in the primitive society" around her (5). Schreiner thus asserts her authority to speak about contemporary sexual matters among Europeans by asserting that she has knowledge of Africa and Africans. That she was a child when she began to gather this information further assures readers of the purity of her insights. Also by taking the role of scientific observer of African life, and thus positioning herself as superior to the objects of study, she fends off potential challenges to her authority based on the fact that she is a woman as well as an African herself.

This introduction to *Woman and Labor* also positions African women's untutored genius as both the intellectual origins of the modern women's movement and the justification for it—proof of the potentially salubrious effect on humanity of observing African life and straining those observations through the filter of a European analysis. Schreiner writes that speaking to a "Kaffir woman still in her untouched primitive condition made a more profound impression on [her] mind than any but one other incident connected with the position of woman has ever done" (5). This "woman of genius" eloquently described the subjection of women of her race with a "stern and almost majestic attitude of acceptance of the inevitable." The conversation, claims Schreiner, "forced upon me the fact, which I have since come to regard as almost axiomatic, that the women of no race or class will ever rise in revolt or attempt to bring about a revolutionary readjustment of their relation to their society, however intense their suffering and however clear their perception of it, while the welfare and persistence of their society requires their submission." From this it also follows "that, wherever there is a general attempt on the part of the women of any society to readjust their position to it, a close analysis will always show that the changed or changing conditions of that society have made woman's acquiescence no longer necessary or desirable" (6–7). This anecdote reveals Schreiner's assumption that information universally applicable to all women is available (even to an audience who has to have that information "forced" upon them) from an African source. Furthermore, such information also proves the soundness of the modern women's movement. The women's movement wouldn't be happening if it were not to the benefit of society because women by nature, she knows from listening to a so-called primitive woman, will not act in ways that are not to the advantage of their people as a group. Additionally, the New Woman is not new at all. Rather, "we who lead in this movement to-day are of that Old Teutonic womanhood, which twenty centuries ago plowed its march through European forests and morasses beside its male companion" (146). The old woman who is celebrated as a model, here, is a historically old European woman. Schreiner's introductory material implies, however, that this old European woman's counterpart is the contemporary African woman who, while terribly oppressed by the forces of colonialism and by the men of her society, labors meaningfully for her people. Both the primitive, old European and the present-day African are the models for the European New Woman who wants to participate in modern society as fully and productively as her ancient European sisters and her contemporary African sisters, in their respective premodern societies.

Many of the ideas Schreiner first develops in *Woman and Labor* become kernels for ideas she takes up again in her much longer work, *Thoughts on South Africa,* although the latter book is not directly about questions of gender, labor, and equality. Organized as a series of portraits of the elements of South African society, *Thoughts on South Africa* begins with a brief

introduction about the distinct native "races" of southern Africa, an opening structure mirroring that of *Woman and Labor.* "The Hottentots," are the
"eternal children of the human race" (107). The South African Bushmen
are "not so much a race of children as a race caught in the very act of evolving into human form" (108). The Bantus are the most developed and "in
place of [the Bushman's] childlike abandon have a proud reserve" (110).
Her descriptions make a verbal version of a graph of panoptical time in
which individual heads represent different epochs of human development.
These descriptions serve, in the context of the larger book, to emphasize
Schreiner's colonial Englishness rather than her femaleness, and thus grant
her the authority to speak about Europeans in the rest of the book, which
culminates with a chapter on the Englishman. As an author who analyzes
all so-called races beginning with the first, or oldest, Schreiner takes a position among the most developed, or newest, race despite the fact that, in
the context of anachronistic space, the most developed race is male.

Schreiner's description of Boer society as peaceful and just, much longer
than her introductory descriptions of black African groups, develops her
idea that the New European woman is similar to the Old. The crux of her
argument is that Boer men and women have egalitarian gender relations
because their labor is equally necessary for the survival of the Boers as a
people. Boer women farm and fight alongside their men; if they don't, as
all concerned are aware, the whole group is likely to die. This is in turn
because, Schreiner believes, the race of Boers are stuck developmentally
in the seventeenth century—a lack of development which is really to their
credit given the fact that they are Europeans in Africa. The only alternative
to their determinedly staying-put developmentally, Schreiner argues, would
have been to slide backward toward the developmental level of the African
races who have surrounded them since they first came from Europe. As a
result, Boers are not as intellectually advanced as they might be, she admits. But individuals from Boer families who move to urban areas and pursue education catch up to the modern era in one generation. This claim
contains echoes of her assertion, in *Woman and Labor,* that as European
societies have become technologically more developed and some parts of
the population have amassed wealth, the role of women in the meaningful
labor of society has shrunk. Not so for Boer women, however, because they
live in Africa in the same manner in which they lived in Europe of the sev-

enteenth century and fight and labor alongside their husbands as a matter of survival.

The point of the descriptions above is to show that for Schreiner, in both *Woman and Labor* and *Thoughts on South Africa,* African women provide the intellectual raw material of the European women's movement: African women provide evidence of human nature with regard to gender; African women are also inspirational models for New Womanhood. Significantly, African women are not positioned as the ones who will make the changes in gender relations that can bring humanity into the modern age. Both of Schreiner's books imply that the most important role for African women is to be preserved as they are in order to provide inspiration and knowledge for the race of European New Women who, largely because they can collect and interpret knowledge about Africans, can usher in a modern age based on freedom for women.

The New Woman in Fiction:
The Story of an African Farm

In the nonfiction prose works discussed above, Schreiner is explicit in her claim that New Women and Men are members of advanced societies who can learn equality from studying the so-called old races of Africa. Schreiner relies on the tropes of panoptical time and anachronistic space in order to define a position for New European Women outside of anachronistic space and, instead, alongside New Men at the modern edge of development. She also relies on and simultaneously speaks back to these tropes in positioning herself as an authority on the developmental levels of people around her. She puts herself, an English South African woman, at the apex of human development. She also partially undercuts the logic of anachronistic space by saying explicitly that the characteristics that make the New Women new are their similarities to the old women of anachronistic space, including the Boer and the Bushman. These ideas are also evident, if less explicit, as an aesthetic strategy for narrativizing new, modern womanhood and manhood in *The Story of an African Farm.* Schreiner's fictional New Women and New Men all have carefully delineated affiliations with old men and women.

The Story of an African Farm is above all else a critique of the Cape Colony society in which Schreiner grew up.[12] The novel has been described by many, including Schreiner herself, as realist rather than romantic. Schreiner's description of her process of creating the novel points to attempts to produce realism as an antithesis to romance. She writes in her preface to the novel:

> It has been suggested by a kind of critic that he would better have liked the little book if it had been a history of wild adventure; of cattle driven into inaccessible "dranzes" by Bushmen; "of encounters with ravening lions, and hair-breath escapes." This could not be. Such works are best written in Picadilly or in the Strand: there the gifts of the creative imagination untrammelled by contact with any face, may spread their wings.
>
> But, should one sit down to paint the scenes among which he has grown, he will find that the facts creep in upon him. Those brilliant phases and shapes which the imagination sees in far-off lands are not for him to portray. Sadly he must squeeze the colour from his brush, and dip it into the grey pigments around him. He must paint what lies around him. (29–30)

The "grey" and grim reality that seems to "lie around" Schreiner, all the more evident in the context of her explicit claims about Old and New Women discussed above, is a degenerate and degenerating version of the family of man; each member of this degenerating family is simultaneously visible in the portrait Schreiner sets in the anachronistic space of the Cape Colony.

Waldo and Lyndall are the most developed forms of humanity in *The Story of an African Farm*. Free-thinking, independent Lyndall wishes bitterly to be "born in the future" when "perhaps, to be born a woman will not be to be born branded" (188). Waldo, the inventive, philosophical, skeptical son of the kind but excessively pious and gullible German overseer, is Lyndall's male counterpart. They sympathize with one another: Lyndall kisses Waldo's "bare shoulder with her soft little mouth" to comfort him after a beating, also telling him "we will not be children always; we shall have the power too, some day" (127). Waldo is the person to whom Lyndall turns to explain her bitterness over the scope of women's opportunities. The world tells men, "Work!" she explains, but tells women, "Seem!" (188). In response, he encourages her to "speak," to try to usher in "that new time [that] will be so great" (195). Like Lyndall, Waldo also yearns for knowledge and books. As a man, he can wander safely, Lyndall tells him (189–

190). But his access to learning is complicated by his dependence as a poor man on the wealthy. He does wander and work, eventually returning to the farm to tell Lyndall what he has seen of the world. But Lyndall does not survive her similar pursuit of freedom. She wastes away of no particular cause shortly after she gives birth out of wedlock. Waldo's experiences don't serve him well either. He dies of no particular malady, unless it is grief, a strong young man enjoying a rest in the warm sun after labor. These deaths at the end of the novel form the critique Schreiner makes of the Cape Colony: New Women and New Men are more developed forms of humanity than can thrive in the society in which they are located. As Cherry Clayton writes, together, Waldo and Lyndall "would be complete, but in the imperfect world to which the novel is faithful, that completeness is not attained" (24). Perhaps most tragically in the context of the novel, the deaths of Waldo and Lyndall leave the rest of society with no model for development. Cross-dressing Gregory Rose vacillates between man and woman and shows some potential to become a New Man in the right circumstance. He is the most round character in the entire novel: contact with Lyndall changes his dependency and self-indulgence into a capacity to nurse another. But once Lyndall is gone, his future in Cape Colony society, like Lyndall's cousin Em's, contains little promise for continuing development.

The characters who thrive, by contrast, are the cruel, usurping materialists Tant' Sannie and Bonaparte Blenkins. Schreiner poses them as the degenerate parents of a degenerating South African human family. When Bonaparte first arrives on the farm, he stands outside a domestic scene looking on. Tant' Sannie stands on the "door-step" with black servants posed as children: "At her feet sat the yellow Hottentot maid, her satellite, and around stood the black Kaffir maids." The "old German overseer" is at the "center of the group" but he commands no patriarchal authority. Rather, "all eyes were fixed" on the "newcomer," Bonaparte, who himself "ever and anon . . . cast a glance . . . to the spot where the Boer-woman stood, and smiled faintly" (51). Subsequently, Bonaparte, as usurping patriarch, falsely accuses Waldo's father of theft and gets Tant' Sannie to expel him from the farm. In the scene of the confrontation, Bonaparte, Tant' Sannie, and the "lean Hottentot maid" are again posed as a family in a domestic scene, but this time Bonaparte has fully taken the place of patriarch. Schreiner writes, "Tant' Sannie stood before the steps of the kitchen;

upon them sat the lean Hottentot, upon the highest stood Bonaparte Blenkins, both hands folded under the tails of his coat, and his eyes fixed on the sunset sky" (89). Tant' Sannie is a powerful figure here, but Bonaparte stands at the head of this corrupt and corrupting family. The Hottentot maid still sits at their feet as if a child. Lyndall, Em, and Waldo are positioned on the periphery. In the first scene all three are missing. In the second, Lyndall and Em stand by watching, impotent to intervene in the destruction of Waldo's father, who dies seemingly of heartbreak shortly after being dismissed.

As the novel progresses, Bonaparte and Tant' Sannie grow stronger. True to his namesake, after failing to colonize Tant' Sannie and her farm, Bonaparte gets access to the resources of another even more wealthy farm by marrying a different unsuspecting woman. Tant' Sannie's success is figured on her expanding body. She is gluttonous and grotesque the first time she appears in the novel; she "roll[s] heavily in her sleep" and dreams bad dreams (35). Neither of two dead husbands is the source of her unrest, the narrator informs readers; instead, she dreams that one of "the sheep's trotters she had eaten for supper" was "stuck fast in her throat." Schreiner thus compares marriage to eating for Tant' Sannie, and both to wealth. As the novel progresses, Tant' Sannie indeed expands in girth, wealth, and husbands simultaneously. By the end of the novel, she has a new husband with many sheep; she is also so big at "two hundred and sixty pounds" that she is "not easily able to move" and has come to see her step-daughter Em probably "for the last time" (292).

The place of African characters in the family of man headed by grotesque, cruel, and materialist characters is, literally, at Tant' Sannie's feet. Dan Jacobson claims, in his 1995 introduction to the novel, that the black characters exist as "merely extras, supernumeraries, part of the background" in a novel that is really about the white people on the farm (25). But whether or not Schreiner is interested in the African characters explicitly, they are central to her critique of European Cape Colony society as she imagines it. Only by placing Africans as the children to Tant' Sannie and Bonaparte can Schreiner create the disgenic portrait of a family of man on which her critique of Cape Colony society rests. Moreover, the Hottentot maid, described as "lean" almost every time she appears, literally disappears from the novel as if Tant' Sannie has eaten her along with the pig's trotters that make her so heavy and also symbolize her wealth. Tant' Sannie has given birth to a child by her new husband as well, suggesting that in Schreiner's bleak vision, the South Africa of the future belongs to the obese Tant' Sannie and her progeny. African people—the old races of humanity—and variously choate modern European women and men, such as Gregory, Waldo, Lyndall, and possibly Em, alike are all equally threatened with extinction in the Cape Colony Schreiner describes. The only hope for the future, the novel suggests, is that what Tant' Sannie eats will continue to stick in her throat.

Schreiner's critique of Cape Colony society is not pro-African, although the critique depends on African figures. Rather, Africans in *The Story of an African Farm* are part of the hostile environment against which embryonic New Women and New Men have to struggle for existence. Paradoxically, however, African figures are also essential to the delineation of the newness of the enlightened white characters. Partly through their presence, Schreiner points out the artistry, rebelliousness, and independence of Waldo and Lyndall, the prototypes of emerging New Womanhood and New Manhood. Waldo's affiliation with the race of Bushmen points to his status as an embryonic New Man. Lyndall's principled, defiant New Womanhood is defined against a backdrop of quiet African rebellion against colonialism. In the context of the novel, defiance is an African racial characteristic; for Lyndall it is an Africanism through which she can develop a defiant, modern, European womanhood.

Waldo's affiliation with the Bushman is the most carefully spelled out connection between black and white characters in the novel. Waldo and an anonymous Bushman are the artists of the novel and also both evolutionary bridge figures. Just as the Bushman paints figures of animals on the walls of caves, Waldo carves sculptures of wood and makes a model of a shearing machine—an "invention" he dreams of eventually building on large scale. Neither artist can survive in the South Africa of the present specifically because they are developmentally out of sync with the landscape in which they live. The Bushman and his race, who Schreiner will later describe in *Thoughts on South Africa* as "a race caught in the very act of evolving into human form" (108), are becoming extinct, incapable of surviving the violent changes of colonialism. As the Bushman, according to Schreiner, is of a race between—a living bridge from animal to human, dying out when the more developed races overwhelm him—Waldo is a race between. He has developed beyond the level of both his gullible father and the cruel, materialist Bonaparte Blenkins and is capable of reinventing the future. His modernity is evident simultaneously in his interest in machines and in his sympathy with Lyndall's concerns about the inadequacy of women's education. In another place or a future time, the two might have been partners in their newness and brought a modern race of humanity into being. But the Cape Colony of the present is not ready for the New Man or the New Woman of the future.

Waldo is, importantly, not exactly the same as the Bushman; rather, they are of a type, with Waldo the more evolved example. Waldo understands the Bushman and can explain him to Lyndall, thus exhibiting the similarity between them and at the same time asserting his evolutionary superiority over the Bushman. He tells Lyndall,

> The little Bushmen lived here, so small and so ugly, and used to sleep in the wild dog holes, and eat snakes, and shot the bucks with their poisoned arrows. It was one of them, one of these old wild Bushmen, that painted those pictures there [cave drawings of animals that are nearly washed away.] He did not know why he painted but he wanted to make something, so he made these. He worked hard, very hard, to find the juice to make the paint; and then he found this place where the rocks hang over, and he painted them. To us they are only strange things, that make us laugh; but to him they were very beautiful. (49)

Waldo might be describing, here, the impulses and desires that prompt him to sculpt and to invent a shearing machine. Ridley Beeton argues that Waldo's description of the Bushmen's artistic creations "represents" the machine and the carving Waldo is to do later in the novel (42). The Bushman's drawings are laughed at by the children; Waldo's efforts to carve a scene of human striving for knowledge are similarly laughed at by the stranger passing by who sees the crudity of Waldo's carving but is kind nonetheless. Waldo's efforts are derided, as well, by the less kind Bonaparte Blenkins, who crushes the shearing machine with his boot. Waldo's newness is indicated by both his inventiveness and his ability to recognize the inventiveness of the Bushman and to respect it for what it was—a less developed, old race's effort at artistry that is also the antecedent of his own genius. That he names the Bushman as his predecessor, moreover, emphasizes his superiority, since he alone has the capacity and the authority to name the relationship between them.

Another Bushman in the novel also affirms the affiliation between himself and Waldo, although, again, it is Waldo and not the Bushman who has analytical language and can explain the nature of the alliance. In Waldo's last letter to Lyndall, he writes of getting drunk to ease the tedium and sleeplessness of life as a wagon driver and of being rescued by a Bushman. He explains, "When I woke up I was lying by a little bush on the bank of the river. It was afternoon; all the clouds had gone, and the sky was deep blue. The Bushman boy was grilling ribs at the fire. He looked at me, and grinned from ear to ear. 'Master was a little nice,' he said, 'and lay down in the road. Something might ride over master, so I carried him there.' He grinned at me again. It was as though he said, 'you and I are comrades. I have lain in a road too. I know all about it. '" (257).

Waldo thus acknowledges with the Bushman a camaraderie that at the same time asserts his difference. Schreiner has him report and analyze the Bushman's speech, and thus defines the superiority of his position. He throws away his liquor flask, in this scene, in an effort not to become the subject of another news report about a drunken carrier, killed when his wagon rolls over him. But finally, both Waldo and the Bushman are threatened with extinction—a tangible threat to humanity in Schreiner's worldview. In both *Thoughts on South Africa* and a 1896 letter, Schreiner argues that "we" should build a preserve for the Bushman such as Europeans have built for ancient breeds of cattle lest they become extinct (156; *Letters* 285). The Cape Colony society Schreiner describes in *The Story of an African Farm* has become, tragically, according to Schreiner, uninhabitable for the Bushman, who is the bridge figure between animal and human; but, equally tragically, that society has not yet become a place of modernity where Waldo can survive.

Similar to the way in which Schreiner defines Waldo's modernity by comparing him to the black South African race of Bushmen, she also defines Lyndall's defiant New Womanhood by comparing her defiance to the defiance of black South Africans against colonialism, including the quiet rebellions of Tant' Sannie's "lean Hottentot maid" and of two "Kaffir boys" who exist for only one scene in the beginning of the novel. These characters represent unprincipled, undiscriminating defiance that requires no analysis and has no anticolonial effect. None of the European characters surrounding Lyndall defies authority; the black African characters, however, whose perspective is evident only through a few glimpses, are defiance embodied. Lyndall has what Schreiner would later, in *Woman and Labor*, identify as a special capacity of only the most developed European members of the human race: she can take a quality—defiance—that Schreiner sees as naturally characteristic of old races and improve it by working it into a modern social order.

Schreiner first introduces the theme of defiance into the novel in a scene involving "two Kaffir boys" who quietly rebel against colonial authority in the form of Waldo's father. Schreiner writes, "He [Waldo's father] stood out at the Kraals in the blazing sun, explaining to two Kaffir boys the approaching end of the world. The boys, as they cut the cakes of dung winked at each other, and worked as slowly as they possibly could; but the German never saw it" (38–39). Schreiner follows this moment of resistance on the part of Kaffir boys with a similar scene involving Tant' Sannie's "lean Hottentot maid." This maid also defies the German overseer when Tant' Sannie is accusing him of being a thief. In desperation, the naive, benevolent, overseer turns to the Hottentot for help, thinking "*she* was his friend; she would tell him kindly the truth" [emphasis in the original]. The maid responds, however, with a "loud, ringing laugh" and encourages Tant' Sannie to "give it him, old misses! Give it him!" Schreiner adds a line of analysis from the Hottentot's perspective in this example, thus giving the Hottentot more agency than she gives the Kaffir boys. She writes, "It was nice to see the white man who had been master hunted down. The coloured woman laughed and threw a dozen mealie grains into her mouth to chew" (90). It is tempting to celebrate these two scenes as anticolonial elements of Schreiner's novel, as they hint at an African-centered world that includes an organized system of resistance to colonial rule. But Schreiner never takes up the issue of African resistance in a meaningful way. No events unfold from these initial moments of resistance. Very little political or social analysis is attributed to those who resist the German. Instead, the "Kaffir boys" and the "lean Hottentot maid" seem to resist the German as a matter of course, without principles that need to be elaborated, merely as a natural and static mode of behavior. By describing the characters in terms of their race and very little else, the narrative implies that their defiance is a function of biology rather than ideology. Even where Schreiner attributes an analytical anticolonial hatred of "the white man who had been master" to the Hottentot maid, the Hottentot's rebellion is an ineffective anticolonialism in the context of the novel. For the protagonists, it produces only harm: the death of Waldo's father and thus the loss of "the one home the girls [Lyndall and Em] had known for many a year" (54). Nor does the defiance interfere in any way with the tyrannical power of Tant' Sannie or Bonaparte, the real villains of the novel, or with their ability to continue to extract wealth from the labor of the Africans around them, which they both do with a vengeance through the end of the novel.

Moreover, Schreiner characterizes the defiance of the Hottentot as the unprincipled defiance of the naturally dependent—a dependence she might call parasitic were she talking about quiet defiance on the part of married European women such as those parasitic women she derides in *Woman and Labor.* When the Hottentot attacks the German, she risks nothing in scorning him because she follows Tant' Sannie, the real tyrant on the farm, in doing so. Sycophancy is the Hottentot's customary mode: she sits at Tant' Sannie's feet, a "satellite" (51), and persistently takes her cues from Tant' Sannie's behavior. When Bonaparte changes clothes and looks distinguished, making Tant' Sannie revise her initial impression of him, the Hottentot looks to Tant' Sannie in order to develop an opinion. Schreiner writes, "the Boer-woman looked at the Hottentot, and the Hottentot looked at the Boer-woman" (69). Similarly, when the Bible closed with a thud after Bonaparte's sermon, "Tant' Sannie loosened the white handkerchief about her neck and wiped her eyes, and the coloured girl, seeing her do so, sniffed" (73). In another scene, the Hottentot tells a lewd joke that flatters Tant' Sannie's vanity. Schreiner writes,

> "Here," said Tant' Sannie to her Hottentot maid, "I have been in this house four years, and never been up in the loft. Fatter women than I go up ladders; I will go up today and see what it is like, and put it to rights up there. You bring the little ladder, and stand at the bottom."

"There's one would be sorry if you were to fall," said the Hottentot maid, leering at Bonaparte's pipe, that lay on the table.

"Hold your tongue, jade," said her mistress, trying to conceal a pleased smile, "and go fetch the ladder." (128)

In none of these scenes does Schreiner expose the Hottentot's motives. Had she done so, I might be encouraged to believe that Schreiner is celebrating the Hottentot for having subversive politics and for working to ingratiate herself against a time when she might be a more powerfully rebellious force. But Schreiner does not credit the Hottentot with subversive intent, nor does the moral imperative of the novel acknowledge that there might be a place for covert rebellion. Instead, Schreiner derides both the Hottentot and Tant' Sannie, perhaps making them mirror images of one another's degeneracy, and celebrates only characters who are willing to make direct, head-on confrontations against tyrannical people and conventions. The defiance of the boys and the lean Hottentot exist not as an effort on Schreiner's part to celebrate covert anti-imperialism, but rather to introduce the theme of defiance that Schreiner can subsequently develop into a more principled, considered behavior in Lyndall.

Indeed, the scene in which the Hottentot laughs at seeing Waldo's father hunted down because he is "the white man who had been master" is also the scene that first shows Lyndall openly defying Tant' Sannie. As Tant' Sannie curses at Waldo's father's departing back, Lyndall says to Em, "Come. . . . We will not stay to hear such language" (91). Tant' Sannie takes out her fury on Em, the easier target of the two, by beating her and saying, "So you will defy me, too, will you." But Lyndall, still a child, overpowers Tant' Sannie with her force of character. Schreiner writes, "For one instant Lyndall looked on, then she laid her small fingers on the Boer-woman's arm. With the exertion of half its strength Tant' Sannie might have flung the girl back upon the stones. It was not the power of the slight fingers, tightly though they clenched her broad wrist—so tightly that at bedtime the marks were still there; but the Boer-woman looked into the clear eyes and at the quivering white lips, and with a half-surprised curse relaxed her hold" (91).

Lyndall, though still a child, effectively defies Bonaparte as well. In this same scene he stands "in the door" in his pose of usurped patriarchal authority. But in the face of Lyndall's challenge, Schreiner writes, "Bonaparte the invincible, in the hour of his triumph, moved to give her place" (91). Lyndall's defiance, here, is modeled after that of the Kaffir boys and the Hottentot, but, unlike their impotent and misdirected acts, it is discriminatingly applied to tyrannical figures. It also effectively intervenes to stop Tant' Sannie's beating of Em. After this scene, Lyndall expands the realm in which she can defy oppressive people and forces. As an adult, she rebels against the conventions of proper femininity by refusing to marry the man who is the father of her child. She expresses her sexuality, but will not be forced by convention to marry without love. This is the characteristic for which Lyndall is known as a New Woman among late Victorian readers—a character whose determination to live fully as a woman calls for her to adhere to the principles of freedom and equality no matter what the cost. She considers a less principled approach to personal freedom when she considers marrying Gregory Rose, not the father of her child, but a tractable suitor, so that her child can be born legitimately. She ultimately rejects this course, though. The New Woman Schreiner invents with her character Lyndall has room for principles, not for politics of expedience. A society based in such principles of New Womanhood has no room for Africans as women; but, as Schreiner presents them, these principles come from African models. African figures are models for the original, natural, undisciplined defiance that Lyndall makes new.

Four

Empire, Social Rot, and Sexual Fantasy in *The Waves*

The writings of Olive Schreiner and of Victorian sexologists as I have described them both reflect and contribute to the emergence of overlapping, interdependent constructions of racial categories, modern woman- and manhood, and sexual-identity categories. Early twentieth-century artists and intellectuals such as Virginia Woolf inherited and further solidified these emergent constructions. Given this inheritance as well as Woolf's own interest in questions of race, gender, empire, and sexuality, I propose that the anti-imperialism and the Sapphism of Virginia Woolf's *The Waves* (1931) are overlapping themes that need to be examined in relation to each other. In *The Story of an African Farm,* Olive Schreiner defines New Womanhood as a principled, ideological version of natural but undiscriminating African defiance. In *The Waves,* recurring motifs bring Sapphism and anti-imperialism together. These motifs are rot and purulence, rise and fall, the metaphoric description of waves as "turbaned warriors . . . advancing upon the. . . white sheep" (75), and Rhoda's constant reference to darkness, distance, and colonial places where other characters refer to sex or sensuality. Woolf uses these figurations of blackness and colonial place, I argue, to indicate Sapphism as what Roland Barthes would call a third meaning—an "obtuse" meaning that exists like a fold or crease beyond the obvious meanings of communication and signification (55); a meaning that rides "'on the back' of articulated language" but evades description by critics' metalanguage (Barthes 62). The anti-imperialism in *The Waves* is one of its "obvious meanings."[1] Another meaning emerges, beyond intent and symbol, largely through juxtaposition, because of these obvious meanings—because of Woolf's politics, because of the histories and discourses of sexology, anthropology, eugenics, and colonialism—and despite them at the same time. This third meaning reflects a structure of imagination, for Woolf, in which lesbianism is consistent with a nonspecific colonial worldview and inconsistent with British middle-class whiteness. This shows up in pervasive ways in Woolf's fiction: figurations of blackness or colonial places accompany characters' thoughts about lesbianism; characters associate blackness and/or colonial places with acceptance of lesbianism; and Woolf experiments formally with representing nonnormative sexuality by removing characters from England.

One brief passage toward the beginning of *Mrs. Dalloway,* for instance, reflects a linkage between what Woolf appears to imagine as a black and colonial worldview and social acceptance of lesbianism. Reflecting with displeasure about the relationship between her daughter Elizabeth and Miss Kilman, Clarissa realizes with a start that "with another throw of the dice, had the black been uppermost and not the white, she [Clarissa] would have loved Miss Kilman! But not in this world. No" (17). This passage reveals Sapphic primitivism as a key structure of Clarissa's imagination: loving Miss Kilman (or Sally Seton, with whom she shares a passionate kiss but whom she gives up for respectable marriage) is possible in a world in which black is uppermost, a world in which a black worldview (as Clarissa imagines it) dominates. But loving Miss Kilman is not possible for Clarissa specifically because she lives in "this world"—the world of upper-middle-class white women who throw parties in which the invitees either add to or detract from her social status. I would argue that Woolf, in this case, is not commenting on Clarissa's psyche but is, instead, reflecting one aspect of the structure of her own imagination. She uses a figuration of blackness to explain a white character's class-bound homophobia.

This is similar, in some ways, to Woolf's use of a South American setting to try to address a narrative problem for herself as a writer in *The Voyage Out.* In this novel, Woolf takes Rachel to a South American country in order to experiment as a writer with the possibility of writing a young female protagonist out of a marriage plot. Like Schreiner's experiment in *The Story of an African Farm* with a New Woman character whose narrative possibilities are restricted to marriage and death, Woolf's experiment in *The Voyage Out* doesn't work: she still has to kill off Rachel to keep her out of a heterosexual marriage. Also like Schreiner's Lyndall, Rachel's rebellion, such as it is, happens outside of England. Similarly, in *Orlando* Woolf chooses Turkey for the setting of her character's homoerotically charged transformation from man to woman. Below, I discuss this structure of imagination as a central component in the aesthetics of Woolf's novel *The Waves.*

The Waves

Virginia Woolf's *The Waves* is most commonly read as a modernist experiment with form. In its planning stages, Woolf imagined the novel as a "serious, mystical poetical work," a "play-poem" and an "eyeless book"; later she thought it had "resolve[d] into a series of dramatic soliloquies" (*Diary* 3: 131, 139, 203, 312). While it is fiction, it is also part of Woolf's lifelong project to remake "life-writing," as she called biographical as well as fictional accounts of lives.[2] The novel tells seven life stories, but "give[s] in a very few strokes the essentials of a person's character . . . almost like caricature" (*Diary* 3: 300). Bernard, Neville, Louis, Susan, Jinny, and Rhoda speak, one by one, their impressions of the nursery and the classroom, of college, marriage, friendship, sex, death, children, and Percival—the seventh character who never speaks at all. The lives shown in these soliloquies are not lives of the great, nor does the form Woolf develops follow traditions of biography she had inherited from Victorians such as her father, whose major life work was the *Dictionary of National Biography.* Woolf leaves out detail not to glorify, purify, or resolve, but rather to eliminate what she calls the "waste" of the "appalling narrative business of the realist" (*Diary* 3: 209).

Rhythm rather than plot drives *The Waves* (*Diary* 3: 316). A few things do happen: Percival goes to India, falls off a horse and dies; Rhoda makes a suicidal leap from a cliff in response; Louis builds a career; Neville falls in love; Bernard marries; Susan has children; Jinny seduces. But there are no chapters detailing a progression of events and thus moving the novel from beginning to end. Rather, the novel progresses by perpetually "beginning again," as Rachel Blau DuPlessis puts it (105–107), and by repetitions of a motif of rise and fall. In the interludes, the sun rises out of the waves in jeweled brilliance and passes in an arc from a watery horizon into a shadowed, solid, hilly one. Waves "heap" themselves, emerge, and fall repeatedly back into the sea. In the interludes, birds circle high up, "descend like a net," and dive beneath leaves into purulence (*The Waves* 182). A house and garden appear indistinctly at dawn, flash sharp white edges in the midday sun, and finally yield to shadow.

In the midst of this rise and fall, the elements of the novel—the birds, the house, the waves, the characters—as well as the interludes and soliloquies are linked to each other by juxtaposition and parallelism. As the sun crosses the sky, characters progress from youth to old age and death. As individual waves emerge and reintegrate, Woolf momentarily isolates each voice in soliloquy before letting it fall again into silence, finally subsuming them all into the story maker Bernard's summing up. Each character metaphorically "rise[s] into this dim light" among his peers, as Louis says, proud of his own rise from colonial outsider to shipping administrator, and disappears into sometimes painful and sometimes soothing anonymity (35).

Also part of the rhythm of rise and fall, modern humanity itself is depicted as having risen, feebly and temporarily, from a subterranean primal past. When Bernard's future wife accepts his proposal, he imagines that he can "sink down" into a "general life" where "the growl of traffic might be any uproar—forest trees or the roar of wild beasts. Time has whizzed back an inch or two on its reel. . . . Our bodies are in truth naked . . . and beneath these pavements are shell, bones and silence" (113). And there is, squatting in Bernard and causing him "great difficulty sometimes in controlling," a "savage, the hairy man . . . whose speech is guttural, visceral," and who "point[s] with his half-idiot gestures of greed and covetousness at what he desires" (289–290).

The importance of rhythm, juxtaposition, and parallelism in *The Waves* and the corresponding absence of narrative progression can make it difficult to make claims about Woolf's meanings. The Sapphism I discuss below is vaguely suggested; the connections I emphasize are loose ones; Rhoda's references to colony are indirect responses to other characters' references to sex. But embedded in Woolf's title is the suggestion to make much of such vagueness: Woolf's *The Waves* has the French *les vagues* as an echo, and vague connections and references are as ubiquitous in the novel as the rise and fall of waves.[3] Linear progression is not the way details and their significance are revealed. Rather, juxtaposition, repetition, and echo make meanings in *The Waves,* including the Sapphic meanings I will discuss below. Vague connections and distant echoes are important; juxtapositions and references that seem irrelevant in single instances build significance by their recurrence.[4]

Rot and Purulence, Maggots and Intruders

Read with attention to the features I describe above, *The Waves* is a characteristic work of high modernism involving formal experimentation with nonlinear structures and prototypically modernist themes of alienation, fragmentation, and savagery. Beginning with Jane Marcus, however, critics have also focused on the political engagement and anti-imperialism of Woolf's work in general, and of *The Waves* in particular.[5] In "Britannia Rules *The Waves,*" Marcus challenges critical approaches to the novel that charge it with being difficult and elite and recuperates *The Waves* as anti-imperialist. Subsequent to Marcus's essay, it is clear, even to one critic who mostly disagrees with her, that "interpretations of Woolf's novel can [no longer] legitimately ignore its political content" (McGee 631). *The Waves,* as Marcus describes it, is an exploration of the imperialism and the nationalism of canon, of "the way in which the cultural narrative 'England' is created by an Eton/Cambridge elite who (re)produce the national epic (the rise of . . .) and elegy (the fall of . . .) in praise of the hero" ("Britannia Rules *The Waves*" 137). Direct references to India as "dark, dirty, disordered and . . . threatening" occur nineteen times in the novel; each of Woolf's characters expresses distinctly imperialist sentiment, defining themselves as civilized "only by imagining Britain's colonies as savage" (157). And Woolf's incorporation of hundreds of lines of well-known romantic poems is part of an attack on a literary mode fully involved with imperialist aggression and expansion: the "Romantic quest for a self and definition of the (white male) self against the racial or sexual Other" (137).

A few critics have also discussed the subtle lesbian content of *The Waves.* Ruth Vanita argues that Neville and Rhoda are doubles united by their homoerotic interests. Neville studies Greek and Latin as models of homoeroticism and is associated with Shakespeare's homoerotic sonnets in the novel. Rhoda is excluded from the study of Greek and Latin for models of unconventional love, but "is a portrait of a Victorian Sappho" who "articulate[s] her attraction to women in a language drawn from the Romantics, especially Shelley" and who "leaps to her death by drowning, as Sappho did in legend and as Woolf was to do in reality a decade later" (Vanita 205–206). Julie Abraham points out that Rhoda's sense that she often dies "pierced with arrows" is a reference to the gay icon St. Sebastian and thus "underlines the possibility of a reading of Rhoda as matched with Neville" (155). Annette Oxindine argues that Woolf clearly marks Rhoda as a lesbian in the holograph drafts of *The Waves* and leaves traces of this lesbianism in the final version. In early drafts of *The Waves,* Rhoda is enthralled by a girl named Alice at her all-girls' school. A look at Alice is "staggering" and provides material for dreams she enjoys alone in bed at night. In these dreams, Alice's lips always fade "just as she is about to kiss her"; Woolf also lists Rhoda's dream of Alice on the same notebook page on which she writes "love for other girls" (*Two Holographic Drafts* H123, H750).

In the published version of the novel, there are hints and remnants of what might be taken as marks of lesbianism. Rhoda's love for the fellow student, Alice, becomes attraction for the teacher Miss Lambert, whose ring gives off a purple "amorous" light and under whose eyes, everything becomes luminous (*The Waves* 33, 45). Miss Lambert, as does Alice of the drafts, makes Rhoda dream (45). These dreams do not include kisses with girls, but the soliloquy that in early drafts contains kisses with Alice includes explicitly female-centered sexuality. Rhoda says, "There is some check in the flow of my being; a deep stream presses on some obstacle; it jerks; it tugs; some knot in the centre resists. Oh, this is pain, this is anguish! I faint, I fail. Now my body thaws; I am unsealed, I am incandescent. Now the stream pours in a deep tide fertilizing, opening the shut, forcing the tight-folded, flooding free. To whom shall I give all that now flows through me, from my warm, my porous body?" (57). This passage is sensuous in itself as well as reminiscent of the often-quoted and more clearly lesbian passage in *Mrs. Dalloway,* in which Clarissa has a sudden revelation of pressure, yielding, cracking, and flowing followed by the vision of a match burning in a crocus.[6] But without knowing the drafts of *The Waves,* or making comparisons with lesbian passages in *Mrs. Dalloway,* the lesbianism of the final version of *The Waves* is so subtle as to be almost absent. Annette Oxindine attributes this to self-censorship, arguing that Woolf's "fear of being labelled a lesbian, and therefore not being taken seriously, substantially affects the composition process of *The Waves*."[7]

Self-censorship in *The Waves* has everything to do with the 1928 obscenity trial involving Radclyffe Hall's overtly lesbian novel *The Well of Loneliness*. Woolf, among other Bloomsburies, attended the trial to testify on Hall's behalf, though Woolf did not much like Hall's book.[8] Woolf's writings around the time of the trial show that she thought repeatedly about the trial and the censorship of lesbianism it represented.[9] In *A Room of One's Own* (1929), Woolf's narrator pauses in her reading of Mary Carmichael's novel when she gets to the line "Chloe liked Olivia." Before she continues, she wants to be assured that "there are no men present" and that "Sir Chartres Biron is not concealed" behind "that red curtain" (82–83). Sir Chartres Biron was the magistrate who pronounced Hall's novel obscene in November 1928. In her diary, Woolf records her fear of being "attacked for a feminist & hinted at for a Sapphist" over the content of *Room* (*Diary* 3: 262). Also, revisions to the manuscript version of *Orlando* (1928) include excisions of "references to Sappho, to Orlando's 'lusts' and her love-affairs with women."[10]

But if lesbianism is scarce at best in the final version of *The Waves*, rot, corruption, purulence, mixing, and staining are ubiquitous. This motif of degeneracy is central to the novel's depictions of empire and imperialists; it is aligned to male homosexuality as if Woolf were responding to linkages J. M. Wilson and other moral purity campaigners made between male homosexuality and imperial decay;[11] and it is central to Woolf's evocations of lesbianism. Of course Woolf is not invoking degeneracy to inspire fear for the success of empire. Rather, she seems to revel in degeneracy in a way that predicts and invites the fall of empire. If Woolf's characters obsess about "rise" and self re-creation—about figuratively holding themselves up out of the waves of water and time that surround and threaten them with obscurity—Woolf takes perverse glee in degeneracy and obscurity as well as fall. In the context of discourses of empire and sex that are dependent on motifs of degeneracy, Woolf marks her novel as rebellious in a specifically sexual way by filling her anti-imperialist novel with an abundance of corruption, staining, intrusion, and taint.

Much of the anti-imperialism of Woolf's novel comes, as Jane Marcus has described, from the emphasis on *fall* in the repeating *rise and fall* of the novel; in addition, ubiquitous biological corruption amplifies Woolf's anti-imperialist emphasis on *fall.* Rot is densest in the interludes. The birds are vicious invaders into purulence and generate even more rot.[12] They are "ruthless and abrupt," tap snail shells against stones until "something slimy ooze[s]" (*The Waves* 109). One "spike[s] the soft, monstrous body of the defenseless worm," leaving it to "fester." They dig among the roots where flowers "decay," "gusts of dead smells waft," and "drops form on the bloated sides of swollen things"; where matter oozes "too thick to run" from the broken skins of rotten fruit. There is monstrosity as well as decay where "yellow excretions [are] exuded by slugs" and an "amorphous body with a head at either end" sways slowly from side to side (57).

Similarly, in the soliloquies characters talk constantly of biological rot and corruption and are ever-anxious about the corruption of their individuality by contact with others who mix, intrude, disperse, overwhelm, or adulterate. In the nursery, Louis mourns that "all is shattered" when Jinny kisses him (12). Seeing this kiss makes Susan want to "die in a ditch in the brown water where dead leaves have rotted" (15). Neville is ambivalent about Bernard's company on a riverbank: "how painful to be . . . mitigated, to have one's self adulterated, mixed up, become part of another" (83). Susan also resists what she calls "mixing"; she "cannot be tossed about, or float gently, or mix with other people" (98). Louis feels dissolved and overwhelmed by darkness when he comes together with others. At the second dinner party, he mourns, "We are gone. . . . Our separate drops are dissolved; we are extinct, lost in the abysses of time, in the darkness" (225). Also at the second dinner party, Rhoda says that she has "dreaded" humanity, hideous and squalid. She says, "I have been stained by you and corrupted" (203). These fears of mixing (or hybridity), extinction, and darkness reflect imperialist discourse. Woolf emphasizes this when characters' thoughts of rot or corruption are simultaneously an expression of their imperial consciousnesses. In the woods, Bernard makes up a game about being explorers, discoverers of an unknown land where he and his friends "tread on rotten oak apples, red . . . and slippery" and hear "the patter of some primeval fir-cone falling to rot among the ferns" (17). In his summation, Bernard exposes the centrality of stained whiteness to his self-concept.

He thinks of the characters' childhood selves as "virginal wax that coats the spine and melts in different patches for each of us," and then reflects that "our white wax was streaked and stained" (241). Neville imagines that Bernard will tell Susan a story about "the big blade . . . an emperor; the broken blade a Negro" and then reflects, "I hate wandering and mixing things together" (19). This prefigures Neville's adult insistence on imperialist differentiation between himself and Other. Wandering is a reference to Jews and Gypsies as well as imperialist voyages; the hatred for "mixing things" is in accord with imperialist and eugenicist anxiety over miscegenation and racial degeneracy. Later Neville will assert his distaste for "the waste and deformity of the world, its crowds, eddying" (180).

Corruption in general is figured as a characteristic of empire and imperialism throughout the novel. The story Bernard tells Susan links rotting and colony. He says, "Here come warm gusts of decomposing leaves, of rotting vegetation," and "We are in a swamp now; in a malarial jungle. There is an elephant white with maggots, killed by an arrow shot dead in its eye" (22). Corrupting and whitening are the same here, suggesting that the degeneracy often associated with colonized places in imperialist rhetoric is the product, in Woolf's eyes, of white intrusion rather than an inherent quality of Africa, the Americas, or Asia. In Bernard's summation, the elephant reappears as "a rat wreathing with maggots under a rhubarb leaf" and "the rat swarming with maggots" (241).

An animal reminiscent of the shot and rotting elephant/rat reemerges later as a metaphor for London and as a symbol of the interconnectedness of mother country and colony. On a train, Bernard sees "men clutch their newspapers envisaging death. . . . We are about to explode in the flanks of the city like a shell in the side of some ponderous, maternal, majestic animal" (111). London's fate here is the same as that of the pierced elephant rotting in a colony; "we" are the missile which blindly charges. A soliloquy of Rhoda's also suggests that "we" are both the maggots corrupting the colonial beast and simultaneously the torpid, gorged, and endangered beast itself. Reflecting on Percival's death, she says, "We cluster like maggots on the back of something that will carry us on [and] we lie gorged with food, torpid in the heat" (162).

The image of a rotting colonial beast, itself corrupting, fed on by vultures, and corrupting the empire, comes up again when characters think of

Percival's career. Rhoda reflects that because Percival advances heroically down a solitary path, "the outermost parts of the earth . . . India for instance, rise into our purview. . . . Remote provinces are fetched up out of darkness." But Rhoda also sees "muddy roads, twisted jungle, swarms of men, and the vulture that feeds on some bloated carcass as within our scope, part of our proud and splendid province" (137). Percival's reign as a colonial ruler is fraught with decay in Bernard's vision, too: "I see India. . . . I see the tortuous lanes of stamped mud that lead in and out among ramshackle pagodas; I see the gilt and crenelated buildings which have an air of fragility and decay as if they were temporarily run up buildings in some Oriental exhibition" (135–136).

Woolf also figures reprisal from the colonized in racialized images of intrusion and taint. In many interludes, images of waves are personified as turbaned African warriors whose backs curve and who mass themselves, threatening white flocks. In one, "the wind rose. The waves drummed on the shore, like turbaned warriors, like turbaned men with poisoned assegais who, whirling their arms on high, advance upon the feeding flocks, the white sheep" (75). The words "assegais" and "turbaned" mark these figures as dark-skinned others; the use of warriors as opposed to soldiers primitivizes them.

These warriors, as well as the vicious birds and the rot, surround and threaten the house Woolf describes in the interludes. As houses are elsewhere in Woolf's writings, this house is metonymic for imperialism and also for patriarchy and male control of women's sexuality.[13] The sun overcomes darkness in and around this house in early interludes, but the house is finally obscured by darkness. Early on, shadow is but a "blue fingerprint . . . under the leaf by the bedroom window" near a "white blind" that "stirred slightly" (*The Waves* 8). Shadow and "impenetrable darkness" hover, but light repeatedly "drives darkness before it" (110). In bright light, the house has "formidable corners," and white walls "glare" between dark windows; shadows are contained: they "hang" in a specific "zone," "encumber" a few objects, are "heaped up" in "mounds," and only "suggest still denser depths of darkness" (110, 150, 166).

Later soliloquies figure shadows as intruders into the house, successfully overwhelming the "weakening" brightness of the sun. Objects in the darkening house are ponderous; they "portend"; they become obscure rather than distinct and sharp. The shadows that lengthen on the beach suggest progress of those warriors toward the white flocks. Shadows "eddy around" and then "engulf individuals," "blot out" couples, and "cover" girls on verandas looking at snow. Darkness "rolls," "envelops," and "mounts." Blackness shoots, and is "a vast curtain" (208, 236–237).

Woolf's motif of a darkening, invaded house makes a specific critique of the sexual displacement and the control over female sexuality that are both central to imperialism. Critiques of the link between sexuality and empire occur in many of Woolf's writings. Kathy Phillips has described such critiques, arguing that all of Woolf's writings show the displacement of sexuality onto colonized people as a secondary motive, after economics, to colonialism and militarism. Phillips writes that Woolf's "investigation of displacement forms one of her most interesting and original contributions to an understanding of the late nineteenth and twentieth centuries. Throughout her novels, men who are unsure of themselves sexually try to enhance their prowess by positioning themselves next to the immensity of the Empire" (236). Woolf also critiques the use of myths about the chastity of white women and the lasciviousness of colonized people—myths used to justify colonialism. Phillips argues that in *Mrs. Dalloway,* Woolf juxtaposes a colonizer calling for more troops with girls buying white underlinen for their weddings in order to show that "the brawler and his society require pure white virginity as one of the justifications for quelling rebellions" (228). As Phillips also points out, in "The Royal Academy," Woolf says explicitly that "scenes from Rudyard Kipling" give maidens occasion to insist on their chastity and gallant officers occasion to protect it (Woolf, *Essays* 3: 90). In *The Waves,* objects within the house on the beach, in addition to being white or having mass and edge, are also tinted with colors "like the bloom on the skin of ripe fruit" (110). Such coloring—like the bloom on ripe fruit, especially in a whitening house—evoke clichéd phrases (blushing bride, pink-cheeked) praising young white girls for both innocence and sexual desirability. Woolf gives direct expression to the idealization of pink cheeks on white girls in one passage: Bernard reports that Percival thought "Lucy's flaxen pigtails and pink cheeks were the height of female beauty" (243). Woolf thus makes connections between imperialist activity, embodied in Percival, and the idealization of the appearance of women with flaxen hair and pink cheeks. In the context of this critique of the sexual politics of imperialism, Woolf's juxtapositions between whiteness with a ripe bloom, warriors racing on the white flocks, and a house whitened by the sun in the morning and overwhelmed by shadow in the evening—especially shadows that leave fingerprints on white blinds outside bedrooms, blot out couples, cover girls, and mount—figure specifically sexual intrusion and taint.[14] In the context of discourse about empire, sexual intrusion and taint include sexual rebellion on the part of women, including promiscuity, miscegenation, prostitution, high or low reproductivity depending on the racial and class status of the woman one is talking about, and lesbianism. Woolf figures this intrusion and taint both to provoke fear and to mock that fear.

These figurations of corruption, sexual intrusion, and taint in *The Waves* comprise Woolf's critique of the imperial consciousness of those "white flocks" who fear fall and mixing and staining and adulteration throughout the novel. Her figurations of blackness as intrusion into a white house, of primitivized warriors threatening white flocks and polluting the white body—these are what, in Goldberg's characterization of the discourse of race and degeneracy, lead to disease, criminality, prostitution; and are all, in turn, evocative of homosexuality in the context of sexological discourses. A middle-class white woman who celebrates this corruption and intrusion, especially in the context of an anti-imperialist argument, marks her novel as rebellious in a specifically sexual way.

Male Homosexuality in *The Waves*

Woolf's references to male homosexuality more explicitly mark her novel as both sexually rebellious and anti-imperialist by mocking the connections moral purity campaigners made between male homosexuality and the destruction of empire. Sitting in chapel, the homosexual character Neville is irritated that "words of authority are corrupted by those who speak them," by "a brute who menaces [his] liberty" (35). Moral purity campaigners *did* menace the liberty of boys/men like Neville by equating homosexuality with the corruption of religion and empire. But Neville makes connections between homosexuality and religion differently than do advocates of moral purity. "This sad religion," he says, is "tremulous, grief-stricken figures advancing . . . down a white road shadowed by fig trees where boys sprawl in the dust—naked boys" (35). And he occupies himself in chapel by thinking of Percival's perfections, one of which is that "he would make an admirable churchwarden. He should have a birch and beat little boys" (36). Neville understands chapel and the Bible in terms of their homoeroticism and is irritated that the headmaster's reading corrupts his own homoerotically charged versions.[15] Woolf did not believe male homosexuality would bring on the fall of empire, but the idea that it might would have been something to celebrate rather than to fear.

Woolf also makes reference to Shakespeare's homoerotic sonnets, literally corrupting the pages of the poem with decaying flowers and simultaneously making those decaying flowers, as well as the poetry, metonymic for homoeroticism. Woolf and her friends saw homoeroticism in the sonnets. Hermione Lee describes a joke cut from the manuscript of *Orlando* in which Orlando's biographer reports having torn up and burned Shakespeare's account of his relations with Mr. W. H. and the dark Lady because "there was much in those pages of an impure nature."[16] In *The Waves,* when the characters are in college, Neville anxiously throws Bernard a poem he has written about loving Percival. In response, Bernard compares Neville's homoerotic poem to "press[ing] flowers between the pages of Shakespeare's sonnets" (88). Later, the pressed flowers literally corrupt Shakespeare's pages. Mourning Percival, Neville mentions "Plato and Shakespeare" and then reflects that "colours always stain the page" of the poem, which is "you," Percival, his lover, and literary heroes (181). Still later, waiting in his room for his lover, he chooses a book from the shelf and reads "half a page of anything." But "one cannot read this poem without effort. The page is often corrupt and mud stained, and torn and stuck together with faded leaves, with scraps of verbena or geranium" (198).

The lover, a homosexual relationship, the poem, and corruption of the flowers are conflated in these passages. This juxtaposition of corruption and homosexuality certainly evokes the rhetoric of moral purity campaigners. It also points to the end of a prior age of British Empire building. But the convergence of male homosexuality and corruption in a novel inviting as well as fearing the decay of empire does not express the same fear of homosexuality that moral purity campaigners sought to inspire. Rather, it mocks the associations they made between homosexuality and corruption.

Colony and Sapphism: Sexual Displacement

If Woolf is often derisive and critical of imperialist ideologies, however, she also seems to be participating in, or simply reflecting, a varia-
tion of sexual displacement that is part of colonialist ideologies: she relies
on figurations of blackness and references to colony and degeneracy to
work as placeholders for Rhoda's lesbianism where it can't be expressed
directly. My argument is loosely parallel to Morrison's theory of American
Africanism: figurations of blackness do not express lesbianism in *The
Waves,* but rather Woolf inserts figurations of blackness as if they will carry
Sapphism as one of their possible meanings—as if Woolf assumes such
figurations have a capacity to replace or stand in for references to lesbianism. She seems, in this way, to reflect one aspect of the overlap between
discourses of sex and empire that she otherwise critiques.

One of the ways in which this displacement is manifest is that where
other characters refer directly to heterosexuality or male homosexuality,
Rhoda mentions, or others mention in relation to her, Africa, India, Turks,
distant places, dark pools, darkness, swallows (significantly, migrating
birds whose path includes England and Africa), tigers, and columns. The
columns are perhaps Roman or Greek, both parts of the Sotadic Zone that
Burton described. In addition, Rhoda is the character most strongly linked,
in terms of her sexuality and in general, to the men with assegais and to
the purulence into which the snails dig in the interludes. In these ways,
Woolf links Rhoda's lesbian sexuality—specifically and importantly *un*spoken sexuality—with colonized places, degeneracy, migration, and distant
places including Greece.

In Rhoda's first long soliloquy, Woolf's use of punctuation suggests a
parallel between lesbianism and the image of a white woman in a primitivized, colonial place: both are what must be spoken indirectly. Playing a
game in which flower petals in a basin of water are ships, Rhoda exposes
an anxious desire to claim untainted whiteness for her self-definition: "All
my ships are white," she says. "I do not want red petals of hollyhocks or
geranium. I want white petals that float. . . . One sails alone. That is my ship."
The others "have foundered, all except my ship which mounts the wave and
sweeps before the gale and reaches the islands where the parrots chatter
and the creepers . . . " (18–19, final ellipses in the original). Jane Marcus
has pointed out that in *A Room Of One's Own,* Woolf uses ellipses to indicate

female desire when it is the object of censorship.[17] The three dots that signify the narrator's pause before reading "Chloe liked Olivia" (83), Marcus
argues, are code for lesbian love. This ellipsis is even more explicitly about
both lesbianism and censorship in an early draft of the scene from *Room* in
which Woolf's narrator reads from Mary Carmichael's book. Woolf writes:
"'Chloe liked Olivia; they shared a ——,' the words came at the bottom of
the page; the pages had stuck; while fumbling to open them there flashed
into my mind the inevitable policemen; the summons; the order to attend
the court; the dreary waiting; the Magistrate coming in with a little bow;
the glass of water; the counsel for the prosecution; for the defence; the ver-
dict; this book is obscene; & flames rising, perhaps on Tower Hill, as they
consumed masses of paper. Here the pages came apart. Heaven be praised!
It was only a laboratory" (Lee, *Virginia Woolf* 525–526). Here, the ellipsis
at the beginning of the passage marks the deferral of the end of a sentence.
In the space left by this deferral, scenes from the obscenity trial against the
publishers of Radclyffe Hall's *Well of Loneliness* flash through the narrator's
mind, temporarily filling the ellipsis with censurable lesbianism. Comically,
the deferred word turns out to be "laboratory." Woolf's narrator, to her relief, needn't read the unmentionable; Woolf herself has referred to lesbianism and at the same time left it unnamed except as an elliptical something
that might have been said.

Similarly, in Rhoda's soliloquy quoted above, Rhoda represents that
which can't be said as what a white girl/woman imagines she does after
reaching a colonial place.[18] If Woolf's use of ellipses in general is suggestive of lesbianism, and more arguably so in this case considering the fact
that lesbianism is literally what Woolf has repressed in Rhoda, then in
Rhoda's soliloquy the image of a white woman in a colonial place is coupled
with lesbianism through the trope of ellipsis: both are that which can't be
spoken.

What Rhoda *does* say makes a similar correlation: when other characters talk of sex or sensuality, Rhoda talks of Africa or India or decay or
men with assegais. This is apparent in soliloquies about the dance party
Jinny and Rhoda attend together. Jinny characterizes the party as both titillating and sexually important: it is "rapture," "relief," "ecstasy," "risk," "adventure"; she is "admitted to the warmth and privacy of another soul" (104).
But for Rhoda, the party is terrifying, and her description is full of references

to colonial places. Tigers leap and pursue. A million arrows pierce her. She sees "the wild thorn tree shake its shadow in the desert" (104). An English thorn tree would be a Hawthorne, but Woolf specifies a desert thorn tree, which is the African thorn tree, ubiquitous in eastern and southern Africa. African thorn trees do make a striking, large, shaky shadow since they grow solitary on relatively flat ground and spread out flat at the top like a table. The shadow looks shaky—wispy and shifting—because it is made of many thin twigs and long thorns which permit light to mix with the shadow. Also during the party, Rhoda thinks of herself as whiteness amidst the waves, which have become, by this point in the novel, always a reference to warriors with assegais racing on the white flocks. Significantly, she is not being pursued by the waves/warriors here, as she is elsewhere, but is amidst them. She is "the foam that sweeps and fills the uttermost rims of the rocks with whiteness" amidst the breaking waves (107).

Among the images Rhoda calls up to protect herself are also suggestions of darkness and distance: "Pools lie on the other side of the world reflecting marble columns. The swallow dips her wing in dark pools" (105). And she thinks back to the game she played with petals in basins and being mistress of her fleet of ships (106). These "treasures" she has "laid apart" are inflected with lesbianism (105). They support her very like the dreams of kissing Alice support her in the drafts. The swallow dips *her* wing in pools. The tiger, while terrifying, is also sensual when Rhoda compares it's "leap" to "tongues with their whips . . . upon me" (106).

In memories of the party, as in the original experience of it, Rhoda speaks of colonized places where Jinny speaks of sex. For Jinny, the party is an event full of glitter and flirtatious socializing. She recalls, "Rhoda and I, exposed in bright dresses, with a few precious stones nestling on a cold ring round our throats, bowed, shook hands and took a sandwich from a plate with a smile." Rhoda's corresponding soliloquy contains images evocative of darkness, migration, and colonialism. She says, "The tiger leapt, and the swallow dipped her wings in dark pools on the other side of the world" (126). Later, Jinny again recalls the party excitedly: "He comes; he crosses the room to where I sit. . . . Our hands touch, our bodies burst into fire" (140). Rhoda describes what she sees in the eyes of her titillated friends, including Jinny, by evoking wild animals and the men with assegais: "horns and trumpets . . . ring out. Leaves unfold; the stag blares in the thicket. There is a dancing and a drumming, like the dancing and drumming of naked men with assegais" (140).

What I want to emphasize here is that Rhoda's thoughts of tigers, waves/warriors, ships carrying white petals to islands where parrots chatter, a swallow dipping her wing in a dark pool, and thorn trees in the desert are evocations of Burton's Sotadic Zone and the people and animals who live there. Woolf juxtaposes references to these figures in Rhoda's soliloquies with explicit, aggressively heterosexual references in Jinny's soliloquies. In addition, each time the party is referred to, Jinny's soliloquy precedes Rhoda's. In this way, the structure of the novel puts Rhoda's references to colonized places literally in the shadow of Jinny's aggressive heterosexuality. Placing the two of them together at these parties also aligns Rhoda's lesbianism to Jinny's sexuality, which, if heterosexual, is nonreproductive and also primitivized by her description of a sexual encounter as animalistic: she hears the "crash and rending of boughs and the crack of antlers as if the beasts of the forest were all hunting" and "one has pierced me. One is driven deep within me" (177).

Other characters' soliloquies about eros or sensuality are also juxtaposed with Rhoda's references to colony. The whole section of soliloquies at Percival's farewell is highly charged sexually, each character's sexuality often the subject of either her own or another's reflection. In one series of six brief soliloquies, one after another, all but one character—Neville—speak a sexual or sensual memory. Jinny and Louis think of the scene in which Jinny bursts in on Louis masturbating and kisses him.[19] Bernard remembers water from Mrs. Constable's sponge sluicing down his body as the moment when "we became clothed in this changing, this feeling garment of flesh." Susan remembers that "the boot boy made love to the scullery-maid in the kitchen garden, among the blown-out washing." Rhoda's recollection is also of the scullery-maid and the boot boy, but her memory exposes a clear link between sexuality and a colonial image. For her, "the breath of the wind was like a tiger panting" (124). This tiger is a place marker for the sexuality between the boot boy and the maid. And Rhoda is expressing fear of the heterosexual kiss in terms of a fearsome creature, a tiger. But her response to the kiss, given in terms of her comment about the wind and the tiger, is also hot and excited. The wind, while it is compared to a tiger's panting, is merely a "breath." The "panting" of the tiger is at least as suggestive of excited panting as it is of anything threatening, especially since Woolf chose panting instead of a more unequivocally fearsome word such as leaping, clawing, growling, hissing. In addition, this is the same tiger that just prior is compared to "tongues with their whips upon me" (106). Even to the degree that Rhoda is expressing fear as well as excitement here, again, she is making metaphors for sex out of a tiger—a reference evocative of a colonial space and savage, animalistic energy. Significantly, the only character whose memory on this page is not of sex or sensuality is the other homosexual character, Neville. Though he does speak directly of sexuality elsewhere, here, where his friends have erotic memories, his soliloquy is about death. He recalls the moment when he heard of "the man [who] lay livid with his throat cut in the gutter" (124). His reference to death and a corpse in the gutter where others talk of sex is another example of Woolf's expression of homosexuality in terms of degeneracy, evoked by both death and gutter.

More references to physicality, sensuality, and potentially erotic intimacy are scattered throughout the section of soliloquies about the characters' first reunion. Bernard tells us that he is engaged to be married, and that Percival loves Susan (118, 123). Susan describes her desire as passion for maternity: "I shall be debased and hide-bound by the bestial and beautiful passion of maternity" (132). In addition to her remarks about the party, Jinny notices of all her friends that "beauty rides our brow" and then points to her beauty and Susan's in particular: "There is mine, there is Susan's. Our flesh is firm and cool" (141). Louis describes the language of the others as speaking "a little language such as lovers use" and says that "an imperious brute possesses them. The nerves thrill in their thighs. Their hearts pound and churn in their sides" (143). Neville arrives early at the restaurant to extend both his agony and his pleasure over the anticipation of Percival's arrival (118–122). And after Percival arrives, Neville describes his meal sensuously: "delicious mouthfuls of roast duck, fitly piled with vegetables, following each other in exquisite rotation of warmth, weight, sweet and bitter, past my palate, down my gullet, into my stomach, have stabilized my body" (138). His description of eating and food segues into a more overtly sexual description of nerves trembling in the roof of his mouth and of sensation spreading into a cavern overlooking what he calls the "mill-race" of his unnamed passion (138).[20] He also imagines an intimate scene with Percival which mirrors his anguished wait at the restaurant: "his slippers. . . . And his voice downstairs in the hall? And catching sight of him when he does not see one? . . . He is with some one else. He is faithless, his love meant nothing. . . . And then the door opens. He is here" (139–140).

In the midst of all this sensuality, Rhoda's sexuality is identified—if not named—as lesbian, and at the same time is explicitly compared to her constant looking into a colonial distance. Neville identifies Rhoda as a lesbian by imagining she will help him name *his* homosexuality. During the dinner, Neville describes his violent feelings for Percival as "these roaring waters" and a "mill-race that foams beneath" "our crazy platforms" of identity. And, when trying to discover "by what particular name are we to call" those feelings, he proposes to "let Rhoda speak, whose face I see reflected mistily in the looking-glass opposite" (138). Neville's belief that Rhoda will help him name his love and his vision of her in the looking glass opposite both reveal that Neville and Rhoda have homosexuality in common.[21] Neville cannot, however, "let Rhoda speak" the name of his love as he proposes to do. As if explaining to himself why he can't imagine Rhoda finding a name, he suggests that love, for Rhoda, is looking into the distance beyond India. He says, "Love is not a whirlpool to her [as it is to him]. She is not giddy when she looks down. She looks far away over our heads, beyond India" (138–139). Through syntax here, Woolf makes Neville's male homoerotic love different from, but parallel to, Rhoda's looking into the distance beyond India.

Rhoda's soliloquy follows immediately. She seems to respond to Neville directly, beginning with "yes," as if to agree that love is not a whirlpool to her, but is, instead, looking over her friends' heads to India. She also makes reference to the distance into which she looks, to whiteness in a dark place, and to the dreaming that, in the drafts of *The Waves,* is specifically lesbian-sexual dreaming. She says,

> Yes, between your shoulders, over your heads, to a landscape, . . . to a hollow where the many-backed steep hills come down like birds' wings folded. There, on the short firm turf, are bushes, dark leaved, and against their darkness I see a shape, white, but not of stone, moving, perhaps alive. But it is not you, it is not you, it is not you; not Percival, Susan,

Jinny, Neville, or Louis. When the white arm rests upon the knee it is a triangle; now it is upright—a column; now a fountain, falling. . . . Behind it roars the sea. It is beyond our reach. Yet there I venture. There I go to replenish my emptiness, to stretch my nights and fill them fuller and fuller with dreams. (139)

Here, Rhoda puts herself amidst darkness and columns specifically in order to replenish those dreams that are the strongest marker of Rhoda's lesbianism in the drafts: her desire to "stretch her nights" and fill them "fuller with dreams" echoes her comments in the drafts about how dreams of Alice fill her nights (Woolf, *Two Holographic Drafts* H123).

In another soliloquy in *The Waves,* Susan places Jinny's heterosexual posing alongside, and in opposition to, the distance into which Rhoda looks throughout the novel. Susan says, "Something has formed at school . . . not Rhoda's strange communications when she looks past us, over our shoulders; nor Jinny's pirouetting, all of a piece, limbs and body" (98). This distance into which Rhoda looks here is not specifically colonial. It is, however, a distance often described elsewhere as containing tigers and swallows, sometimes India and Africa, and sometimes columns and hills. In this novel of repetition and echo, mention of waves also invokes warriors, and mention of warriors also invokes waves whether or not both are made explicitly present in any given scene. Similarly, each time a character refers to Rhoda's "distance," Africa and India and columns and hills are also invoked by echo.

In yet another soliloquy, Rhoda imagines darkness, drumming, and Turks when she sees her friends in sexual interactions. After their second reunion, the six characters walk in three heterosexual couples who all make reference to sex or love. Bernard goes off with Susan, "who has always loved [him]." Neville takes Jinny's hand and the two of them say "love, love" to each other (229). Louis says, of Rhoda, "We have sacrificed the embrace among the ferns, and love, love, love by the lake, standing, like conspirators who have drawn apart to share some secret, by the urn" (233). As the others talk of sex or love, Rhoda watches her friends in pairs and sees "darkness clos[e] over their bodies" (230). She also hears "drumming on the roofs of a fasting city when the Turks are hungry and uncertain tempered." Furthermore, the sounds of Turks change into the sound of a bride eager for sex. Rhoda hears Turks "crying with sharp, stag-like barks, 'Open, open.'" A few lines later, the sound is a bride who has "let her silken night-dress fall and come to the doorway saying, 'Open, open'" (230).

Rhoda also fantasizes the freeing of her lesbian sexual desire as something she will do in a colonial place. Walking on an embankment with her withered violets for Percival, she sees "ships that sail to India" and says immediately afterward,

> I will walk by the river. . . . I will pace this terrace and watch the ships bowling down the tide. A woman walks on deck. . . . Her skirts are blown; her hair is blown; they are going out to sea; they are leaving us; they are vanishing this summer evening. Now I will relinquish; now I will let loose. Now I will at last free the checked, the jerked back desire to be spent, to be consumed. We will gallop together over desert hills where the swallow dips her wings in dark pools and the pillars stand entire. Into the wave that dashes upon the shore, into the wave that flings its white foam to the uttermost corners of the earth I throw my violets, my offering to Percival. (164)

In this passage, Rhoda sees a woman with whom she fantasizes letting loose her previously "checked" desire. The woman's blowing skirts and hair add to the sexual importance of the scene, since they hearken back to the kiss the children saw amidst the blowing laundry. But the sexuality of the scene is at first intertwined with references to colony and perhaps Greece, and finally expressed entirely in terms of what Rhoda will do in a colonial place. Even before Rhoda sees the woman, she sees the ship bound for India. Once the ship departs for India, "now" Rhoda can begin to loose her desire. When Rhoda actually gets to describing the fantasy, it is only very obliquely, if at all, spoken in terms of sex. Instead, it is very specifically about being and doing in the colonial-sotadic place Rhoda has been describing in dreams and fantasies from the beginning of the novel: they will ride in the desert where the swallow dips her wings in dark pools and where the pillars are. Rhoda also imagines herself following the woman's ship on the backs of waves (warriors) which fling white foam (elsewhere identified unambiguously as Rhoda herself) to uttermost corners of the earth (107).

Rhoda is also the character most closely aligned with the warriors/

waves, often fearing them, sometimes amidst the waves, sometimes the waves themselves. As a child having a nightmare, she longs to wake from dreaming: to "pull myself out of these waters. But they heap themselves on me; they sweep me between their great shoulders; I am turned; I am tumbled; I am stretched among these long lights, these long waves, these endless paths, with people pursuing, pursuing" (28). The people pursuing are, of course, those same figures described in the interludes as men with assegais, and also described as tigers at the party. Rhoda's dreams in the draft are of kissing Alice, and thoughts of those dreams help her hold up during the day; it is no coincidence that Rhoda's dreams in the final version are nightmares involving drowning amidst waves/warriors/tigers.

Later, when she is coming home from school, Rhoda blends the tiger and the waves in her imagination and then attaches herself to them as well as to wildness. She says, "So I detach the summer term. With intermittent shocks, sudden as the springs of a tiger, life emerges heaving its dark crest from the sea. It is to this we are attached; it is to this we are bound, as bodies to wild horses" (64). And during what is probably Rhoda's suicide, she pictures Africa (as Sappho leaping from her cliff might have seen the North African coast), hears drumming, and describes herself as white petals being darkened with sea water. Riding a mule in Spain, she says, "The ridge of the hill rises like mist, but from the top I shall see Africa," and then, "We launch now out over the precipice. Beneath us lie the lights of the herring fleet. The cliffs vanish. Rippling small, rippling grey, innumerable waves spread beneath us. . . . We may sink and settle on the waves. The sea will drum in my ears. The white petals will be darkened with sea water. They will float for a moment and then sink" (206). Toward the end of the novel, Louis says that Rhoda has gone "like the desert heat." And Rhoda exclaims that she has hated humanity—that they have stained and corrupted her. She says this, however, from the perspective of refuge, as if she is regretful about what *has* been. Her relief seems to come equally from being separate from humanity on a mountain and also from being able to see Africa. She reflects on how hideous humanity has been—"now as I climb this mountain, from the top of which I shall see Africa" (203).

In a few passages Rhoda is closely aligned with the purulence—the oozing snail and the festering worm—of the interludes and at the same time to images of colonialism. She is described as having eyes "the color of snail's flesh" by Louis, who also says he thinks of her "when the dry leaves patter to the ground; when the old men come with pointed sticks and pierce little bits of paper as we pierced her" (200, 203). Additionally, in his summation, Bernard suggests that the children who pierced Rhoda and the birds who pecked the snail are one when he describes the "tap tap tap of the remorseless beaks of the young" (288). This makes a link between Rhoda and India/Africa, as well. A worm that is pecked in the interludes becomes a hooded cobra in one of Bernard's stories. He imagines that "the birds pick at a worm—that is a hooded cobra—and leave it with a festering brown scar to be mauled by lions" (23). Reference to cobras and lions evokes both India and Africa and, by alliance, places Rhoda there, pecked and left to fester.

A description of Rhoda in Bernard's summary similarly aligns her with corruption as well as with colonial places. He says of her that "the willow as she saw it grew on the verge of a grey desert where no bird sang. The leaves shrivelled as she looked at them. . . . Perhaps one pillar, sunlit, stood in her desert by a pool where wild beasts come down stealthily to drink" (252). There is also a parallel between Bernard's image of sexual love and Rhoda's image of rot and blackness. Mourning Percival's death, Bernard walks into a picture gallery to avoid being drawn back into daily life—what he calls "the sequence of things" (155). He is grateful to see pictures that stop the flood of images, in his mind's eye, of Percival's death. In his search for "something unvisual" he says, "Here are gardens; and Venus among her flowers. . . . [These pictures] expand my consciousness of him and bring him back to me differently. I remember his beauty. 'Look, where he comes,' I said" (156). Following Bernard's soliloquy is one of Rhoda's. She too mourns Percival; she too walks in the street; she too considers going into a museum; she too entwines her memory of Percival (her tribute to him) with flowers. But where Bernard sees Venus—love—among flowers and remembers Percival, Rhoda sees "oaks cracked asunder and red where the flowering branch has fallen"; and she picks violets to offer as a tribute, violets that by the end of her soliloquy are "withered violets, blackened violets" (159, 161). The parallel between Bernard's and Rhoda's responses to Percival's death emphasizes this contrast between Bernard's thoughts of Venus among her flowers and Rhoda's thoughts of blackened and withered violets. This parallel is part of the general pattern of Rhoda's reference to darkness and degeneracy where others mention sex (reference to Venus is certainly a reference to sexual love). As Woolf stains and corrupts the pages of Shakespeare's homoerotic sonnets with decaying flowers, Rhoda's tribute to Percival is worship mingled ambiguously with corruption.

Not one of the instances of Rhoda's sexual-lesbian connection with darkness, colonial place, or corruption is very striking. It is the mass of connections, the accumulation of juxtapositions, that draws my attention and suggests that there is something significant in Woolf's linkage between Rhoda, in whom lesbianism is repressed, her responses to sexuality, and her references to colony, blackness, tigers, cobras, India, Turks, drumming, warriors, assegais, and ships that cross oceans. If juxtaposition is significant anywhere, it is in Woolf's *The Waves,* where relatively passive juxtaposition rather than overt, active interaction of people or ideas makes the meanings. It isn't that Woolf is making a claim that lesbian sexuality is equal to primitivized images; but the number and frequency of primitivized references to blackness, savagery, tigers, and islands with creepers all build up an impression left on the mind, like the film left on the bottle that Woolf uses as a metaphor to describe the action of the waves racing down the beach and back to the sea, leaving foam and bits of black in their path down the sand.

Five

Class, Race, and Lesbian Erotics in *Summer Will Show*

Sylvia Townsend Warner, like Virginia Woolf, is a British novelist who writes about imperialism and lesbian erotics. Warner's evocations of both, however, are much more direct than Woolf's. Also unlike Woolf, Warner is persistently absent from literary histories. For all twenty-one years of the halting revival of her work, beginning with the 1978 Women's Press of London reprint of her first novel, *Lolly Willowes* (1926) (J. Marcus, "Sylvia T. Warner" 531), critics writing about Warner have repeatedly had to explain who she was, catalog her many accomplishments, and exclaim over her absence from literary history. In 1985, Eleanor Perenyi noted that Warner's obituary read like "a passport to respectable oblivion" (27). In 1990, Gillian Spraggs claimed Warner as "arguably one of the most neglected twentieth-century English writers of stature" (110). And in 2002, "Sylvia who?" is the most common question I get asked about her.[1] Warner's anonymity persists despite her incredible productivity, the generally positive reception each work received when it appeared, and the continuing devotion of loyal readers. In her long lifetime (1893–1978), Warner published seven novels, six collections of poetry, and thirteen collections of short stories, many of which were first published in the *New Yorker.* Her first two novels, *Lolly Willowes* and *Mr. Fortune's Maggot* (1927), were nominated for prizes and selected as book-of-the-month by American book clubs.[2] Among contemporary Warner readers, according to Maroula Joannou, "it is axiomatic that she is among the most accomplished and versatile of early twentieth-century English writers" (89).

Many of these readers have sought to rewrite Warner into histories from which she has been excluded. She has often been left out of discussions about the Communist Party, left politics, and the Spanish Civil War because she was a woman, but critics have worked at redressing this problem.[3] She is not included in the *Norton Anthology of Literature by Women,* Gilbert and Gubar's *No Man's Land,* or Lillian Faderman's *Chloe Plus Olivia,* but she is included in Bonnie Kime Scott's *The Gender of Modernism,* and she has been the subject of several essays and one book, Gay Wachman's *Lesbian Empire: Radical Crosswriting in the Twenties,* by critics who put her feminism and/or her lesbianism at the center of her writing.[4] Other critics have de-emphasized her politics to celebrate the beauty, passion, humor, and rich literary allusiveness of her work.[5] Two biographers have also sought to revive Warner studies. Wendy Mulford's *This Narrow Place: Sylvia Townsend Warner and Valentine Ackland: Life, Letters, and Politics, 1930–1951* is excellent though limited by the fact that Mulford didn't have access to all of Warner's papers. Clare Harman's more recent *Sylvia Townsend Warner: A Biography* addresses the long span of Warner's life, but de-emphasizes her political activism.

Warner's absence from literary history is partly the result of her left-wing politics, her gender, and her lesbianism. Warner herself thought that her "political commitments" to the Communist Party had affected her reception "very badly." In a 1975 interview, she said she "usually had two or three amazingly good reviews" but never "reviews from the sort of reviewers that *sell* books" (Warner, "In Conversation" 36). As Simon Watney sums it up, Warner was "intensely literary, a far leftist, an intellectual to her fingertips, a woman and a lesbian"; this combination is "hardly . . . likely to ensure her reputation in modern Britain" (56). Warner also seems to have lived the wrong kind of life to have been embraced by scholars of British modernism, left history, or feminist politics. She lived in London in the 1920s, was friends with Bloomsbury's David Garnett and Steven Tomlin, once had lunch with Virginia Woolf, and later became friends with Leonard Woolf.[6] But after the mid–1930s, Warner lived rurally and wrote about rural people, while modernism is often defined as exploration of urban lives and mechanization. Her communist organizing was also among rural agricultural workers rather than factory workers.[7] And though Warner was a feminist and a lesbian, neither feminism nor sexuality were the principles around which she organized her political activism or her writing.

The last paradox of Warner's neglect is that it is exacerbated by an incredible diversity that makes her writing impossible to categorize.[8] Her work includes both realistic and fantastic fiction, involving talking cats, elves, and witches,[9] as well as historical realism. Even the most realistic work, *Summer Will Show,* has buried references to Cinderella and witchery that contribute a great deal of ironic humor to an also serious and political book. Her work is full of modernist experimentation, but isn't described by any characterization of modernism I have ever seen. Rather, Warner experiments with realism itself. For instance, her novels *After the Death of Don Juan* (1938), *The Corner That Held Them* (1948), and *The Flint Anchor* (1954) involve many characters in realistic and historical settings, but Warner denies the reader easy identification with any one central consciousness. Stylistically, Warner is compared to Virginia Woolf and to Jane Austen, sometimes in the same essay.[10] If her poetry is experimental in some ways, formally it is traditional.

For all these reasons, though, a full-scale revival of Warner's works—getting them all back into print, into libraries, and onto syllabi—is important. Analysis of her and Valentine Ackland's contributions in Spain and her work for the Communist Party would go far toward clarifying women's participation in left-wing political movements of the 1930s and 1940s. Her long and fairly public sexual partnership with Ackland, who wore pants when and where it was not common for women to do so, as well as Warner's friendships with gay men, makes her important to lesbian and gay history of the twentieth century.[11] Her private theorizing about sexuality and gender—she called her relationship a marriage, asserted the masculinity of her mind, analyzed sexological studies—and her stories involving incestuous, interspecies, and intergenerational as well as homoerotic love demand that Warner be written into the history of contemporary queer studies, a field too often imagined as not having a history involving women intellectuals who lived and worked rurally, theorized about sexuality, and had a good time in bed sixty years ago. Her lecture about women writers, during which she refers back to Virginia Woolf's lectures published as *A Room of One's Own,* as well as her own comments about women in letters to Nancy Cunard, among others, locates her firmly in the history of feminism. For feminist activists and scholars, she raises questions about how a genteel daughter of a master at a famous English boys' school—the kind satirized in *The Waves*—became a communist activist constantly aware of her class. Her modernist experimentation with fantasy and realism and her use of history in fiction will necessarily shift accounts of modernism. Not the least, new Warner studies would emphasize how much humor and passion there is in Warner's work, as well as the sheer fun of reading her.

My focus in this chapter is the way in which Warner's political and erotic passions are inextricably blended. Warner was deeply committed to political action against injustice all her life. She writes against abuses of power, from capitalist exploitation of the working class, to fascism in Spain, to fox hunting, to patriarchal exploitation of women. She is sharply critical of romantic and primitivizing notions that work to keep hierarchies in place, her critique often taking the form of antagonism toward middle-class ardor for a "picturesque" working class. But she relies on primitivism when she represents homoerotics: she figures homosexuality always in terms of white middle-class contact with members of the working class or people of color. This is connected to the way in which sensuous love and political activism against oppression are enmeshed for Warner; but it also follows the pattern set by Richard von Krafft-Ebing, Havelock Ellis, Edward Carpenter, John Addington Symonds, Sigmund Freud, and Bronislaw Malinowski, among others, who each sought to take the measure of middle-class British homosexuality by writing comparative sexology.

Warner and Class Primitivism: The Picturesque

At least as passionately as Olive Schreiner did, Sylvia Townsend Warner embraced political activism as part of her role as a public intellectual and writer. Warner and Ackland joined the Communist Party in 1935 and worked as local leaders organizing among the rural workers in Dorset (Mulford, *This Narrow Place* 58–60). Warner never gave up her membership in the Communist Party, though Ackland did in 1953 and encouraged Warner to do so also. Warner's political rage during this period was directed at the landowning class for its part in creating the despicable living conditions of the working class in rural Dorset. She was convinced that those conditions could be remedied only when the British working classes, rural and urban, made alliances with each other and with "their fellows in other countries, and other continents" (Warner, "The Way" 486). Warner and Ackland were also aggressive fund-raisers for the Republican side during the Spanish Civil War, went to Barcelona with a Red Cross unit in 1936, and visited Valencia and Madrid with the Second International Congress for Writers in Defense of Culture in 1937. At the Third American Writers Congress in New York in 1939, Warner condemned fascism with characteristic contempt: it is "as deadly to those it would cherish as to those it would destroy, . . . teaches race hatred to children, . . . says to women, Be fruitful and multiply and replenish the battlefield, [and] drives out its artists and thinkers" ("Review and Comment" 22).

More than any other of the writers I am discussing, Warner is overtly critical of primitivizing and romanticizing ideas especially about the people to whose cause she is politically devoted. Warner writes most critically about class primitivism in her journalism. Her first published work, "Behind the Firing Line: Some Experiences in a Munition Factory by a Lady Worker" (1916), critiques middle-class views of working-class lives as "picturesque" from the point of view of a temporary, middle-class, factory worker. The essay is mostly lighthearted and reflects Warner's excitement about participating, as a woman of leisure, in a wartime scheme to relieve regular workers in a munitions factory. But the essay also has a political charge. She notes that harsh conditions—including dangerously bad air quality, a lack of adequate tools, inadequate time for eating and drinking, and dirty bathrooms—make difficult and tedious work more difficult and tedious, and she challenges employers to improve conditions. Of the wages, she writes, "I am not doing [the factory work] for a livelihood, but if I were, I doubt if I should think it good pay" (204). She juxtaposes her remarks about harsh working conditions and inadequate wages with a remembrance of "the large fortune that [her] employers were making" (200).

The essay is also self-ironic and mocking of the narrator's own romantic view of working-class experience. The narrator, Warner, confesses that "between signing on and beginning my training I went about telling my acquaintances joyously enough how hard I was going to work, and wondering inwardly what manner of thing I had let myself in for" (191). She notes of herself and the other women who had been recruited, "It was natural to be sprightly while the dirt could still be washed off, and the aches slept off without much difficulty, and while the idea of the extreme picturesqueness and daring of such an adventure as ours still upheld one. True that no one else seemed to see in our blue overalls anything but a uniform: we knew them, secretly, as a vestment" (195). Warner is having fun here. But the "picturesqueness," "daring," and "adventure" with which she describes the situation of the relief workers are representations of working-class labor that Warner is critiquing seriously. Employers and owners, she suggests, rely on romantic notions about labor as a justification for complaisance about conditions. Later, in a 1939 essay, "The Way by Which I Have Come," written after Warner became involved in labor organizing, she reports being embarrassed to have participated in what she later realized was a scheme "devised to avoid the payment of overtime rates to the regular workers" (475).

"The Way by Which I Have Come" challenges romantic views of rural working-class lives. Intended to chasten landowning farmers and motivate farm workers to join the Communist Party, the article begins with a description of Warner's childhood as that of a "happy and innocent little townee" who thought of the country as a place where "one was taken in wagonettes, with a clattering picnic-basket, to see the beauties of the district" (473). But the essay charts her gradual exposure to the realities of country life and her move, as an adult, to rural Dorset. Warner details the inadequacies of the tied housing in Dorset, asserting that "houses that have gone bad weigh heavily on those who live in them" (478). She catalogs "the average weekly mileage covered by the labourer's wife who fetches all her water from the well and carries all her slops to the ditch . . . the amount of repairs done to cottages and the amount that should be done; the average number of sleepers per bedroom and of rats per sleeper" (483). Warner also describes the house she bought in Dorset—Miss Green's cottage—as attractive for its slate roof. Sod was the norm, and the source, according to Warner, of constant leaks and illness. The house is attractive, as well, for having "no claims to be picturesque." This is important because she was, by then, "exceedingly wary of that falsification of values which puts week-enders into sunbonnets and causes genuine regrets at any proposal to pull down a vermin-ridden, sixteenth century nuisance and build a sound dwelling in its place." She says that she still "proposed to be a week-ender, though unsunbonneted," thus differentiating herself from those middle-class people who would idealize the bad housing the working class had to live in (480–481).

Thirty years later, after Valentine Ackland's death, Warner still emphasizes her own difference from those who value working-class housing for being picturesque. In a narrative she wrote as part of *I'll Stand by You: Selected Letters of Sylvia Townsend Warner and Valentine Ackland,* Warner writes of Miss Green's cottage that it had been attractive because it was "freehold: An unevictable tenure" and not a tied cottage, as were most in the village, and that it had had "nothing to be said in its favor except that it was totally unpicturesque and stood by itself" (5).[12] A letter to Nancy Cunard also evidences Warner's antagonism toward the middle-class glorification of bad housing, a glorification that she referred to as a desire for the picturesque. Warner writes that Cunard will like some cottages she is trying to rent for Cunard's visit because of the landscape, and because the cottages "are weatherproof, and not picturesque" (*Letters* 83).

In one of her later novels, Warner is also critical of the kind of primitivism that enables middle-class displacement of sexuality onto the working class. *The Flint Anchor* (1954), set in the first half of the nineteenth century, is about the relatively unhappy and loveless lives of John Barnard, owner of a shipping business that makes money in Baltic trade, and his family of many children. Toward the end of the novel, Barnard observes the public displays of physical affection between his daughter and her new husband and realizes "he was an old fogey. He had grown up in an England which had the precision and balance of an engraving: good and bad, heaven and hell, Whig and Tory, Queen Charlotte and Queen Caroline. In that world modest women behaved modestly, and what they might lack in ardour was supplied by women who had ceased to be modest" (282). This passage marks the beginning of Barnard's somewhat insightful old age, but Barnard's insights are extremely limited. He never realizes he has used cultural beliefs about the "modesty" of respectable married women to avoid confronting sexuality altogether, his own homosexuality in particular. Julia will, he anticipates, be a "wall, . . . her breasts like towers" that will defend him against "mothers of Loseby families" who are "continually jostling their daughters against him." Similarly, a wife will protect him from his "maid-servants" who "did not directly menace his chastity" but "exercised an oblique pressure against his bachelor quiet" (8). Accordingly, Barnard has no desire for Julia in particular. He wishes before his wedding that he did not have to take her maidenhead (16). And after Julia's death, the narrator comments that Barnard had begotten his children halfheartedly: "Only Julia knew how discreditable to them both those occasions had been; how little love there had been on his side, how much unwomanly prompting on hers to rouse that little love into a brief lust, and how difficult it had been afterwards to conceal the resentment felt by both parties" (271). Barnard's belief in the "modesty" of some and the ardorousness of others is part of a larger reliance on divisions that Warner critiques in his character—divisions symbolized from the beginning of the novel by the high spiked wall that surrounds his house, keeping it and his family always in partial shadow and separate from the rest of the surrounding town. The twin assertions of sexlessness among middle-class women and excessive sexuality among the working class is one aspect of a large-scale reliance on divisions that destroy Barnard's life.

Warner's *The True Heart* (1929) reflects her hostility to the arguments of eugenicists who categorize blacks, homosexuals, criminals, and the mentally ill as those who should be prevented from reproducing in defense of the strength of the empire. The novel also reflects Warner's awareness and rejection of myths of black hypersexuality. The novel tells the story of Sukey Bond, a young servant, and her quest to marry Eric, a young gentleman and an "idiot," against the wishes of just about everyone else in the novel. Two minor characters exchange the following remarks after they overhear Sukey reporting that she is with child: "'Fancy an idiot getting a girl that way,' remarked the housemaid, filling her mouth with currants. 'I shouldn't have thought it hardly possible.' 'Oh, they're wonderful at it. Like the blacks. If you must wolf all the currants, all I say is, wolf those you've picked over yourself.' 'Well, I call it disgusting'" (98). Warner points to the harm and absurdity of these ideas about black hypersexuality in several ways. The characters who make the remarks about the sexuality of idiots and blacks are among the many who work against Sukey in her quest to find Eric, save him from life in an institution, and marry him. More important, assertions of black hypersexuality are made parallel—similarly clownish and unthinking—with a peevish exchange over the number of currants picked versus those eaten.

Homosexual Primitives

If Warner is overtly critical of ideology that displaces sexuality onto working-class women and black people, and overtly critical of primitivizing middle-class ideas about picturesque working-class lives, however, her critique of primitivizing stereotypes also has a blind spot. When it comes to representing homosexuality and representing characters discovering homosexuality, Warner relies on class- and race-primitivist stereotypes that she critiques when homosexuality is not involved, stereotypes created and perpetuated in writing by Olive Schreiner and the sexologists discussed earlier. In *The Flint Anchor,* working-class sexual mores, as opposed to Barnard's rigid walling out of homosexuality, are idealized as entirely free and openly inclusive of homosexuality. Warner is blatant in making this suggestion in the second half of the novel when Crusoe, a young fisherman, admits having written on a public wall "Tomas Kettle goes with Dandy Billy," characteristically misspelling "Thomas" to reveal his identity, and thus get an opportunity to tell Thomas he loves him (197). To Thomas's assertion that "for a man to love a man is a crime in this country," Crusoe replies, "Not in Loseby, Mr. Thomas, not in Loseby. Nor in any seagoing place, that I've a-heard of. It's the way we live, and always have been, whatever it may be inland. I can't say for inland. I never went there, and wouldn't want to particular. But in Loseby we go man with man and man with woman, and nobody think the worse. Why, they darsn't even preach against it" (205). The Barnards later receive a letter from Thomas, who has been shipped off to some foreign destination for not denying that he "goes with Dandy Billy." The letter says he is on his deathbed and is accompanied by a death certificate. But there is also the suggestion that Thomas has had a chance to live more fully than John Barnard manages specifically because Thomas has affiliated with fishermen and because he is eventually sent away from England: both of these moves enable him to see homosexuality as a possible kind of love. That Warner has a fisherman explain acceptance of homosexuality to a middle-class man and that she writes the passage in Crusoe's working-class dialect—the only passage written in dialect in the entire novel—all locate homosexuality in the working class and attribute middle-class discovery of homosexual possibilities to contact with working-class people and culture.

Crusoe's reply to Thomas also confirms the suspicion generated by other aspects of the novel that Barnard's own unhappiness is the result of excluding the possibility of homosexual love by walling himself off from any contact, except to give charity, with the working class. At the beginning of the novel, the narrator explains that John Barnard is applauded for a speech, though

> not for what he had said, but for how he looked while saying it. They [the Loseby fishermen] had not realized till now what a handsome young man they had got. . . . He was revealed as very handsome indeed, romantically handsome, with such glossy dark hair, such large bright eyes, and such well-made legs. Among Loseby fishermen it was taken as a matter of course that men should feel amorously towards a handsome young man. John Barnard on his twenty-first birthday was the image of a man's young man (women might feel that his forehead was too narrow and his nose too sharp), and Job Ransom, bellowing out his toast of "Mr. Barnard— bless his flesh!" summed up the mood of the occasion. (8)

Barnard is, himself, oblivious to the fishermen's homoerotic responses to his appearance. But the novel suggests that were John Barnard as capable of admitting homoeroticism as the fishermen of Loseby, or were he able to make friends, as Thomas does, with the fishermen, and thus be exposed to the possibility of homoeroticism, he might have avoided many of the "error[s] in love" by which he made himself and everyone around him miserable (309).

In *Mr. Fortune's Maggot,* homoeroticism is similarly positioned as accessible to an Englishman among Pacific Islanders. In this novel, Timothy Fortune, an English missionary, goes to the Pacific island of Fanua, marked as a primitive place by the fact that Mr. Fortune's watch, by which he has previously organized every aspect of every day, stops running shortly after his arrival. On a Pacific island, he is, Warner suggests humorously, in an anachronistic space. It would also follow, given Freud's explanation of the development of human sexuality, that Fanuans, stuck in the early phases of human development, are bisexual. Whether or not Warner read Freud, his ideas, as well as popularizations of primitivizing anthropology, were in wide circulation by the time she wrote *Mr. Fortune.* Consistent with these anthropological and psychological constructions of dark-skinned people and their geographies, Mr. Fortune is transformed by Fanua. He submits, under the pretense of relief for an injury, to sensual massage over increasingly numerous parts of his body. His masseur, Lueli, is a young Fanuan who befriends him and who Mr. Fortune thinks is his one convert to Christianity. In fact, it is Mr. Fortune who is converted, finally, to sensual and homoerotic partial self-awareness—as well as to anti-church and anti-imperialist sentiment—by his contact with Lueli, and Fanua itself.

Warner's representation of the way in which middle-class white people get access to homoerotic influence is not a product of her own imagination. The claim in *The Flint Anchor* that homosexuality flourishes among seafaring men certainly reflects the claim of some sexologists that upper- and middle-class gay men preferred sexual relationships with working-class men. Her representation of the conversion of middle-class whites to homosexuality follows the model established by anthropologists and sexologists who sought to take the measure of Euro-American middle-class sexual behavior by writing comparative ethnographies. Ackland and Warner read sexological writings and Warner described volumes by Havelock Ellis, Iwan Block, and Richard von Krafft-Ebing as "dear possessions." In a letter published in *I'll Stand by You,* Ackland asks Warner to "bring back our Havelock Ellis? Or Block? or Krafft-Ebing?" and in a footnote, Warner explains that "in 1942 we had been told, confidentially, that in the event of an invasion our house would be requisitioned as a machine-gun post—in which case we would have to leave at short notice. So we packaged our smaller dear possessions and housed them with friends in less menaced places. One of these deposits was a crate of 17th cent. folios and Nonesuch editions with Havelock Ellis etc. squeezed in among them, which I had taken to Little Zeal [her mother's house]" (Warner and Ackland 199, 199n). Like the sexologists whose work she valued, Warner can't seem to talk about homosexuality among middle-class whites without there being a working-class or racialized person as part of the scene as a source of the sexuality to which she wants to expose a middle-class white person. She represents homosexuality in terms of contact between middle- or upper-class whites and dark-skinned or working-class characters.

Summer Will Show

Sylvia Townsend Warner's 1936 novel *Summer Will Show,* set in rural England and in Paris of 1848, strongly exhibits this paradoxical combination of primitivism and anti-imperialism. The obvious political goal of the novel is to encourage the rural laborers of Dorset, among whom Warner and Ackland were working as organizers, to join the Communist Party. Warner's and Ackland's experiences showed them that workers were often kept apart, especially women from men, by "deference and fear" as well as "low wages, long hours, and isolation. . . . within communities" (Mulford, *This Narrow Place* 62). As if in response, the novel presents an argument that working-class men and women have common cause against hierarchies—those based on economics and those based on gender—that keep them from uniting and on which exploitation depends. The novel also makes an argument for an international as well as antiracist approach to ending capitalist and imperialist exploitation. The two murders at the end of the novel are a direct result of the failure of Warner's protagonist, Sophia, to make a political alliance with her nephew Caspar, a fourteen-year-old Caribbean "half-caste," as part of her developing communist economic and political analysis (34). Warner suggests, with these two deaths as examples, other deaths that are also the result of failures in alliance making. The novel claims that unless English workers, including soldiers and potential soldiers, make common cause with one another and with the exploited producers of English capital in the colonies, revolutionary efforts are inadequate at best and likely doomed to failure.

Summer Will Show is also Warner's most obviously lesbian novel.[13] The elliptically presented lesbianism between Sophia and Minna Lemuel in the second half of the novel is foreshadowed by Sophia's naively homoerotic response to her neighbor Mrs. Hervey, as has been noted by both Terry Castle and Thomas Foster.[14] But Warner also writes Sophia's lesbianism as sexual curiosity about the "strange loves" of the working-class lime-kiln man and her romantic interpretation of Caspar's West Indian appearance and origins, which function as metonymy for Sophia's difference—a difference specifically to do with her gender orientation and her sensuality. The combination of politics with depictions of lesbianism in *Summer Will Show* clearly reveals the paradox of Warner's simultaneous critique of and reliance on primitivist stereotypes about the working-class and dark-skinned people, including Jews. In *Summer Will Show,* the tropes of access to sexuality are specifically working-men's hands,[15] working-class political rage, Caribbean and Lithuanian origins, Jewish features and animalism, Gypsy "wandering,"[16] and the history of Jewish huntedness. By means of contact with these, a white landowning woman fully discovers her political "assignation with the fox" (93) and lesbian-erotic "happiness" (405), as Sophia puts it.

Critics of *Summer Will Show* generally assume that Minna is the agent and source of Sophia's sexual and political transformations.[17] But hints of Sophia's homoerotic inclination abound in the first third of the novel that takes place on Sophia's estate, Blandamer, before Sophia ever goes to Paris or meets Minna. The early lesbian-erotic hints and scenes foreshadow the lesbianism Sophia later experiences with Minna. More significantly for my purposes, in the early part of the novel, Sophia rejects lesbian erotics with Mrs. Hervey explicitly because of Mrs. Hervey's middle-class status. This initial rejection of lesbian possibility emphasizes Warner's consistent use of working-class and dark-skinned figures to explain homoerotic transformation and indulgence. Sophia rejects lesbian-sexual possibility with middle-class Mrs. Hervey, but with Jewish Minna, she is seduced.

Hints of Sophia's lesbianism begin in the first scene. As Sophia walks her children over her parched land toward the lime-kiln to breathe fumes as a cure for whooping cough, their latest malady, she reflects that "it was a pity (for many reasons it was a pity) that she was not a man," as then she "could have known with more assurance how Papa would have brought up a boy" (6). The parenthetical and cryptic "for many reasons" suggests that in addition to wanting to be a better parent to a boy, there is something only parenthetically expressible, such as lesbian desire, in Sophia's wish to be a man. This wish also reflects "sexological discourse of homosexual desire as 'inversion'" (Foster 540).

Lesbianism is similarly hinted at by Sophia's disinterest in her husband, Frederick. His absence is unregrettable; her marriage is "that deplorable mating" (20). Her original impulse to marry at all is only "a sudden imperious curiosity to know what the love of man and woman might be, which at the first learning had shrivelled away and left her cold and unamorous" (255). She describes herself as "opposed" and "frigid" to "wine and the love of man" (77, 78). Over life as a wife, she prefers to husband the life around her.[18] Her concern in the early part of the novel is to ensure reproductivity of life on her estate, from her children to "Dymond's bull" to "Topp's eldest girl" to tomato vines, from which she approves the pinching off of under-developed fruit for the benefit of the more promising (20, 23). This philosophy of husbandry extends even to her daughter Augusta's hair, which is "cropped to make it grow more strongly" (8).

Sophia's belief that freedom is being rid of the conventions of her gender also foreshadows her lesbianism. She enjoys her visit to the Trebennick Academy because the smell of the air makes her feel "absolved back into animal," and she has the impression that "one waft of wind there would blow . . . the petticoats from one's legs . . . leaving one free, swift, unburdened as a fox" (36). She imagines that there she might live "a wild romantic life in which, unsexed and unpersoned, she rode, sat in inns, slept in a bracken bed among the rocks, bathed naked in swift-running brooks, knocked people down, outwitted shadowy enemies, poached one night with gypsies, in another went a keeper's round with a gun under her arm" (36). Here Sophia links both wild animals and Gypsies with freedom from gender, as well as stating her preference for playing the masculine role of "keeper" with a gun.

Sophia's interactions with Mrs. Hervey, the doctor's wife, explicitly foreshadow the lesbian eros of the end of the novel. When Damian and Augusta, Sophia's children, are dying, Mrs. Hervey makes a sympathy call; another time she climbs through a window into Sophia's drawing room, drenched by a storm, to show Sophia the doctor's letter recalling Frederick to his children's bedside (68–72). Mrs. Hervey is outraged that anyone thinks he has a right "to interfere, to discuss and plot. . . . As if, whatever happened, you could not stand alone, and judge for yourself! As if you needed a man!" (72). The language Warner uses to describe the interactions gives the visits erotic subtexts. Mrs. Hervey knows her visit is "indiscreet" and "peculiar" (70, 72). She keeps "redden[ing] as a schoolgirl in fault," speaks "passionately," and confesses something like sexual attraction, though she doesn't know how to name it: "I have thought of you day and night, ever since that first evening . . . my husband sent me to you. You can't understand, and I can't express it" (71, 72, 70). Sophia is irritated by Mrs. Hervey's "genteel" and "boarding-school" manners, but also observes that her company has "a certain reviving quality," and her eyes have a beauty Sophia will "never forget" (57–58). When Mrs. Hervey gives her an awkward embrace good-bye, Sophia notices the feel of her lips—"hot, a little roughened . . . like those of a child"—and thinks, "She might be in love with me" (58).[19]

During the second visit, Sophia is irritated that while her children are dying she must "sit here, dosing this little ninny with port and waiting to hear what fool's errand brought her" (69). But she is also surprised to feel "a sudden dash of tenderness and amusement" and to be "almost glad that . . . Mrs. Hervey was here, blown in at the window like a draggled bird" (70). Sophia is aware that "the letter, lying so calmly on [Mrs. Hervey's] lap, seemed to have no real part in this to-do. Some other motive, violent and unexperienced as the emotions of youth, trembled undeclared between them." She thinks, "We might be two schoolgirls . . . two romantic misses, stolen from our white beds to exchange illicit comfits, and trembling lest amid this stage-rattling thunderstorm we should hear the footsteps of Mrs. Goodchild" (72). Looking back on this visit, Sophia reflects that it was prompted by a "misguided impulse" (89).

Sophia ultimately rejects Mrs. Hervey largely because her pronouncement that a husband isn't necessary agitates Sophia by transgressing her sense of sexual decorum. In response, she reasserts calming heterosexual normalcy: she thinks of things "practical, proper, and immediate" to do, including physically reasserting the semblance of heterosexuality by expelling Mrs. Hervey from her house and determining to send letters—her own and Dr. Hervey's—recalling Frederick. Sophia removes "all traces of [Mrs. Hervey's] extraordinary visit," for "such escapades were intolerable. One could not have such young women frisking round one, babbling as to whether or no one needed a husband, declaring on one's behalf that one didn't" (74).

If in rejecting Mrs. Hervey, however, Sophia calms her mind, she also abandons her body. She feels "round her steadied mind . . . her flesh hanging cold and forlorn, as though in this conflict she had for ever abandoned it" (73). Rejecting Mrs. Hervey means to Sophia rejecting the possibility of sexual contact. She is "frigid to the love of wine and man," but might "be warmed" by traveling with Mrs. Hervey after her children die, she reflects. If "a woman cannot travel alone . . . two women may travel together" (78). But as soon as she considers it, Sophia rejects this "foolish vision," thinking Mrs. Hervey is appealing not for anything she "really is," but only because she offers a "dew of being young and impulsive" to Sophia's "aridity" (78–79). Though this passage is overtly about travel as a preoccupation, Sophia's talk about being "warmed" rather than "frigid" makes it also about sex, as does Warner's use of a metaphor of wetness: dry Sophia will be dampened by Mrs. Hervey's impulsiveness. Warner uses this metaphor elsewhere, as well. Sophia sees Blandamer as "parched" and "barren" when she walks to the kiln with her children. But as she walks Mrs. Hervey home, holding her hand, she hears, louder than the storm's thunder, "the sipping whistle, all around them, of the parched ground drinking the rain" (74).

But even more significant for the progression of the novel than Sophia's erotic response to Mrs. Hervey is Sophia's repression of that response specifically because of Mrs. Hervey's class position. Class-specific behavioral norms are the reason Mrs. Hervey's pronouncement against the need for husbands is so upsetting. Sophia reflects that "from a woman of the village she could have heard such words without offence. Down there in that lowest class, sexual decorum could be kilted out of the way like an impeding petticoat; and Mary Bogler, whose husband was in jail, and Carry Westmacott, whose husband should be, might declare without offence that a woman was as good as a man, and better" (74). A woman of the upper classes can think such things, and even dismiss a husband, but she can't *say* she doesn't need a husband. Sophia continues, "In her own heart . . . unreproved, could lodge the conviction that a Sophia might well discard a Frederick, and in her life she had been ready, calmly enough, to put this into effect. But into words, never! Such things could be done, but not said. . . . In this room, the serene demonstration of how a lady of the upper classes spends her leisure amid flowers and books and arts, words had been spoken such as those walls had never heard before" (75). Sophia says she is prepared to dismiss Frederick silently, but—as "a lady of the upper classes"—she is not prepared to act or speak in an independent way, sexual or otherwise, with Mrs. Hervey, whose suggestion about the irrelevance of husbands is itself evidence of middle-class vulgarity.

Sophia's dislike of Mrs. Hervey is a revulsion of her middle-class status elsewhere, too. Sophia refers to Mrs. Hervey repeatedly in terms of her husband's profession—the wife of a doctor—and calls her disparagingly a "boarding school miss," and a "social minnikin"; Mrs. Hervey has merely "an exasperating gesture of refinement," a "false refinement" (70, 75).[20] The two have walked hand in hand, but "a visiting relationship betwen [*sic*] them [is] neither possible nor desirable" according to Sophia. Mrs. Hervey's house is in a village with "genteel pretensions enough" to support several shops, villas, and a chapel. But "it represented the new world, as Blandamer Abbots, with its mud-walled cottages, tithe barn, and one great house, represented the old" (89). Mrs. Hervey's mother is also of this new world—a vapid "stout matron" who prances and assails Sophia with chairs and unfinished sentences, whose cap ribbons flutter, and who contributes to making the Hervey house a "narrow den of gentility" and an "airless closet" (90).

Resolving Back into Animal: Minna Lemuel

While Sophia rejects the possibility of erotic relations with Mrs. Hervey, however, despite proximity, need of solace, and a seeming—if only partially conscious—willingness on Mrs. Hervey's part, she warms in one day to both wine and "passionate amity" with Minna Lemuel. Sophia's response to Minna is erotic from first contact.[21] More significantly, Sophia is compelled by Minna in a way that she is not by Mrs. Hervey. The erotic subtext of Sophia's interactions with Mrs. Hervey becomes overt erotic text in interactions with Minna. Sophia's first contact with Minna takes place in Paris at a party in Minna's apartment, where Sophia has gone to find Frederick and "beguile" him into giving her another child (99). Minna entertains her guests with a tale about her childhood in Lithuania and the pogrom in which her family was killed. At the first sound of Minna's "siren voice," Sophia thinks, "See her I must" (145, 115). When she does see, it is "as though she had never opened her eyes before" (145). Sophia's gaze on Minna throughout the tale is "faithful," and gets her, in reply, "the smile of the dutiful child" and a swift "confidential grimace" (136, 127, 136). And because of her gaze, when the storytelling is interrupted, Minna tells her, "I was sorry to lose such listening as yours. Yes, as yours. Did you not know that I was speaking to you?" (140). Thoughts of Minna tease intensely after this initial contact. Sophia fears that "she would never know, never know more!" about Minna (138). To go home without becoming pregnant would be disappointing, but worse would be never "knowing more about Minna," departing "as tantalized, as unfulfilled" as previous dreams of Minna had left her (139). Sophia fears sexual loss, in particular. When she falls asleep on Minna's couch and dreams she is headed home, "it was not for the loss of the child she mourned so desperately. Something else was lost, there was some other hope some other promise irretrievably mismanaged and irretrievably lost and it was for this something, this unpossessed unknown, that she mourned in such desolation, having not even the comfort of knowing what was for ever left behind and forfeited" (150). That she can't name precisely what she will lose likens it to the "other motive" that Sophia notices "trembled undeclared between" her and Mrs. Hervey (72). Minna also sparks in Sophia a "curiosity" such as she has "never in her life . . . felt . . . or dreamed . . . possible." Curiosity, here, is the same specifically sexual impulse that leads her to marry Frederick. But if that experiment left her "cold and unamorous," and if she chooses mind over body in her exchange with Mrs. Hervey, the curiosity over Minna directs Sophia back to the body. This curiosity "went beyond speculation, a thing not of the brain but in the blood. It burned in her like a furnace, with a steadfast compulsive heat that must presently catch Minna in its draught, hale her in, and devour her" (145).

Without ever being explicit, Warner elaborates on the erotic connection between Sophia and Minna for the rest of the novel by reference to passion, compulsion, warmth, sensual textures, throbbing, stroking, womanhood, kisses, caresses, and bewitchment. Sophia wants to "unburden herself" to Minna and to "explain passionately"; she is "compelled" by Minna (147). When Sophia falls asleep on Minna's couch, she lies "passive under the hands that untied her bonnet-strings and took off her shoes, and covered her with something warm and furry, stroking her, slowly, heavily, like the hands of sleep, stroking her hair and her brow" (150–151). Talking to Minna, Sophia "felt the weight of her whole life throbbing to be recounted, . . . her womanhood rose up crowded and clear before her" (156). The image of Minna "thoughtfully licking the last oyster shell" invites a sexual reading, as Terry Castle and Thomas Foster have noted (274; Castle 79; Foster 544). At various other times, Sophia and Minna pace "arm in arm," and get "too excited to finish a meal" (276). Sophia admires Minna's eyelashes, or "caresses" Minna to warm her and take her pulse when she is ill (252, 250, 254). Sophia professes to love her for her "odd mixture of nobility and extravagance" (290). While Minna's body is "heavy, ill-framed, and faintly grotesque" by day, at night it "achieved an extraordinary harmoniousness with its bed, became in suavity and sober resilience the sister of that exemplary mattress" (299). Sophia's "whole being" is "ravaged with love and tenderness" watching Minna eat a biscuit in bed at night (301). Sophia remarks with some amazement that Minna had "freed her from" ideas about how and why "one ought to love" and granted her "one flower, liberty" (290–291).

Minna's influence over Sophia, in stark contrast to Mrs. Hervey's more mundane attractions, has the power of witchery. Sophia is under "some extraordinary enchantment" from the time Sophia gets wind of Minna's voice (261). The pogrom narrative that captivates Sophia once she meets Minna in person is a "spell broken" when the concierge interrupts with his announcement that the revolutionaries want carriages for the barricade (141). And when Sophia is temporarily back under the influence of her Aunt Leocadie and aristocratic feminine decorum, she suspects Minna of having "laid some spell on her common sense" (184). Minna claims her role in Sophia's transformation, too, saying, "I've encouraged a quantity of people to run away, but I have never seen anyone so decisively escaped as you," and again, saying, "I have converted Sophia now" (225, 281). Sophia is indeed transformed. Waking up on Minna's couch, Sophia thinks "she could do anything, go anywhere, if she could spend a day in such passionate amity with her husband's mistress. Hers was the liberty of the fallen woman now" (156). Accordingly, she moves in with Minna, collects scrap metal for revolutionary bullets intended for use in carrying out the threat of the slogan "bread or lead," delivers copies of a pamphlet that turn out to be the *Communist Manifesto,* and eventually fights behind a barricade alongside revolutionaries.

Just as Warner makes it clear that Sophia rejects erotic engagement with Mrs. Hervey specifically because she is middle class, Warner makes it clear that Sophia is "bewitched" and transformed by Minna largely because Minna is a Lithuanian Jew and, as such, behaves like a hunted animal. I believe Warner sets out to underline the limitations of Sophia's worldview by making her incapable of considering a middle-class woman's sexuality, as she also points out Barnard's similarly limited conception of middle-class women's asexuality in *The Flint Anchor.* But Warner also relies on a corresponding set of conceptions about hypersexuality and race. Her plot turns on the stereotype of the primitive Oriental, a stereotype that says Minna's erotics will be especially powerful, compelling, and transformative even to the point of bewitchment. In her reliance on this trope, Warner follows the model employed by sexologists.

Sophia's responses to and descriptions of Minna emphasize both repulsiveness and sensuality as products of her darkness and her Judaism. When Sophia first sees Minna, she is both repelled and attracted, first describing her face as "ugly, uglier than one could have believed, hearing that voice. A discordant face . . . for the features with their Jewish baroque, the hooked nose, the crescent eyebrows and heavy eyelids, the large full-lipped mouth, are florid, or should be; but the hollow cheeks forbid them and she is at once a heavy voluptuous cat and a starved one" (123–124). Sophia also imagines Minna making a gesture that conforms to stereotypes of Jews as avaricious, but that also "caresses" provocatively. Minna "savors" those listening to her story as if they were "money-bags," Sophia thinks: "Our ears are your ducats. You are exactly like a Jewish shopkeeper. . . . In a moment you should rub your hands, the shopkeeper's gesture. . . . Then, as though in compliance, Minna's large supple hands gently caressed themselves together in the very gesture of [Sophia's] thought" (127). Warner is marking Sophia's limitations here, in Sophia's expectations of stereotypically Jewish behavior. But to whatever degree Warner is being ironic about Sophia's belief in Jewish stereotypes, she is also mixing up references to Minna's Judaism with Sophia's compulsive attraction to her. The sources of Minna's simultaneous compellingness and sensuousness are persistently her Judaism and her darkness. Minna has a "siren voice" housed in a "thick, milk-coffee coloured throat" (145). Sophia wants to talk to her "as though the Jewess's impassive attention had been a dark sleek-surfaced pool into which, as one is compelled to cast a stone," Sophia wants to "cast her confidence" (147).

Warner also marks the erotic change Minna effects on Sophia by having Sophia warm to wine and Minna simultaneously. This refers back to Sophia's remarks that she was "frigid to the love of wine and man" (77, 78). But the scene in which Sophia warms to wine and to Minna makes a direct assertion that Sophia's frigidity thaws to some specifically Jewish essence. In their first interaction, Minna offers Sophia hot wine that both smells of Lithuanian forests and feels to Sophia like a caress. Sophia thinks, "The warm spiced scent, slightly resinous, as though the Jewess had mixed all the summer forests of her childhood in the cup, was like a caress." And "round the first sip she felt her being close, haggard and hungry" (139). The next morning, Minna's glance is inextricable from the wine: Minna takes Sophia's hand and gazes "at her with a possessive earnest glance, a glance that instantly recalled the taste of the mulled wine offered overnight" (154). And later, having taken Minna to dinner and ordered a Beaujolais following "an axiom of Papa's," Sophia "yield[s] again to that wine-like sensation of ease and accomplished triumph which had been with her all day" (160).

As Minna is marked racially, she and her apartment are also outfitted with a garishly tattered, colorful mishmash of oriental and occidental objects. When Sophia stares at Minna, she sees "sleek braids of black hair and the smooth milk-coffee coloured shoulders, the drooping yellow scarf lined with rather shabby ermine" (138). The sofa on which Sophia sleeps is "a gilded sofa upholstered in pink brocade." And the clothes she wakes up in include a "yellow ermine-lined scarf," a "scarlet dyed sheepskin," and "a pair of sky-blue woollen slippers." "It was," she thinks, "like waking up in the bosom of a macaw" (151). In addition to this reference to a tropical bird, the apartment's furnishings include "what looked like the beginnings of a curiosity shop. . . . A mandoline leaned against a mounted suit of armour, a Gothic beaker, ecclesiastically embossed with false gems, stood on a Louis-Seize trifle-table and propped an Indian doll with tinsel robes, beaded nose-ring, and black cotton features of a languishing cast. Dangling over a harp was a Moorish bridle. On the walls hung scimitars and bucklers, pieces of brilliant embroidery, tapestries, and a quantity of pictures" (151). This mix of oriental and occidental objects, brilliantly colored, is in contrast to the whiteness with which Warner characterizes Blandamer. The "Bland" in the name points both to tiresomeness and to whiteness. In addition, coming home with Frederick from their aborted honeymoon, Sophia "beheld the chalk cliffs of Kent whose whiteness promised her the chalk downs of Dorset" (27). The oriental mishmash of Minna's apartment is also in direct contrast with Doctor Hervey's prim neighborhood and house. His neighborhood is full of nursemaids, "beribboned children and fat pug-dogs"; his house is described by its "green-painted trellis, . . . white front," and "pocket-handkerchief lawn" (89). Similarly, Minna's voluptuousness is in contrast to Mrs. Hervey's mother's incessant babbling, prancing, fluttering, and stoutness (90).

Minna's Jewishness also contains animalism, which is, like the reference to wine, one of the ways Warner marks Minna's erotic and compelling effects on Sophia. At the Trebennick Academy, Sophia imagined that freedom from gender constraints meant being "absolved back into animal" and being "as unburdened as a fox" (36). Minna is a Jew who can "extend a paw" for Sophia (145), releasing her from constraints about gender and sex and from the constraints of her class as well. Before Sophia even meets her, Sophia compares Minna, as a Jew, to a dog and a creature. She is "a byword, half actress, half strumpet; a Jewess; a nonsensical creature bedizened with airs of prophecy, who trailed across Europe with a tag-rag of poets, revolutionaries, musicians and circus-riders snuffing at her heels, like an escaped bitch with a procession of mongrels after her; and ugly; and old" (31). Here, Sophia imagines Minna's sexuality in particular as that of an animal. Moreover, while it is the people who desire Minna rather than Minna herself who are "mongrels," Sophia's description still suggests that Minna's sexuality has to do with inferior mixing of breeds in a way antithetical to Sophia's early preoccupation with improving the strength of her own and other lineages through selective breeding.

At other places in the novel, Minna is a "vital creature" with a "dispirited tail" (145). She resembles "a heavy voluptuous cat and a starved one" (123). She makes "no more claims on one's moral approval than a cat" and "her flashes of goodness were as painless as an animal's" (291). Sophia compares her to a sheep being sheared when she is ill, and she watches Minna's face "for some kindred sign of animal strategy" (250). During the pogrom narrative, Minna is a hunted creature pursued over the snow by Christians, misnamed by Frederick "Wolves" (130). This Jewish huntedness associates Minna with the fox who is, in Sophia's imagination, "unburdened,"and, more significantly, to the hunted fox with whom Sophia feels an "assignation" during a hunting party. And certainly this fox is reminiscent of the orphaned fox, with paws soft as raspberries, that Warner describes in her letters (*Letters* 169).

Minna's likeness to animals, sometimes warm and senuous, partly reflects the genuine affection with which Warner created Minna. But Warner is also underlining the limitations of Sophia's character by her blatantly anti-Semitic ideas of what makes Minna ugly and deceitful, including animalism, avariciousness, and a "complexion that could look greasy" (291). But however much Warner is intentionally creating Sophia's offensiveness by constructing a hyperbolic anti-Semitism, Warner also relies on Minna's

Judaism for narrative coherence and to justify why a Sophia previously frigid to Frederick, wine, and Mrs. Hervey can undergo a liberating thaw. Minna's exceptionally transformative power, her compelling erotics, are products of her oriental Jewishness. Sophia's "thaw" doesn't happen with Mrs. Hervey because Mrs. Hervey is a middle-class white woman; it does happen directly as a result of contact with a Jew, in a country not her own, away from the whiteness of Blandamer, and in the context of revolution. Warner's plot of sexual transformation turns on contact between characters who are marked as racially different.

The Lime-Kiln Man

This trope of homosexual transformation via contact with sexualized, racialized others is also at play in *Summer Will Show* in terms of class. Critics of the novel very reasonably attribute Sophia's transformation to Minna because of the eros between them and because Sophia meets the revolutionaries through Minna. But Warner also makes the lime-kiln man at least as pivotal to Sophia's sexual and political transformations as Minna is. Specifically, it is his working-class status that makes contact with him so powerfully transformative. If Minna is a spell-caster and the instrument of Sophia's transformation, she is an agent conjured by the lime-kiln man, a Satan-like figure similar to the Satan who contributes to Laura's liberation in *Lolly Willowes*. Though the kilnman never reappears after the beginning of the novel, it is he, not Minna, who first sets Sophia's transformation in motion and whose political analysis resonates through the novel. His character and the "red winking eye" of the kiln are symbols of Marxism and of the revolutionary fire Warner worked to keep alive among rural workers. Most importantly for my purposes, his sexuality sparks the sexual curiosity that Sophia later satisfies with Minna. Just as Warner relies on contact between Sophia and the compelling, hunted Jewishness to explain Sophia's sexual change, she also relies on contact between Sophia and reputed working-class hypersexuality, embodied by the kilnman (a man similar to those among whom Warner spent her political time organizing), to set that change, as well as Sophia's political transformation, in motion.

The most obvious way in which Sophia's transformation and the plot of the novel turn on the kilnman's presence is that the children contract smallpox from him, which prompts Sophia's desire to become pregnant with another heir, and, in turn, prompts her trip to Paris. But Warner makes much more of the kilnman than she might have if she were only looking for an accident to propel Sophia to Paris and/or to Minna. He is exceptionally powerful from his first appearance—both "priest-like" and demonic (16). To Hannah, the children's nurse, approaching the kiln is like "advancing towards an altar of Moloch"—a Canaanite idol to whom children were sacrificed and one of Milton's chief fallen angels. Hannah thinks, "The look of the kiln, too, was ecclesiastical in a heathen way. . . . The fumes trembled upon the air, glassy, flickering, spiritual, as though they were rising up from the power of a mysterious altar" (15). The kiln itself is a burning hell over which the kilnman presides. Damian has to be "returned to earth" after looking into it. Augusta thinks it must look like Hell, and Damian raves that "that's hell sister" in his feverish hallucinations. Sophia imagines that both children are possessed by devils when they are ill (56), and Damian suggests that the lime-kiln man is Satan when he rants, "O Devil don't drop me. *That's Satan, you know*" (64, emphasis in the original). The kilnman behaves oddly, too, sick himself when Sophia and her party arrive. He is "sullen" and "dull." He claims that the sores of smallpox are bug-sores, though on Sophia's second visit he proves himself fully aware of the diseases, including smallpox, which threaten his community. Augusta also says he is "auspicious," which is odd since she is afraid of him (16). Warner further draws attention to his odd "auspiciousness" by having Augusta struggle to find the word. The departure from the kiln also affirms the kilnman's spiritual power. Warner writes, "The little party moved away, slowly and religiously, as they had approached. . . . The fumes must have made us sleepy, [Sophia] thought, suddenly conscious that there was something odd, something pompous and bewitched about the way they were all behaving" (17).

This powerful, satanic kilnman speaks the critique of class injustice and upper-class hypocrisy that Sophia takes on as her own ideology by the end of the novel. When Sophia visits the kilnman a second time, hoping to become pregnant by him, he is angry rather than sympathetic. He is "dull and proud" at first, knowing that she is a lady and that she has come for reproductive sex; his "sullenness strengthen[s] to wrath" when she hints that he is guilty of killing her children. Sophia, he rails, is a hypocrite to expect sympathy from him over the deaths of children when she has never had any concern over the many working-class children who die—often of poverty-related illnesses—on her estate. "Children do die hereabouts," he rages. "There's the smallpox, and the typhus, and the cholera. There's the low fever, and the quick consumption. And there's starvation. Plenty of things for children to die of" (96). Nor will he provide the sexual-reproductive services Sophia thinks she can demand. If the gentry say about the poor that there are "plenty more children . . . where the dead ones came from," if the poor are expected to "die like cattle" and "breed like cattle too," then, he reasons, "rich and poor can breed alike" (97).

This is the last time the kilnman is physically present in the novel. But Sophia speaks words very like his when she and the other revolutionaries are waiting to be shot. The kilnman's importance to the scene, and to Sophia's political transformation, is first signaled when the jailed revolutionaries wake up suffering from "a raging thirst" (384), as Damian and Augusta had died "begging for water" after their contact with the kilnman. Sophia has come to resemble the kilnman himself: she is "cramped, parched, aching all over" and "sullen and dull-witted" as he is repeatedly described. And she echoes the kilnman's language with her sullenness, like his, strengthened to wrath over hypocrisy. When a priest comes to hear the confession of one of Sophia's comrades but "cannot consent," he says, "to the death of a woman," Sophia castigates him for claiming to defend her based on her gender: "Death of a woman! And how many women are dead already, and how many more will be, with your consent and complaisance? Dead in besieged towns, and towns taken by storm. Dead in insurrections and massacres. Dead of starvation, dead of the cholera that follows starvation, dead in childbed, dead in the workhouse and the hospital for venereal diseases. You are not the man to boggle at the death of a woman." He concedes, and "with a bow" rephrases his objection: he "cannot consent to the death *of a lady*" (390, emphasis in the original). As the kilnman had once castigated Sophia's hypocritical concern over the deaths of only upper-class children, she now castigates the priest's concern over the deaths of only upper-class women. Though the kilnman has nothing to do in any physical way with her experiences in Paris, his language, once flung at her, becomes her own and enables her to make an attack, like his, on class-based injustice.

Warner also emphasizes the kilnman's transformative significance by having Sophia recognize him as the initiator of her experiences in France. The night before her journey she pays homage to him: she "looked towards the ruddy star on the hillside, and nodded to it briefly, the acknowledgment one resolute rogue might give another. The determination set in her by the kilnman had never wavered or bleached into fantasy" (100). When Sophia decides to travel alone, she remarks that "only the world was against it. But since her visit to the lime-kiln Sophia was against the world." She remembers "the kilnman and his ruddy signalling star" when she is finally out at sea looking toward the lights of Calais (101). She acknowledges the kilnman as the progenitor of her experiences when she longs to tell Minna her story beginning with "the expedition to the lime-kiln" (146). And when Sophia walks through Paris to find Minna a second time, after an aborted reconciliation with Frederick, she understands her journey as another of the kilnman's making: "The red winking eye of the lime-kiln," she reflects, "had let her off on just such another journey" (206).

Most significantly, from his first appearance to his last, the kilnman exists specifically as a working-class man, in an always-sexualized field. I would argue that the kilnman is an icon of working-class hypersexuality and deep pagan spirituality; as such, his function in the novel is to prompt Sophia's shift from sexually uninterested (except when it has to do with reproduction) to erotically awake. Contact with first the kilnman, and later Minna, catapults Sophia into sexual curiosity while even Mrs. Hervey's fairly aggressive pursuit of Sophia fails. The kilnman also awakens her class consciousness as a human being and world citizen.

Sophia's first mention of the kilnman is erotic and is an eros based on the class difference between them. As she walks her children to the lime-kiln, she recalls her childhood encounter with a kilnman—not necessarily the same man, but a man in the same job—with great detail about the man's hands and where they touched her: "Sophia's own whooping-cough had been dealt with by the traditional method of being dangled over a lime-kiln to inhale the fumes; she could recollect the exciting experience, and the hands of the man who had lifted her up—hard hairy hands, powdered with lime, the fingers with their broken nails meeting on her bosom under the fur-edged tippet" (5). Though the memory of a child, this is erotic—a fetishistic response to dirt, hair, work, and animal fur—and not consistent with Sophia's later self-assessment as "frigid to . . . the love of man" (78).

Frederick, an upper-class man, might leave her "cold and unamourous," but the kilnman is "exciting" in a way that has largely to do with class difference: Sophia recalls being touched under garments that mark her upper-class status by hands that signify the working-class status of the man who holds her. The kilnman's hands—hard, dirty, bruised, and exciting—are also in direct contrast to Frederick's constantly disparaged constitution and his "sloping shoulders" and weaknesses (8).

Sophia's second visit to the kiln is specifically for reproductive sex. She chooses him because she realizes that he is the source of the smallpox that kills the children, but also because she remembers Hannah saying that other women went to the kilnman for sex, "stealing to him by night, guided by the red glare of his kiln upon the dark hillside" (68). She imagines that she too can "go to him, as those other women do" (94). Here, Sophia begins to identify getting what she wants sexually in terms of behaving like someone outside of her class—a working-class woman. This trip initiates her sexual transformation. Though the kilnman rebuffs her, he affects her sexual imagination, makes her curious about the "strange loves . . . up there on the hill, canopied by the wavering ruddied smoke; loves bitter and violent as the man's furious mind, but in the upleaping of that undaunted lust of a strength which could outface violence and bitterness" (99). The love and sex that can stir Sophia are love and sex that occur in the politicized realm of work, symbolized by ruddied smoke in this case. It is "strange" and "undaunted" working-class love, timeless, primeval, and primitivized as well as especially strong for having to compete with violence and bitterness also connected to class-based oppression.

Sophia is terrified at the man's rage when he rebuffs her and forgets her lantern in her haste to get away from him. But she ends up thinking the visit a good thing. As her contact with Minna does later, the kilnman's verbal attack returns her to pleasure in her body—a sharp difference from her abandonment of her body in her effort to avoid Mrs. Hervey. She reflects that "the outrage had left her neither shocked nor angry. Indeed it seemed to have done her good; for after the moment of terror had blown off she found herself tautened and stimulated, as though a well-administered slap in the face had roused her from a fainting-fit. Her blood ran living again, her wits revived, her natural vitality, which seemed to have died with the death of her children, returned to her, and once again thinking was a satisfaction, and the use of her limbs a pleasure" (98–99). Furthermore, Sophia compares working-class women with foxes—the same creatures that Sophia idealizes for being free from gender constraints and that she also associates with Minna. When Sophia is running away from the kilnman, she hears the laugh of a woman. The "chuckle sound[s] out over the silent field, coarse and freehearted, a sound as kindred to the country night as an owl's tu-whoo, or the barking of a fox" (99). This woman, she also thinks, must be the kilnman's "vixen."

This "vixen" desire, and that of other women who "trudge up to the lime-kiln," and the "strange loves" on the hill in general spark a "prosaic" desire in Sophia. Her practical desire is for a child, but as she leaves the kiln, chased by the vixen's laugh, a "wish, half truly, half ironically felt, arose in her that she could know what manner of love it was that would take one out on a November midnight to lie embracing on the soggy turf" (99). For Warner, the manner of love that would take one out to lie, hunted like a fox, embracing on soggy turf was her love for Valentine Ackland. After the night they first went to bed together, Warner wrote in her diary: "It was a bridal of earth and sky, and we spent the morning lying in the hollowed tump of the Five Maries, listening to the wind blowing over our happiness, and talking about torpedoes, and starting up at footsteps. It was so natural to be hunted and intuitive" (*Diaries* 70). Sophia eventually does share this "manner of love" with Minna—a kind of love that can lead one to lie not on the soggy turf, but on a cold floor. When Minna is ill with emotion, cigars, and liquor, Sophia wants to warm Minna, but, "measuring Minna's weight against her own, measuring the distance from floor to bed," decides bed is too far away. Instead, "fetching blankets and eiderdowns she padded Minna round with them, and then laid herself down alongside in a desperate calculated caress" (250).[22]

Parallel to the way in which Warner opposes middle-class sexual "foolishness" (going away with Mrs. Hervey is just a "foolish vision") with Jewish siren-like sexual allure, she relies for the coherence of her plot on reputed working-class hypersexuality. In Sophia's mind, behaving like a working-class woman gives her access to a man's sexual-reproductive services. Warner here is making use of literary tropes used by Ellis and Carpenter: working-class sexuality can make a rigidly procreative upper-class woman long to know about the "manner of love" that would make one embrace on cold turf, outside of the patriarchal house—specifically lesbian love for Warner. Working-class sexuality is "violent," "lustful," and "strange" enough to propel an upper-class woman who can't imagine sex with a middle-class woman toward the Jew with whom she can.

Caspar

Caspar is the most disturbing and the most interesting presence in *Summer Will Show.* Warner's references to Caspar in early scenes contribute to the novel's condemnation of the fact that much British wealth comes from the exploitation of colonial and slave labor. Warner also uses Caspar's murder of Minna and Sophia's subsequent murder of him to press the political point that divisions across gender, race, and nation cripple the struggle to change oppressive relationships between labor and wealth.[23] But Caspar's racial designation is also key to Warner's invention of Sophia's lesbianism. Warner places Sophia's primitivist adoration of Caspar's body in opposition to the more hostile racism of others at Blandamer. Her adoring fascination with Caspar is meant to be one redeeming feature of her character amidst her more general upper-class snobbery and her belief in the rightness of a system in which everyone labors for her benefit. Sophia's adoration of Caspar thus functions in the novel as a hint of compassion that makes Sophia's gradual political transition narratively coherent. More significantly, Sophia's initial adoration of Caspar is also metonymic with her sensual difference from others around her as well as her masculine gender orientation, both of which foreshadow her lesbianism. Sophia's eventual rejection of Caspar also has implications for her newly discovered lesbian-erotic life: her effort to expel him because he is no longer entertaining has as its most important affect Sophia's loss of "happiness"—the end of her lesbian affair with Minna.

Early references to Caspar contribute to Warner's critique of upper-class English assumptions of superiority. Among Sophia's social responsibilities is "that boy from the West Indies that Uncle Julius [Rathbone] was sending"—"that Caspar, Gaspar, whatever the child was called" (19, 20). From Sophia's view, Caspar warrants some "human[e] consideration" like any other of Sophia's living charges, from bulls to peasants to children to tomatoes (35). But Sophia's refusal to know Caspar's name exactly, or give much thought to his accommodations ("the red dressing-room would do"), is her pointed effort to identify publicly his exact, subordinate socioeconomic status (20). Warner also critiques Britain's economic dependence on money made through imperialist exploitation and the slave trade by showing that Sophia's and Frederick's wealth comes from the Caribbean. Frederick's family sneers at Sophia over her "commercial and suspect" source of wealth—"ownership of an estate in the West Indies." But Frederick also brought a "dowry of debts" to the marriage (27). He and his family may sneer, but his upper-class status, Warner points out, is maintained by the same tainted, imperialist money that is also the source of Sophia's family wealth.

Details Warner includes about this West Indian estate emphasize the fact that if it is from a Caribbean source, Sophia's Aspen-family wealth would have been produced by slave labor through Sophia's childhood, and increased by wage labor in near-slavery conditions after 1833.[24] Uncle Julius is "part-owner and manager of the estate in the West Indies that supplied the Aspen wealth." This estate produces sugar to sell, presumably, as well as edibles for use at Blandamer: twice a year, Rathbone sends "large consignments of guava jelly, molasses, preserved pineapple, and rum" (34). Caspar, Julius's "illegitimate son, a half-caste," is fourteen years old when the novel opens in June 1847, which puts his conception approximately a year before the slave trade was officially declared illegal throughout the British Empire. Caspar's mother had been a slave; in Sophia's fantasy she is "an unknown quadroon, passionate and servile her gold ear rings swinging proudly, and the marks of the lash maybe on her back" (40). Before 1833, Caspar would have added his number to the slave labor force; in 1847, Rathbone treats Caspar as a byproduct of Caribbean sugar production to be used, like molasses, in a way advantageous to the capital-owning class. Rathbone gives instructions concerning Caspar at the beginning of a letter and then turns, "as though with a waving of the hand, . . . to a more detailed account of the guava jellies, etc., which would accompany the boy across the Atlantic" (35). Like the edibles, Caspar should enrich the lives of the ruling class: the edibles will be eaten; Caspar will flesh out the ranks of the managerial class. Julius sends him to Sophia, far away from his "elegant sharp-nosed wife and his three plain daughters," so Sophia can place him "in a moderate establishment where he [can] receive a sound commercial education" without getting "false ideas into his head" (34).

Sophia's and Rathbone's expectations about Caspar's proper station in life are part of Warner's critique of English notions of racial superiority. Sophia approves of the shift from slave to wage labor in the Caribbean specifically because it perpetuates her wealth and status (34).[25] She tells Damian and Augusta that "rational humanitarianism . . . forbids that any race should toil as slaves when they would toil more readily as servants" (37). Warner's critique extends to British education, in service to the upper class, when she writes, with deep sarcasm, that answers to Sophia's advertisements for a school for Caspar "came in hundreds, it seemed as though England's chief industry was keeping boarding schools where religion and tuition had united to put into the heads of bastards all the suitable ideas and no false ones" (35).

But if Warner critiques Sophia's "rational humanitarianism" and her sense of superiority; if she critiques upper-class dependence on wealth produced by exploited labor; if she makes Sophia a mostly reprehensible character in order to press the argument that the working classes must unite against the ruling class across lines of gender, nation, and race, Warner also makes primitivism a redeeming quality that marks Sophia's difference from others around her and foreshadows the erotic transformation she will undergo. The narrator's early descriptions of Caspar, given from Sophia's point of view, make him an entertaining spectacle and are designed to show that Sophia's views about race and blood—views shared by Sophia's neighbors and servants—are disrupted when she actually sees Caspar. Sophia expects Caspar to be "no more than a wooly negro," because black blood is stronger than that of the English races. But instead she is enthralled: "before his extreme beauty and grace she felt her mouth opening like that of any bumpkin." She can't believe his "beauty is for her eyes alone" and says to herself, "Fools!" when she hears a servant whisper "what a little blackamoor!" (37). She is enchanted by Caspar's athletic abilities as well. He "was always the readier, the more agile, the more daring" than Damian (42). He was "anxious to please" and, when he did well, displayed "his chattering teeth . . . in a smile of pleasure" (41). Though Sophia lacks his "instinct for music," she enjoys Caspar's singing and playing. He sings enchantingly in a "thrilling over-sweet treble . . . as a bird sings, his slender fingers clawing the wires with the pattering agility of a bird's footing" (42–43).

It is tempting, and perhaps somewhat justifiable in light of the sharp satire with which she often treats Sophia, especially in scenes involving Caspar, to read here a critique of Sophia's adoration of Caspar for being a mimetic primitive—almost monkey-like, naturally musical, athletic, and pretty—instead of a brutish one. But I think Warner's point is to differentiate Sophia from others at Blandamer who think of him as *exactly* monkey-like and who despise him for it. While Sophia appreciates him, others "must need call out some achievement, as people prod monkeys at a fair; and then, angered by the brilliant response, sulk, grumble and belittle it" (41). The rector derides Caspar for not knowing his Catechism, then derides his effort to learn it as "very glib, remarkable quickness" but inadequate, as "such facility . . . is not altogether desirable. Light come, light go, you know." In response, Sophia amuses herself by taking the rector to the conservatory and apologizing for being able to offer only "a bouquet of her gaudiest and most delicate tropical plants" because "there are no violets left." She further enjoys the fact that he doesn't "perceive the insinuation" (42).

Warner's critique in these scenes is not for Sophia, but rather for those whose hatred for Caspar is more overtly hostile. When the narrator reports that it "was no more than natural" for "the child [to] be viewed askance because he was coloured and a stranger," Warner is, in her usual style, being sarcastic about Sophia's household's idea of "natural" racism. Sophia—perhaps the only time in the novel—is approved of because she sees, while the servants and the neighborhood disparage "a little blackamoor," that Caspar is "not more black than vivid, not more of a stranger than of a phoenix" (41).

Warner also makes Sophia's response to Caspar metonymic for her masculinity, thus using him to foreshadow her lesbianism. Though Sophia is generally obsessed with managing the reproduction on her estate to perpetuate status-quo wealth and class relations, she finds herself pondering, with "unexpected approval," her Uncle Rathbone's behavior—the "scrapes, financial and amatory," one of which is the "scrape" that produced Caspar. Sophia's approval, the narrator reports, comes from the "masculine toleration" she inherited from her father. Furthermore, Sophia imagines Caspar's mother in sensual orientalizing detail suggesting that Sophia's erotic interest is in line with Rathbone's. What Warner represents, here, is less approval of Rathbone than desire in common with him for a woman of mixed race with limited power to defend herself against uninvited sexual advances. This, in turn, links Sophia's fantasy about Caspar's mother with her erotic response to Minna: Caspar's mother's victimization foreshadows Minna's tale of her suffering in a Lithuanian pogrom.

Warner also links Sophia's fantasy about freedom from the constraints of gender to Caspar's appearance. Just before Caspar arrives, the narrator reports that Sophia fantasizes living free from gender constraints while visiting Trebennick and that she savors those fantasies by reinvoking them at will in the midst of her mundane tasks. This fantasy is a private one of "darkness stranger than any star has pierced"; it is a "personal darkness, an unknown aspect of Sophia as truly hers as one may call the mysterious sheltering darkness of one's eyelid one's own." Immediately following this passage, Caspar makes his first appearance. Sophia thinks "the boy who stepped from the carriage and walked toward her up the sunlit steps might have come, not from any surmisable country, but from a star" (37). Warner suggests by this juxtaposition that Sophia's own darkness is not so strange as to be impenetrable, and that this "star" from which Caspar is imagined to have come is perhaps the one that can illuminate Sophia's "stranger darkness."

Caspar is the first in a trio—including the kilnman and Minna—who disrupt Sophia's routine, change her point of view, wake up her sensuality and sensual curiosity. Being of the party listening to Caspar play his guitar, Sophia is "caressed by the outer wave-lengths of a world into which she could not enter; and while the music lasted she would stay, gazing at the picture the children made—the picture of two white cherubs and a black" (43). As she is later by Minna and the kilnman, Sophia is spellbound, caressed and warmed and loosened by Caspar. With Caspar, the narrator reports, "something came into her life which supplanted all her disciplined and voluntary efficiency, a kind of unbinding spell which worked upon her lullingly as the scent of some opiate flower" (43). Sophia's response to Caspar even suggests that there is an affinity between Damian and Sophia based on mutual homosexuality. Before Caspar arrives, Sophia worries that Caspar will "tease Augusta and corrupt Damian." Why she fears that Caspar will affect her son and her daughter differently is unexplained, but both words suggest sexual affects, and "corrupt" carries a specifically homosexual meaning. Warner elaborates this suggestion by suggesting that

Damian does fall in love with Caspar. From the beginning of the novel, Sophia worries over Damian's failure to be properly masculine. He is uninterested in hunting and carpentry, though he is given guns and tools. Despite having been given a pony, he is "fast becoming that ignoble kind of rider who knows how not to fall off" (7). While a wide patch of green is cleared for him to play sports with the local boys, he becomes an idol rather than a leader among his peers. Sophia is infuriated when a boy shows up with the gift of a hawk that Damian had been unable to catch for himself. And Damian seems to be in love with Caspar from the minute Caspar arrives. While Augusta smiled prettily when she first saw Caspar, following instructions, Damian "had both stared and been shy" (38). About Caspar's effort to learn Catechism, Warner suggests provocatively that Caspar and Damian do private things together: "Damian only was privy to what followed" (42). Warner also writes that Caspar's music alone is enough to "birdlime" Damian—"birdlimed" is a phrase Warner uses to describe the way in which a young woman immediately attracts an older man with whom she becomes a lover in the short story "The Foregone Conclusion." Damian also weeps inconsolably when he isn't permitted to say goodbye to Caspar (42, 48).

More significantly, Sophia feels affinity with Damian over his feelings for Caspar; just as Caspar stirs Sophia, "it was obvious that this dusky piece of romance had stirred [Damian] deeply" (38). In response, Sophia is, for the first and last time in the novel, "moved towards her son not as a child but as a companion. His admiration for Caspar corroborated hers, sanctioned it almost; she was knit to Damian not by the common bond that tethers a mother to her child, but by the first intimation of that stronger link that time might forge, the close tremulous excited dependence of the woman upon the male she has brought forth" (38). It is possible, here, that Sophia approves Damian's love of Caspar because it is like her own love of Caspar and her fascination with the woman she imagines is his mother; it is possible as well that she identifies with Damian because his love is homoerotic, like her love for Minna. Sophia even compares Minna with Caspar; she realizes she is taking Minna to see the revolution and to dinner "as though she were a child to be given a treat—as though she were Caspar" (160).

The end of the novel also makes Caspar central to both Sophia's political stories and her lesbian stories. Caspar is the tool by which Warner turns the violence of Sophia's own beliefs back at her and thus chastens Sophia out of the remnants of her solidarity with the upper class. This links the death of Caspar with the disappearance of Sophia's possibility to enjoy sensuality. Sophia effectively expels lesbian love from her life when she expels Caspar, as in ridding herself of Casper, she inadvertently contributes to the development of the situation in which Caspar kills Minna. Here, Warner makes the point that race, like gender, is used to divide potential allies against ruling-class oppressors.

In the last third of the novel when Sophia and Minna are struggling to feed themselves in revolutionary Paris, Caspar shows up, having run away from Trebennick, with outgrown clothes, adolescent ugliness, and interminable hunger. Most irritatingly to Sophia, he intrudes on their privacy. At one point Sophia literally pushes him out of their apartment and slams the door in his face (317). Every effort of Sophia's to push him out, though, rebounds and leads inexorably toward tragedy. Because she pushes him out of the apartment, he spends nights with Madam Coton, who feeds his jealousy of Minna until it becomes full blown anti-Semitic hate. (This is doubly ironic, since Minna defends Caspar to Sophia from the minute he shows up.) Sophia can't find a commercial school for Caspar with no money to pay up front, so she hands responsibility for his maintenance to Frederick, who has taken her money. He, in turn, enlists Caspar in the *guardes mobiles,* the government forces against whom the revolutionaries will fight in June 1848.

Eventually Sophia's many efforts to keep Caspar in his place—the last gasp of her solidarity with the upper class—deprive her of "the only happiness she has ever known": Caspar leaps the barricade behind which Sophia and Minna are fighting and thrusts his bayonet into Minna's breast, yelling, "Drab! . . . Jewess! This is the end of you" (382). Without hesitation, Sophia calmly shoots him in the head before herself being dragged away with the other revolutionaries to be shot herself. Critics who focus on the lesbianism of the novel have criticized this ending for its melodrama. Terry Castle calls it "a problem [that] cannot be denied," though she also tries to explain the implausibility of the ending as a characteristic of lesbian fiction: "precisely because it is motivated by a yearning for that which is, in a cultural sense, implausible—the subversion of male homosocial desire—lesbian fiction also characteristically exhibits, even as it masquerades as 're-alistic' in surface detail, a strongly fantastical, allegorical, or utopian ten-dency. The more insistently it gravitates toward euphoric resolution, moreover, the more implausible—in every way—it may seem." The "prob-lem" with the novel, Castle concludes, "is not so much that it forfeits plau-sibility at the end but that it forfeits plausibility from the start" (88). Julie Abraham calls the ending of *Summer Will Show* a formulaic "punishment" indicating that Warner, like many other writers of lesbian fiction, couldn't end the novel with a lesbian couple intact (6). Wendy Mulford argues that the writing sinks to bathos at the end of the novel and that the end is "tinny realism" (*This Narrow Place* 119, 121). Thomas Foster argues that the "plot twist" at the end "strains the novel's plausibility" (553). The end of *Sum-mer Will Show* is unquestionably melodramatic. But it is not, I argue, a cop out—a reading encouraged by identifying Minna alone as the force be-hind Sophia's transformation. Rather, the end is Warner's utterly coherent propagandistic warning. Because Sophia does not incorporate Caspar and racism into her class analysis soon enough to prevent tragedy, she suffers the loss of Minna, the source, as she says, of everything that has ever made her happy. Warner seems to be saying that lesbian love doesn't exist in a vacuum, that you can't have a revolution in love without taking responsi-bility for the past—family lands, houses, and prosperity based on slavery. Also, if you leave the racial other, who might well be one's own nephew, to be cared for by the right wing, he is very likely to be turned against you. As Foster argues, "*Summer Will Show* suggests the possibility of feminist intervention around issues of sexuality and pleasure in the Marxist narra-tive of revolution, while at the same time it demonstrates the need for women's stories of liberation and narratives of same-sex desire to come into contact with narratives of class, race and colonialism, beyond their own borders" (554). The depiction of lesbian love and lesbian revolution-ary heroines in *Summer Will Show* clearly reveals the paradox of Warner's simultaneous critique of and reliance on primitivist stereotypes. Warner's protagonist, Sophia, makes a political transformation from landowning aris-tocrat—a snob who believes that her superior place in the world is a result of her superior ability to prudently husband all her creatures and re-sources—to communist activist; this political transformation is simulta-neous with a sexual transformation from "frigid" wife to sexually awake lesbian (78). Warner attributes these changes to Sophia's contact with the working-class lime-kiln man, Jewish Minna, and Caribbean Caspar. For Warner herself—a middle-class white woman—it was possible to engage in lesbian sex and emerge into a lesbian identity with Valentine Ackland, another middle-class white woman, specifically in the context of activism against injustice.[26] In her fiction Warner relies on contact with working-class and dark-skinned figures as tropes of access to lesbian sexuality for her heroine, a white upper-class character for whom the idea of lesbianism is otherwise "intolerable" (75). In Warner's vision it is the lived experience of comradeship in revolutionary struggle that inspires love between women. The scene of love and death on the barricades may be melodramatic, but it is one that appeals to radicals in Warner's era and now.

Six

Jezebel and Sapphira

Willa Cather's Monstrous Sapphists

Willa Cather's *Sapphira and the Slave Girl* (1940) has obvious differences from *The Story of an African Farm, The Waves,* and *Summer Will Show,* including the fact that its author and setting are American rather than British or South African. But *Sapphira* is as fully involved with Sapphic primitivism as a mode of lesbian representation as the novels discussed earlier. *The Story of an African Farm, The Waves,* and *Summer Will Show* reflect Olive Schreiner's, Virginia Woolf's, and Sylvia Townsend Warner's reliance on figurations of blackness and physical markers of working-class status to represent sexual autonomy for women—specifically lesbianism in Woolf's and Warner's cases. For all three writers, this sexual use of figurations of blackness and working-class status takes place, perhaps paradoxically, in the context of anti-imperialist national critiques. *Sapphira and the Slave Girl* reflects a similar reliance on figurations of blackness to represent lesbianism, but in the context of a more ambiguously critical depiction of nation and nation building. *Sapphira* is set in a rural, antebellum Virginia peopled with enslaved African Americans, slave-owning whites, and abolitionists. The central character is a white woman obsessed by the bodies of the black women she owns. Cather critiques unequal power relations in slavery, especially in relationships between white and black women. But she also looks back to the antebellum south nostalgically and writes an alliance between white and black women characters to explore the possibility of authoritarian, erotic relations between white women, such as the relation Sophia fantasizes with Caspar's mother. Cather's novel also provides a curious gloss on Olive Schreiner's *The Story of an African Farm*. Both novels embody tyranny as gluttonous white women who grow more monstrously huge the more they exert power over others and the more they accrue wealth at the expense of people whose labor they exploit. Schreiner's Tant' Sannie grows to a nearly immobile 260 pounds by seeming to ingest husbands, African lands, and African people who work those lands. Cather also figures tyranny as gluttony; her protagonist Sapphira swells to death, seeming metaphorically to ingest the bodies of the slaves over whom she desires to wield complete power. Moreover, in both novels the characters who are the objects of desire and/or the victims of despotic control shrink to death or disappearance as if they have indeed been gobbled up. Schreiner's principled, defiant Lyndall becomes increasingly "shriveled," "shrunken," and "a little crushed heap" as she approaches death (*Story of an African Farm* 273, 276, 282); and the Hottentot maid who is her naturally defiant African double is consistently described as "lean" until she disappears from the novel without comment. Like Lyndall and the lean Hottentot maid, Sapphira's African double, Jezebel, shrinks to child-size as she dies in Cather's novel.

My argument, here, is meant to complement the claims of many writers who, in the last ten years, have rescued Cather's novel from oblivion by analyzing it as an exploration of relations between white and black women in slavery. But compounding the problem of Cather's nostalgic treatment of slavery, I want to argue, is her use of figurations of blackness to suggest, where she doesn't name, homoerotic relations. Cather's primitivism, here, reflects the interdependence of figures of sexuality and race discussed by cultural critics and scholars of literary modernism, but with an additional specificity about lesbianism and sexological sciences of homosexuality. That the homoerotic presence is unnamed in *Sapphira* warns us to make more rather than less of it. In her often-quoted essay about realism and fiction, "The Novel Demeuble," Cather writes, "whatever is felt upon the pages without being specifically named there—that, one might say, is created. It is the inexplicable presence of the thing not named, of the overtone divined by the ear but not heard by it, the verbal mood, the emotional aura of the fact or the thing or the deed, that gives high quality to the novel or the drama, as well as to poetry itself" (*Not under Forty* 50). This statement has encouraged queer readings of Cather's work, in part because "the thing not named" echoes the Oscar Wilde's reference to homosexuality as the "love that dared not speak its name."[1] Sharon O'Brien argues that in "The Novel Demeuble," Cather writes as both "a modernist writer endorsing allusive, suggestive art and inviting the reader's participation in the creation of literary meaning" and at the same time as a "lesbian writer forced to disguise or to conceal the emotional source of her fiction, reassuring herself that the reader fills the absence in the text by intuiting the subterranean, unwritten subtext" ("The Thing Not Named" 577). With regard to *Sapphira and the Slave Girl*, Cather's belief in the aesthetic value of the unnamed in fiction, combined with her familiarity with Wilde's work and his trial,[2] insists that the unnamed be attended to carefully.

Willa Cather and the Critical Response

Over the last hundred years, critics have paid varying degrees of attention to Willa Cather and her work.[3] She was well received during her lifetime, fell into near obscurity in the two decades after her death in 1947, and has been the object of steadily increasing attention since the early 1970s. Her first novels, *Alexander's Bridge* (1912) and *O Pioneers!* (1913), attracted positive reviews and widespread attention (Murphy, *Critical Essays* 2). Her fifth novel, *One of Ours* (1922), which first made her the subject of controversy, was criticized sharply for its depictions of the war, but also won a Pulitzer prize. Through the 1930s, critics on the left railed against the escapist and nostalgic qualities of her fiction, which made it, Granville Hicks charged in 1933, antimodern and politically conservative.[4] But also in the 1930s and 1940s, critics began to write of Cather as a major American writer. By the end of her life, Cather lived well off book sales, though her later works have consistently earned less praise than her early works. Shortly after her death in 1947, several partial and full biographies of Cather appeared.[5] These were followed by relative silence until new biographical and critical works began to appear again in the early 1970s.[6]

By the mid–1980s, John Murphy could introduce his collection *Critical Essays on Willa Cather* by saying triumphantly that she had "survived her season of neglect" (1). And from the perspective of the end of the 1990s, Cather seems to have done better than merely "survive." She is described as "one of America's most important writers" by an anonymous critic on the cover of the 1988 paperback edition of Sharon O'Brien's biography, *Willa Cather: The Emerging Voice*. In the 1990s, *My Ántonia* and *O Pioneers!* were made into television movies (Lindemann 8, 144n), and Cather has repeatedly been a subject of popular journalism. In the *New Yorker,* for instance, John Gregory Dunne recounts details from Cather's life to emphasize the tragedy of the murder of Brandon Teena, a transgendered teenager from Nebraska. Dunne relies on readers' affection for Cather's writing, as well as on our familiarity with her life story, reminding us that she, too, cross-dressed and called herself William.[7] Cather is being taken increasingly seriously in academic settings as well.[8] Significantly for my purposes, for instance, Hermione Lee takes up Cather's modernist primitivism. About *The Professor's House,* "published at the height of the modernist movement," Lee writes that Cather's "recognition of a primitive, instinctual self brings Cather extraordinarily close to some of her contemporaries" in their search to find enduring truths "in the instinctual, the primitive, and the mythological."[9]

Cather's rise in stature in both popular and academic settings is primarily a result of feminist scholarship—including critical writing and agitation over canonical boundaries—that began in the 1970s. Feminist scholars of the 1970s and 1980s focused on Cather's depictions of women characters and on her manipulations of conventions about gender and sexuality.[10] Specifically lesbian-feminist analyses of the 1970s and 1980s often focused on the presence or absence of encoded lesbian themes or figures in Cather's fiction.[11] Following the publication of Sharon O'Brien's 1984 essay "'The Thing Not Named': Willa Cather as a Lesbian Writer," and O'Brien's 1987 biography, most scholars have taken Cather's lesbianism as a given.[12] O'Brien makes an excellent case for calling Cather a lesbian writer based on an analysis of early 1890s letters to Louise Pound, on whom Cather had a passionate crush when the two were in college in Lincoln. Careful to note that Cather would not have called herself a lesbian because the word was not in common use in the 1890s, O'Brien claims that Cather's "self conscious awareness that her involvement with Louise Pound placed her in a suspect category sharply distinguishes her from women who enjoyed romantic same-sex friendships earlier in the century" (*Willa Cather* 132). More recently, Marilee Lindemann seconds O'Brien's claim, arguing that Cather's use of the word "unnatural" to describe her friendship with Pound reflects a "self-conscious sense of the deviant nature of the relationship" that "places it on the modern side of the line historians of sexuality have drawn between romantic friendship and lesbianism" (19).[13] In what is both a 1990s continuation of feminist and lesbian-feminist scholarship but also a new area of study, Judith Butler, Eve Sedgwick, and Marilee Lindemann, among others, have contributed queer-theoretical analyses of Cather's work. These critics, unlike many of their predecessors in Cather studies, stay clear of biographical readings, interested instead in Cather's literary treatment of sex and gender as key aspects of her engagement with main currents of twentieth-century American literature and culture. Butler, for instance, argues that one of the persistent features of Cather's texts is "the destabilization of gender and sexuality" through her use of names.[14]

Additionally in the 1980s and 1990s, a handful of critics influenced by studies of race in America and/or by Toni Morrison's discussion of *Sapphira* in *Playing in the Dark: Whiteness and the Literary Imagination* (1993) began to talk about race and ethnicity in Cather novels.[15] Morrison uses *Sapphira* as a key example of the ways in which white American writers have employed figurations of blackness. Until Morrison's book, very few critics had addressed Cather's treatment of race. Deborah Carlin argues that "race has frequently been an unspoken issue in criticism of Cather's fiction because . . . Cather's racial sensibilities are likely to strike the modern reader as less than enlightened, to say the least" (150). Since Morrison's book, however, there has been both a small flurry of interest in *Sapphira* and an increased willingness to discuss the ways in which Cather incorporates racially as well as ethnically marked characters in her other works.

In my examination of Cather's last novel, I am concerned most with work by critics who discuss race and sexuality together. In *Willa Cather: Queering America,* Lindemann productively takes up both Cather's lesbianism and her engagement with questions of race, ethnicity, and the politics of nation building. Lindemann examines Cather's writing for the work it does toward simultaneously shaping the constructions "queer" and "American." In some novels, Cather seems to police the boundaries of citizenship and identify only specific, unqueer kinds of bodies as assimilable.

In other writing, Cather resists boundaries, making room for varieties of queer figures within the concept of citizen. About *Sapphira and the Slave Girl* in particular, Lindemann argues, "in Sapphira's white aging female disabled body, Cather figures the paranoid subjectivity of a nation of free and equal people that had systematically denied the freedom, equality and personhood of women and African Americans (135). The novel "allegorizes the making of America as inherently and inevitably terroristic, a process in which [queer] bodily differences . . . whether they are differences of race, sex, gender or physical ability provoke fear and loathing rather than cultural dynamism and a creative instability successfully negotiated through love and translation" (Lindemann 136). In this regard, Cather's vision of America as a place where queer bodies suffer disintegration has a great deal in common with Olive Schreiner's bleak vision of colonial Southern Africa as a place of terror within which queer figures—the New Woman and New Man of Schreiner's age—cannot, or chose not to, survive.

In "'The Pull of Race and Blood and Kindred': Willa Cather's Southern Inheritance," Lisa Marcus discusses the ways Cather's earliest fiction and poetry and her last novel address her southern heritage and reflect the intersections of race and gender in American history. Marcus argues that by writing herself as narrator into the end of *Sapphira,* Cather "implicates herself in the problematic genealogy of white southern womanhood" (117). Also in *Sapphira,* Cather explores the narrative possibilities of powerful white female desire through the African American character Nancy, thus displacing lesbian desire onto the body of the black woman (L. Marcus 115–116). Naomi Morgenstern writes, more generally, that "Cather often used racially othered people, if not ancient and 'vanished' ones to write stories of sexual awakening" (191n). Lindemann argues similarly that "desire is displaced onto the body of the black female (Nancy)" (169n). But Lindemann adds that it is "grossly reductive" to understand *Sapphira* through the masquerade model that writers such as Judith Fetterley have used to explain how Cather negotiated "the dilemma of the lesbian writer."[16]

I seek to build on the work of Morrison, Lindemann, and Marcus by focusing on the ways in which Cather uses the figure of Jezebel in her evocations of lesbianism. As southern African Bushmen enable Schreiner to narrativize New Womanhood and New Manhood in *The Story of an Afri-*

can Farm, Jezebel is an icon of savagery that enables Cather to narrativize lesbianism in *Sapphira and the Slave Girl.* Judith Butler argues that "substitution is a condition for [the] sexuality" figured in Cather's texts. This, she argues, is the "historically specific consequence of a prohibition on a certain naming, a prohibition against speaking the name of this love that nevertheless and insistently speaks through the very displacements that that prohibition produces" (*Bodies That Matter* 162). Butler is not using what Lindemann calls a masquerade model here, talking about lesbianism as a presence encoded or disguised by the use of tropes such as giving her narrators male names. Rather, Butler describes substitution as a characteristic of lesbian representations in Cather's work. I am arguing that in *Sapphira,* Cather substitutes savagery for lesbian erotics and figures white women's sexual desire as the product of violent, controlling relationships between white and black.

Cather and Modernist Primitivism

All of Willa Cather's work involves a strong element of primitivism that marks her as a modernist engaged, as were many others, in orientalist and primitivizing fantasy. At the mythic centers of her novels, from first to last, are figures representing formidable human and natural force—force that is timeless, essential, and original as well as variously dangerous, erotic, or pure—an American version of the creative and essentially old African power that Schreiner hoped would push new European humanity into a healthful modern age. Cather writes this force as supremely creative, capable of pushing nations and opera singers up out of prairie and rock;[17] supremely destructive as well, it brings death and ruin to miscreants and heroes alike. Such force can be thwarted, colonized, or vanquished in any single manifestation, and Cather's novels mourn its loss in the nostalgic manner for which she is known. But her works taken as a whole also testify to the continuous, triumphant, and terrifying presence of such power.

The primitive erotic force in Cather's first published novel, *Alexander's Bridge,* is an incessantly rushing, violent river "with mists and clouds always battling about it" (17). Bartley Alexander's bridges seem to evade the force of the river. They are brilliantly engineered "slender skeleton[s]," "delicate as a cobweb," arching over the water (17, 117). But Bartley's most ambitious bridge fails, and the river remains, a deadly "forc[e] which men direct but never circumvent or diminish" (117–118). Cather's vision of this primeval force is notably more hopeful than Schreiner's. In Cather's novels, tragedy comes when one character loses contact with his own force and, as in Bartley's case, is overcome by primitive power greater than any individual. Schreiner, on the other hand, can conceive of wholescale collapse. Her bleak vision is of a modernity in which men and women whose newness has the vitality of the primitive cannot survive.

Timeless, immutable forces like that in Bartley's river and in Schreiner's Africa are the myths around which all Cather's novels revolve. Such force is in the soil, the rocky canyons, and the red grass that pioneers in many of her novels do battle against. The land in *O Pioneers!* is a "wild thing" marked as primitive by being outside time—its "history" doesn't begin until Alexandra Bergson sets her face "toward it with love and yearning" (20, 21, 118, 65). It has a "fierce strength," a "savage kind of beauty," and a "free spirit" untamed since it "emerged from the waters of geologic ages" (15, 65). Heroic human force moves pioneers to do battle against such powerful land. Those who succeed are those most like the land in nature: wild, powerful, vigorous. Alexandra's ability to finally bend the land to her will is the result of her strong affinity with it. From the beginning of the novel, she feels her own heart hiding among the other "wild things" "under the long shaggy ridges" and feels "in her own body the joyous germination in the soil" (71, 204). By the end of the novel, the narrator presents Alexandra's body itself as virile, earthly vigor—a force that pushes up "yellow wheat," "rustling corn," and "shining youth"—while the land becomes the domesticated, vanquished, maternal body that will eventually take Alexandra "into its bosom" (308). Alexandra is successful as a farmer because she is vital like the land, close enough to it in nature to be moved by it and to coax it into new forms.

In *The Professor's House,* Cather celebrates pure, originary, potent creativity and mourns its vulnerability to corrupt, modern materialism. Tom Outland is the novel's unsullied primitive, raw human energy in contrast to the clerks he sees in Washington, D.C., "all more or less" the same, "stream[ing] out of the Treasury building and the War and Navy . . . like people in slavery, who ought to be free" (211).[18] His exceptional intellectual abilities are produced "by nature and early environment" rather than

schooling (39). And his purity remains unsullied because he dies young before his brilliant invention begins to draw material rewards. In Cather's
Death Comes for the Archbishop, the untamed New Mexican landscape is
a vital force, variously wild, terrible, and sensuously beautiful or fragrant
(see 130, 182, 207). The wind of the desert has the power to make Bishop
Latour "a boy again" every morning (275). Latour fears that such rejuve-
nating power exists "only on the bright edges of the world" and will "dis-
appear from the whole earth in time, perhaps," destroyed by the "moisture
of plowed land, the heaviness of labour and growth and grain-bearing"
(275). But this is an enduring, prehuman force, its source "a great underground river . . . perhaps as deep as the foot of the mountain, a flood moving in utter blackness under ribs of antediluvian rock" (130).

This ubiquitous force is variously gendered in Cather's work. In early
journal articles, Cather, like Olive Schreiner, champions forceful, heroic,
sexually pure masculinity as a necessary component of both football and
poetry: both "appeal to the crude savage instincts of men" (*The Kingdom
of Art* 212). If the nation loses "brute force, or an admiration for brute
force" such as that required by football, poetry and art will be "forever dead
among us," she warns; football forwards the causes of art and poetry because it is "manly," "purifies the living of young men," is not conducive to
"unnatural excitement," and opposes "tendencies toward effeminacy,"
"chappieism," "dissipation," and "soft-handed-" and "soft-headedness" (*The
Kingdom of Art* 212–213).[19] Even in women characters, power is also often expressed as a degree of masculinity; the gender ambiguity thus created is a source of the homoerotic suggestiveness of many Cather works.
In the opening scene of *O Pioneers!* Alexandra Bergson is a "tall, strong
girl" who walks "rapidly and resolutely" (6). She wears a man's coat "as if
it were very comfortable and belonged to her; carried it like a young soldier." As she walks, she hurls "a glance of Amazonian fierceness" at a man
on the street who comments on her hair (8). Her dependence on Carl to
get Emil's kitten down from a pole in this scene seems contradictory at
first, but Carl's slimness and vulnerability further define Alexandra's masculinity. He darts, head down, while Alexandra strides resolutely; he is "tall"
and "slight" in contrast to her "tall" and "strong" (9). These ambiguously
gendered characters and the chaste love that develops between them contribute a generally queer texture to the novel. This in turn provides a

sympathetic context for the more specifically lesbian eros Cather writes into her descriptions of the wild landscape that becomes fertile under Alexandra's hands and finally takes her "into its bosom" (308). Landscape is often homoerotic in Cather's work. As the once-wild land in *O Pioneers!* takes the Amazonian Alexandra "into its bosom" in a lesbian-erotically suggestive way, in *My Ántonia* Jim and Ántonia "slid[e] down straw-stacks, . . . climbing up the yellow mountains over and over, and slipping down the smooth side into soft piles of chaff" (172). Marilee Lindemann argues that in both these novels, the prairie is a "sit[e] of youthful eroticism" where "pastoral language evokes the fantasy of a space that is erotically charged but also precarious and vaguely threatening" (28). Similarly, in *Death Comes for the Archbishop,* the New Mexican desert is sensuous, feminine, threatening, and a place where love between men can flourish. The cave in which Bishop Latour hears the antediluvian river is a vaginal "orifice," entered between "two great stone lips, slightly parted." Bishop Latour is "struck by a reluctance, and extreme distaste for the place," which he thinks "fetid," "disagreeable," and "rank" (127, 129). Latour's anxiety over feminine sexuality as well as his naivete about why he is anxious contribute to Cather's depiction of his unconsciously homoerotic love for Father Vaillant. And Latour's anxious response coexists with the narrator's sensuous depiction of New Mexico in general—including the lips of the cave, strong scents, dry heat, reviving air, and hidden spots of wet, life-sustaining, green canyons. New Mexico is powerfully feminine and erotic at core; if it horrifies Bishop Latour occasionally, it also nurtures and protects his sensuousness, including his love for Father Vaillant.

Cather's most well-known character, Ántonia, is also ambiguously gendered. By the end of the novel, she is powerful in her maternal, reproductive capacity, but she has a degree of masculinity early on that foreshadows her success as a pioneer. During the time that she works the farm with her brother, Jim Burden finds her "disagreeable" because she eats "noisily . . . like a man" and yawns and stretches at the table. She is also "too proud of her strength," and provokes "farmhands around the country [to joke] in a nasty way" by doing "chores a girl ought not to do" (*My Ántonia* 120, 121). Later, a more mature Jim reinterprets Ántonia's physical vigor as both feminine and erotic. As in *O Pioneers!* Ántonia's ambiguous femininity queers the novel. This in turn supplements the lesbian-erotic suggestion of the novel explicated by critics who take the masculine voice of the narrator as a displacement of lesbian erotics.[20] Other Cather women are corrosively rather than productively forceful. Marie in *O Pioneers!* "spread[s] ruin . . . by being too beautiful, too full of life and love" (304). Myra's power in *My Mortal Enemy* is a "savagery" that compels Oswald's and Nellie's attention, not necessarily to the benefit of either (68). Oswald possesses "some kind of courage and force which slept"; in another sort of world he might "have been a soldier or an explorer" (43). But because he falls in love with Myra, he bends himself to work that enables him to marry her.

Most significantly for my purposes, Cather racializes this ubiquitous force. Where antediluvian, wild, savage, corrupting, or erotic force pulses in Cather's writing, racialized, primitivized figures are nearby, not the source of force themselves, but consistently marking the presence of force. In *Alexander's Bridge,* Bartley's passionate, youthful, and self-annihilating force breaks out of its constraints because he reestablishes contact with Hilda, who is pointedly Irish. Her success in the theater is attributed to this Irishness: She is a Burgoyne, Irish people of the stage "for generations" with an "Irish voice" and a laugh never heard "out of Galway"; part of her beauty is her "Irish skin" (43). Her Irishness is accented by the London setting of her affair with Bartley and by her difference in "background" from Bartley's elegant and refined Bostonian wife (3). Specifically as a racial other, Hilda is the condition that enables Bartley's youthful, erotic, passionate self to re-emerge and take over, corrupting his masculine productivity.[21]

This kind of pairing between ethnic and racial others and the emergence of force—both productive and destructive—is a constant in Cather's novels. In *The Professor's House,* Cather marks Tom Outland's purity and his status as a primitive—an untutored, natural, inventive genius, also naturally appreciative of beauty and art—by giving him an affinity with an ancient native American civilization. He is spiritually in tune with the location and remains of the cliff city he finds, and his life is a mirror image of the story he pieces together of the city's former inhabitants. The cliff city has never been invaded because of its remote site. Similarly, Tom's purity of mind is a result of isolation: he has no formal schooling and spends a lot of his youth herding cattle with only a few other men. The inventiveness manifested by the architecture of the cliff city parallels Tom's scientific inventiveness; both the cliff dwellers and Tom die prematurely in wars started by someone else; and both the city and Tom's work are plundered after their deaths for others' material gain. In *The Song of the Lark,* Cather similarly marks Thea Kronborg's powerful musical artistry, by replacing her affinity with her family for an affinity with Mexicans who, as Cather depicts them, are naturally superior musicians and dancers (206–208). Spanish Johnny claims that the quality of Thea's singing is something he never sees in "a child . . . outside Mexico" (206). Her success as a singer is foreshadowed by the dance in Mexican Town, where Spanish Johnny and others first appreciate her voice and where she is "one white head moving among so many dark ones" (209).[22] Spanish Johnny's musical sensibility is also the "only commensurate answer" to Thea's talent at the end of the novel (411).

Erotic force is racialized in *O Pioneers!* The powerful lover of Alexandra's fantasies is first "yellow" and "bronze" in contrast to Alexandra's "gleaming white body" (206). Toward the end of the novel, he is simultaneously darker and stronger: "His shoulders seemed as strong as the foundations of the world. His right arm, bared from the elbow, was dark and gleaming, like bronze" (282–283). Destructive erotic force in this novel is also racialized, the product of Emil's trip to Mexico City, where he goes to escape his increasing erotic attraction for Marie, but which she imagines as essentially about eros: a "gay, corrupt old city" where Emil will live "among . . . temptations" and serenade "all those Spanish girls dropping flowers from their windows" (201, 193). As Marie's imagination foreshadows, Emil comes back from Mexico erotically changed. He kisses her for the first time immediately after his return, wearing the Mexican outfit he brought home with him. Emil's kiss also has an erotic, Mexican symbolic double—"a handful of uncut turquoises, as big as marbles" that he takes from "the pocket of his velvet trousers" and drops "into [Marie's] lap" (224). This gift and the sexuality it symbolizes destroys both Emil and Marie; it leads to the assignation in the garden, over which Frank shoots them both. If Emil is the "shining youth" that Alexandra has pushed up out of the Nebraskan soil with her vitality, the erotic power of old Mexico is the destructive match to Alexandra's creative force.

Similarly, sensual and erotic force is a racial characteristic in *My Ántonia.* Blind Samson d'Arnault is an icon of racialized primitivism and exists in the novel for no reason other than to signal the awakening of Ántonia's powerful sensuality. Lisa Marcus writes that with d'Arnault,

"Cather, like other white American writers, embodied her Africanist characters with a vital sexuality and utilized them to dramatize carnal pleasure and transgression" (113). D'Arnault's piano playing is instinctual rather than learned. It comes from "animal desires" and is "barbarous" and "wonderful." It is "abominable" piano playing, but "real" music, "vitalized by a sense of rhythm that was stronger than his other physical senses" (182, 183). D'Arnault "enjoys himself as only a negro can" and looks "like some glistening African god of pleasure, full of strong, savage blood" (183, 185). D'Arnault, here, is reminiscent of the black musicians in Radclyffe Hall's *The Well of Loneliness*. In *The Well*, Hall describes the savagery and musicality of the musicians as innate in order to mark what she argues is a similarly innate homosexuality in her white characters. Hall writes that Henry is "not an exemplary young Negro; indeed he could be the reverse very often. A crude animal Henry could be at times . . . just a primitive force rendered dangerous by drink, rendered offensive by civilization. Yet as he sang his sins seemed to drop from him, leaving him pure, unashamed, triumphant"; he and his brother are "carried away . . . by their music" and seem to sing "a kind of challenge; imperious, loud, almost terrifying, . . . a challenge to the world on behalf of themselves and of all the afflicted," including the homosexual characters listening to the musicians play (363). The scene in *My Ántonia* in which d'Arnault plays and his listeners dance is a turning point in the novel after which Jim focuses on Ántonia's sensuality. He describes her passion for dance and compares her to town girls, as he calls them, whose "bodies never moved inside their clothes; [and whose] muscles seemed to ask but one thing—not to be disturbed." Sensuality makes Ántonia seem *racially* different: she and other ethnic girls who had "helped to break up the wild sod . . . were almost a race apart" from the assimilated town girls. Out-of-door work had given them a vigor that "developed into a positive carriage and freedom of movement, and made them conspicuous among Black Hawk women" (192).

Ántonia and Lena and the other country girls are, importantly, not the same as d'Arnault. While Cather's depiction makes d'Arnault clearly a race apart—musical, pleasure loving, necessarily an untaught genius if a genius at all, because of his African heritage—they are only almost a race apart. But at the same time that she makes this careful distinction, Cather also relies on the primitivist notion that Africans and African Americans are erotic powerhouses—gods of pleasure if gods of anything—to show that Antonia and her ethnic friends are erotically different from other Black Hawk residents. If they are not made racially the same as d'Arnault, they are not made entirely white either; they are racially like d'Arnault specifically by virtue of their sensuality.

Just as d'Arnault signals the not-quite-white erotics of Ántonia and the other ethnic immigrant girls, in Cather's *The Lost Lady* a statue of "a scantily draped figure, an Arab or Egyptian slave girl" signals Mrs. Forrester's corrupt erotics, as well as the end of Niel's innocence. The girl in the statue holds "a large flat shell from the California coast" where "letters for the post were always left," including, toward the end of the novel, Mrs. Forrester's letter to her lover (97). Mr. Forrester draws Niel's embarrassed attention to the letter, discussing the envelope and Mrs. Forrester's fine penmanship before he lets Niel take it to mail. If Niel has believed he might be wrong about Mrs. Forrester, or that he is chivalrously keeping her secret from Mr. Forrester, the statue seems to hand him horrifying sexual truth. Cather writes, "Niel had often wondered just how much the Captain knew. Now, as he went down the hill, he felt sure that he knew everything; more than anyone else; all there was to know about Marian Forrester" (99).

Cather's status as a modernist has been the subject of debate in criticism of her work since the 1930s.[23] If the debate is resolved now, that is mostly because the question has been discredited by critics who fracture a monolithic canonical modernism into multiple modernisms by taking the histories and arts of women and people of color as starting points for literary investigation. But even in the context of an older and more narrow definition of modernism, and despite her oft-discussed nostalgia, her political conservatism, and her own repudiation of the modern in art and literature, Cather's use of racialized images to signal overwhelming force, purity, corruption, and sensuality is of a kind with modernist primitivisms by D. H. Lawrence, E. M. Forster, Virginia Woolf, Joseph Conrad, Pablo Picasso, Igor Stravinsky, Sigmund Freud, T. S. Eliot, Ezra Pound, and James Joyce; as do these artists and others, Cather uses icons of primal humanity to represent evil, eros, power, corruption, and revitalizing energy. Cather and many other modernists imagine an originary human core, attached to the earth, that can be stifled or set free, twisted into ugliness or pressed into the service of civilization and materialism. This originary humanity is repeatedly represented or marked by the presence of dark-skinned figures.

Sapphira and the Slave Girl

Here I want to reassess Cather's last novel in terms of the trope I have traced though all her work: her use of racialized figures to mark supremely creative and supremely dangerous force, often erotic, gendered either productively masculine or corrosively feminine, and implicated in the nation-building ethos and the homoerotic suggestiveness of Cather's fiction. Cather's last novel is her most in-depth examination of corrosive feminine force. It is also her most direct representation of lesbian erotics. Cather often identifies desire for women through heterosexual relations or male narrators, but in *Sapphira* she "creates a female character who desires a woman" and "makes her authorial identification with this character explicit by entering her own text as a character in the final pages of the novel."[24] Likewise, if racialized figures are present in all Cather's novels, they are more prominently figured in *Sapphira* than they are in any other. I argue that Cather's use of dark-skinned figures—four generations of African American women—has everything to do with her depiction of Sapphira as a powerful, lesbian-erotic, and corrupting feminine force. If, as the examples in the preceding section show, Cather participated in the kind of orientalist modernist fantasy often discussed by cultural critics, in *Sapphira* this primitivism takes a distinctly lesbian form.

Sapphira and the Slave Girl is often discussed in terms of its autobiographical and historical content.[25] The novel tells a fictionalized version of events that took place in ante- and postbellum Back Creek, Virginia—in 1856 and 1881—on the mill and farm where Cather spent the first nine years of her life. The story involves Sapphira Colbert's plot to have her nephew Martin rape Nancy, the slave girl of the title, in order to maintain control over Nancy's sexuality. With the help of Rachel, Sapphira's daughter, Nancy escapes rape and slavery by running to Canada via the underground railroad. Cather's rendition of the story is based on stories Cather heard women in her family tell. That its source and setting are biographically important suggests to many that the novel is Cather's nostalgic return to familial—particularly matrilineal—origins. Sharon O'Brien, for instance, reads the novel as Cather's treatment of her relationship with her mother and other female forebears, depicting her mother's complex mix of harshness and generosity. At the same time, according to O'Brien, Cather explores and values her own matrilineal artistic inheritance more fully than she has done before (*Willa Cather* 45–48).

The novel is nostalgic. Cather's formal experimentation involves mixing chapters that progress the plot with chapters describing ancestors and land grants that lead to Cather-family ownership of land on Back Creek. Cather also includes parenthetical narrative explanations of Virginia traditions as if to rue their loss. There is, as well, plenty of nostalgic content, including flower-filled descriptions of pastoral scenes and scents and devotion on the part of loyal slaves. Both this nostalgia and the monstrosity of the novel are consistent with a southern tradition of pastoral writing about United States slavocracy.[26] This nostalgia is a problem for critics who focus on the historical context of the novel. To some degree, Cather seems to expose slavery's brutality, its distortion of human relationships, and its specifically sexual violence. Toni Morrison's assertion that Cather is the first white writer to try to explore relations between white and black women in slavery has been taken up by many critics.[27] Cather's plot does expose Sapphira's absolute power over Nancy and Nancy's corresponding vulnerability. But most agree that Cather's nostalgia as well as her limited ability to develop the inner lives of the black characters she introduces seriously flawed her novel.

Such analyses based on the novel's southern antebellum context are extremely valuable. To add to rather than replace these readings, I read the novel through the literary and historical contexts of the sexological writings that are largely responsible for the emergence of the modern category "lesbian," a category that became part of public discourse in the United States during Cather's youth and young adulthood.[28] If the novel is part of the southern tradition of pastoral writing about slavery and, paradoxically, part of a tradition of post-emancipation exposure of the sexual nature of violence perpetrated upon enslaved people, it is also, as reading the novel through the sexological discourse shows, part of the tradition I am calling Sapphic primitivism.

Cather was familiar with the racialized discourse about homosexuality discussed in chapter 2. In an 1896 article printed in the *Nebraska State Journal*, Cather praised Sir Richard Burton's "matchless translation of those glorious Arabian romances, *The Thousand Nights and a Night.*"²⁹ This suggests that she would also have read Burton's concluding essay in which he describes the Sotadic Zone as an area characterized by homosexuality. That Cather doesn't mention the essay specifically indicates less that she didn't read it than that she didn't think it especially noteworthy that Burton characterizes various parts of the world as a zone where homosexuality is "an established racial institution" (Cory 208). Whether or not she also read Richard von Krafft-Ebing, Havelock Ellis, or Sigmund Freud directly, Cather's fiction "is clearly and deeply marked by the medical and juridical discourses that pathologized nonprocreative sexualities" (Lindemann 6). Krafft-Ebing's *Psychopathia Sexualis* was first published in 1882, and Ellis's *Studies in the Psychology of Sex* in 1897, when Cather was nine and twenty-four, respectively. As a drama critic in Lincoln, Cather associated with relatively avant-garde groups of people who "would have been among the first to be aware of the emerging conceptualization of homosexuality" (O'Brien, *Willa Cather* 135). And Cather's letters to Louise Pound reflect characterizations of intimacy between women as unnatural and perverse, a characterization that is a product of sexological and medical literatures that relied on comparative ethnography to make their arguments about homosexuality among whites in England and the United States.

Cather's letters to Pound also reveal her incorporation of an orientalist fantasy about unconventional sexuality in general. In the same letter that acknowledges the "unnatural" quality of her relationship with Pound, Cather discusses FitzGerald's *Rubáiyát of Omar Khayyám,* which she had given to Pound as a gift. Marilee Lindemann argues that Cather gave the book as "a kind of fetish, a substitute for [her] soon to be absent body," and as an invitation to revel in the fantasy of the Orient as a space of sexual promise (21, 22). The letter, with its convergence of sexological ideas about homosexuality and its reliance on orientalist fantasy to evoke risqué sensuality "stands . . . as an early important example of the mingling of racial and sexual inflections in Cather's figuring of queerness and the queer."³⁰

Cather's journalism also reflects her participation in orientalist fantasy. In an 1895 newspaper column, Cather praises a "new Hindoo play called *Aspara*" because its author, Judith Gautier, "has followed her father's eastern studies and gone beyond him." This "eastern" quality of Gautier's work, she says, is a result of hot winds blowing up from the south. Because of these winds, all French writers—Theophile Gautier, Daudet, and Flaubert—are "full of oriental feeling [sic]," and France is a place where "the great passions never become wholly conventionalized" (*The Kingdom of Art* 138). The passions described here as "never wholly conventionalized" include the lesbian passions of Gautier's famous *Mademoiselle de Maupin* and Daudet's *Sapho*. O'Brien writes that these two novels "gripped Cather's imagination in the 1890s" (*Willa Cather* 136).

Finally, an anecdote about Cather suggests that she believed she could step out of conventions about gender-appropriate behavior for young white girls by stepping into blackness. In her memoir *Willa Cather Living,* Edith Lewis recounts that Cather "once told of an old judge who came to call at Willow Shade, and who began stroking her curls and talking to her in the playful platitudes one addressed to little girls—and of how she horrified her mother by breaking out suddenly: 'Ise a dang'ous nigger, I is!'" (13). As a secondhand account, Lewis's description of an interaction between the judge, Cather, and her mother is to be viewed skeptically. It may show the young Cather trying to cross into maleness and forbidden sexuality by claiming blackness to the degree that "dang'ous nigger" connotes hypersexual, perverse masculinity. Sharon O'Brien interprets Cather's outburst as her "first rebellion against patriarchy," represented by the judge, and also a rejection of "her mother's standards of propriety and hospitality" in favor of assuming "the identity most opposed to the one her mother had fashioned for her" (*Willa Cather* 43). Similarly, Lisa Marcus describes the outburst as a "ventriloquized performance of blackness [that] reveals an urgent desire to disrupt the veneer of Southern social customs and marks her entrance into racial othering" (98). Lewis's account is even more important as a firsthand description of the adult Cather telling a story, however. Even if Cather never spoke to the judge at all, the story she told Lewis about herself shows Cather deploying a figuration of blackness in order to mark—and celebrate—her own rebellion against "the smooth unreal conventions about little [white] girls"—conventions that include narrowly defined heterosexuality. Also, when Cather explains her outburst, as Lewis says she does, as "the only way that occurred to her *at the moment*" to resist those conventions (13), Cather also suggests that she has, since she was a child, discovered other methods of resisting.

I suggest that Cather reveals one of these other ways to resist gender-sex conventions, still involving figurations of blackness, in *Sapphira and the Slave Girl*. Reading the novel through this personal anecdote, through the history of the discursive construction of homosexuality, and through Cather's participation in primitivist and orientalist literary modes underlines the homoerotics that seep into the novel via Cather's deployment of the minor character Jezebel. Cather makes Jezebel a mythic savage African—a cannibal whose dying wish is to eat the hand of a girl, and perhaps also a female version of the "dang'ous nigger" of Cather's anecdote—and Sapphira's closest ally in the novel. This alliance is figured in many small ways that give Sapphira's monstrosity—her swollen, dropsical body and her abominable abuses of Nancy and Till—a savage mirror image. As an adult storyteller, Cather marked her rebelliousness against sex-gender conventions for white girls by using a figuration of blackness—by telling a story about a girlhood claim to be black and dangerous; similarly, as a novelist, she marks Sapphira's sexual perversity and her resistance to patriarchy by allying her with Jezebel. Jezebel and Sapphira both express perverse appetites for girls that Cather seems to both celebrate and abhor.

Jezebel's Mythic Savagery

Cather makes Jezebel an icon of mythological savagery in the section of *Sapphira and the Slave Girl* that gives her "history." She is the "only one of the Colbert negroes who had come from Africa"; specifically, she comes from a "fierce cannibal people." She is also "anatomically . . . remarkable" according to the captain of the slave ship on which she is brought to the United States (90, 91). He does not say outright that she is long in the clitoris, as do captains who write the early-modern travel narratives Valerie Traub discusses. But he does say that Jezebel is anatomically as good as "the best of the men": "tall, straight, muscular" and "long in the legs" (93, 94).

Jezebel's savagery involves dangerous sexual behavior as well. Cather hints at this sexuality but leaves it mysterious and, significantly, unnamed. For Cather to suggest that there was anything sexy for captives of a slave ship is obviously offensive; but, especially because it is so inattentive to historical reality, it is an indication that Cather's primary concern in this novel is not slavery or the enslaved. Rather, she is using the antebellum context for purposes of making homoerotics "felt upon the pages" but not "specifically named there," an "overtone" suggested by both hints and ambiguities, as Cather says in "The Novel Demeuble" (*Not under Forty* 50). In the slave ship, Jezebel causes some kind of "row" in the "women's quarters" after the sailors have "seen that all the females were lying in the spaces assigned to them" (92). The row is not, as might be expected, a resistance to slavers: they have gone on deck to "take air." It does, however, disrupt women in all female "quarters." Also, in the aftermath of the row Jezebel bites the "thumb" of the first mate. That a "thumb," here, isn't just a thumb is suggested by the fact that the sailors give Jezebel "the name she had borne ever since" as a result of the row (92). This naming shows that the sailors perceived what they saw to be sexual: "Jezebel" is the name associated with the slave-rooted caricature of dangerous black-female sexuality (Morton xiii, xiv, xvi, 10) as well as the name of the murderous biblical wife of Ahab.

Jezebel's cannibalism recedes as she becomes American but reappears at the end of her life. The only thing that would tempt her to eat, she tells Sapphira, is "a little pickaninny's hand" (89). Specifically, she seems to want the flesh of her great-granddaughter. Nancy is too old to be described as a "pickaninny," but her hands are characterized by their youthfulness and even their appetizing bonelessness earlier in the novel. They are "slender, nimble hands, so flexible that one would say there were no hard bones in them at all . . . like a child's" (18). Nancy herself assumes that she is the object of Jezebel's fantasy: she jumps up in terror immediately after Jezebel speaks, crying out, "Oh, she's a-wanderin' agin! She wanders turrible now. Don't stay, Missy! She's out of her haid" (89). This is Cather's clearest depiction of Jezebel as an ultimately unregenerate savage.

Sapphira's remarks, in this scene, also suggest that Sapphira is Jezebel's savage double. "No need," Sapphira rebukes Nancy, "for you to be speaking up. I know your granny through and through. She is no more out of her head than I am" (89). As Naomi Morgenstern points out, "Sapphira's utterance aligns her with Jezebel. . . . Jezebel would eat her young, and Sapphira who understands her perfectly appears to be seated at the same table" (201).[31] Sapphira claims both familiarity and accord with Jezebel's most savage desires. If Jezebel is a mythic savage African, anatomically remarkable for being long in the "leg," cannibalistic, and interested in consuming Nancy in particular, Cather makes it clear that Sapphira is no less savage and no less interested in consuming Nancy. Sapphira is distinctly cannibalistic, elsewhere, too. Cather repeatedly mentions Sapphira's "very plump white hands" and her swelling, dropsical, pale body (6, 7, 53, 100, 32). This white plumpness is contrasted with Till's "spare" frame and "small feet," and Nancy's oft-mentioned thinness (31, 32, 13, 18, 45). Sapphira also swells out of her clothes and shoes while Jezebel "wither[s]" into them (32, 86). In death, Jezebel is so diminished that "one of the embroidered night-gowns [Sapphira] wore as a girl" is "big enough" to shroud the once "tall, strapping woman" (98). These contrasts suggest that Sapphira has grown plump on the bodies of Nancy, Till, and Jezebel, among the others who are her slaves. It also echoes Olive Schreiner's depiction of colonialization as a process by which white women grow fatter as black Africans grow lean to the point of disappearing.

Sapphira is Jezebel's double in other subtle ways. Jezebel arrived at the Dodderidge home on "the day Sapphira was born" (96). Hence, Jezebel professes to have special knowledge of Sapphira even though Sapphira and her motives are a mystery to everyone else (22). "Of course I know you," Jezebel says, as Sapphira enters her cabin. "A'int I knowed you since de day you was bawn" (86). Sapphira's visit to Jezebel suggests that despite the master-slave relationship between them, Jezebel is Sapphira's peer in a way that none of the other characters are. Everyone else who has contact with Sapphira comes to her. Martin comes to the farm at Sapphira's invitation. Henry is occasionally summoned for tea and he regularly goes to Sapphira's table for breakfast although he sleeps at the mill. Rachel bursts in on her mother as Nancy is dressing her. Even when Sapphira goes out in her carriage, her grandchildren, the postmistress, and merchants come to her window to talk or do business. But Sapphira goes to see Jezebel in her cabin. Cather draws attention to Sapphira's visit, too, by making it a production—the "boys" have to come, dressed nicely, with poles to carry Sapphira in her chair across the yard (85–86).

Also, as Jezebel is anatomically as good as "the best of the men" in the past of the novel, so Sapphira is "the Master" in her marriage to Henry. The novel opens with the breakfast-table battle in which Henry asserts his husbandly authority and refuses to sign for the sale of Nancy (4). But Henry's masculinity is qualified from the beginning. He is "a solid, power-ful figure of a man in whom height and weight agreed," but has "eyes that were puzzling. . . . reflective, almost dreamy" with "long lashes [that] would have been a charm in a woman" (4–5). And he later says to Sapphira, approvingly, "You're the master here, and I'm the miller" (50).

Other links between Jezebel and Sapphira include that they are both approaching the ends of their lives. "I've been housebound for a long while now, like you," Sapphira tells Jezebel. "We must take what comes to us and be resigned" (87). Names also mark both as sexual transgressors: if Jezebel's name refers to a caricature of dangerous sexuality, "Sapphira" is reminiscent of Sappho, whose poetry Cather read and liked, and who is also a dangerously sexual character in some of the French literature Cather enjoyed. Merrill Maguire Skaggs encourages readers to make much of Cather's choice of names. "Cather's reliance on symbolic or meaning-full names to define her characters," she writes, "is so marked that one generally does well to assume a name has meaning until all attempts to find one have failed" (14).

Most significantly, Jezebel's monstrous desire to eat Nancy's hand is parallel to Sapphira's monstrous scheme to rape Nancy by making use of Martin as her surrogate.[32] Sapphira is obsessed, in general, with being at the center of the sexual lives of all of Jezebel's female descendants. She marries Till off to old Jeff, "a Capon man," as if to secure even more exclusive control over Till's sexuality than she already has as owner (43). When Till becomes pregnant anyway, Sapphira speaks as if she were the injured but forgiving party, telling Henry, "Till was within her rights, seeing she had to live with old Jeff. I never hectored her about it" (9). Sapphira also gets pleasure from thinking of Till's sexuality. In an exchange with Henry over whether Nancy's father is "that painter from Baltimore" or one of Henry's notoriously rakish brothers "hanging around" Back Creek at the same time the painter is there, Sapphira "laugh[s] discreetly as if the idea amused and rather pleased her" (9). Cather even leaves open the possibility that Sapphira orchestrated Till's rape just as she tries to orchestrate Nancy's. It is unclear what "idea" about Till's pregnancy amuses and pleases Sapphira. Syntax and juxtaposition suggest that she is pleased to have gotten "the portraits out of" the painter "and a smart yellow girl into the bargain," as she says (9). But if we imagine that she behaved in the past of the novel as she does in the present, she may have invited the rakish brothers to disrupt a romance she believed to be going on between the painter and Till, as she later invites Martin, another rakish Colbert, to break up a romance she imagines is taking place between Henry and Nancy. Till's own ambiguous remarks don't rule out this possibility. She recalls only that the "Cuban painter came along to do the portraits" and "was a long while doing them" (72–73). This mournful remark neither confirms the identity of Nancy's father, nor rules out the possibility that Till was raped by the painter, or a Colbert, or both. Furthermore, the discrepancy about whether the painter is "from Baltimore" or "Cuban" or both draws attention to Till's ambiguous remarks about Nancy's parentage. The possibility that the white members of Sapphira's household think that the painter is "from Baltimore" while Till identifies him as "Cuban" suggests that Till has private information about him and thus adds evidence for an argument that Till and the painter were in a love relationship that Sapphira intentionally broke up.

Cather suggests that Sapphira's effort to orchestrate Nancy's rape is an erotic escapade for Sapphira, too. Some critics have assumed that jealousy over Henry's wandering affection motivates Sapphira's plot to have Nancy raped.[33] But this assumption leaves Cather's plot seeming illogical; rape would certainly punish Nancy, but in the context of American chattel slavery, as Toni Morrison points out, Nancy's rape would not make her less available to Henry. As a slave, she can't be "ruined" as far as Henry is concerned; "ruined" implies a loss of marriageability, and there is never any marriage to Henry in Nancy's future (25).

Sapphira might see Nancy as a rival, but Cather never encourages this interpretation. Much detail, however, suggests that Sapphira sees Henry as a rival for Nancy's affection. Both Nancy and Till are welcome in Sapphira's bedroom to brush her hair and dress her, while Sapphira's daughter Rachel is an unwelcome intruder and Henry never appears in Sapphira's bedroom at all. Sapphira invites him to stay once, but only as a ploy to assess his level of involvement with Nancy. The only moment of satisfaction Sapphira experiences in the entire novel is when Nancy and Till, believing Sapphira ill, rush into her room "sooner than she thought possible." Cather specifies that Sapphira is "comforted by the promptness and sympathy of" Till and Nancy. Till sits on the floor "rhythmically stroking her mistress's swollen ankles and knees, murmuring: 'it's all right, Missy'" (107). Henry isn't mentioned as a source of comfort at all.

The scene in which Martin traps Nancy in the cherry tree and grabs her legs is clear in its suggestion that Sapphira's motive in plotting the rape includes Sapphira's erotic desire for Nancy's body. Martin draws Nancy's "two legs about his cheeks like a frame" and smells something "sweet—like May apples" (181). The orality of the scene and the vaginal rather than phallic suggestiveness emphasize the fact that Sapphira has orchestrated the rape; Martin is present more as a surrogate than as a body with desires in his own right. In addition, the seductive language suggests that Sapphira's interest in Nancy is erotic if also angry. The orality of the scene also furthers the connection between Sapphira's desire for control over Nancy's sexuality and Jezebel's cannibalism. As Jezebel wants access to Nancy's body in a prohibited way, so does Sapphira.

Complicating Sapphira's erotic interest in Nancy's sexuality, Sapphira seems also to want to play patriarch. If she wants to consume Nancy, she also wants to locate herself in relation to Nancy as if Nancy were a white woman over whom Sapphira had the authority of brother or father. This is evident in the language with which Cather describes Sapphira's anxiety over the possibility that Henry and Nancy are sexually involved: she is afraid of being "befooled," "hoodwinked," "deceived," and "mocked" by members of her household (105–106). Sapphira's fear is thus explicitly connected to the way in which several white women are "fooled" in the novel: Mandy Ringer's daughters are fooled when they become pregnant by men who can't be forced to marry them; Martin has an ugly false tooth because he fools a girl whose brothers beat him unconscious in retaliation. To be fooled, as to be ruined, is something that happens to white women but cannot happen to black women in the context of slavery, as it relies on the idea that a woman is tricked out of rights that enslaved black women do not have—specifically, the right to marry the fathers of their children and gain in status by virtue of their relation to a man.

White fathers and brothers, like white husbands, are also fooled—proven inadequate—when their female charges become pregnant. Martin understands his beating to be a fair exchange: he takes something from the brothers when he fools their sister. They seek to take back their stolen authority by giving him a beating: they "put their mark on him by knocking out one of his white teeth" (163). But they also recognize him as one of themselves when they agree to fight "fair"—with fists rather than a whip—and "let his horse go home to give the alarm" (163). Mandy's son Lawndis, however, can't participate in this exchange of women and power. Because he is lame, other men make free with his sisters. "Fooling" seldom happens twice in one family, the narrator reports, "even in the most shiftless households" (120). But Mandy Ringer's daughters have no one "to see [they] git [their] rights" (122). Lame Lawndis can't force a marriage when one sister and then another become pregnant. Sapphira will prove as inadequate a patriarch as Lawndis if Nancy, like Till, becomes pregnant in ways Sapphira does not authorize.

Sapphira's anxiety over Nancy's sexual status is illogical given the historical context, as Morrison points out: Sapphira treats Nancy as a white man might treat a white daughter or sister who can be fooled and understands that potential fooling as a slight upon herself. This is one of the reasons *Sapphira* makes so many readers angry. Cather seems, as Toni Morrison says, to be writing about the relationship between white and black women in slavery. But in a substantial way she isn't writing about black women or slavery at all. Rather, she is using slavery as a context through which to write about white male authority over white women, and to explore the possibilities of sadistic, controlling, lesbian-erotic freedom for white women equal to the erotic freedom of white men. These freedoms, as Cather writes them into being in *Sapphira,* come at the expense of black women's freedom. Cather explores the possibility of sexual freedom for white women who have to struggle for equality with white husbands, fathers, and brothers—but who also stand to gain more control over black women the more they succeed in gaining equality with white men. As she professes to do in the anecdote she tells Edith Lewis, Cather explores possibilities for white women's erotic lives by making a white woman character cross into patriarchal masculinity and by giving her a double who is not the "dang'ous nigger" of Cather's anecdote, but is, instead, a "dangerous" black woman.

Sapphira's monstrous cannibalism might be construed as Cather's critique of slavery. Her cannibalism might be read as a metaphor for white exploitation of black labor and bodies, as Hermione Lee proposes.[34] Cather may be suggesting that slave-owning in America is akin to eating one's young. This is an apt metaphor for the legacy of slavery in the United States, where white women's wealth has been gained at the expense of the bodies of enslaved Africans. Cather might be imagining the covert war against whites that the grandfather in Ralph Ellison's novel *The Invisible Man* (1947) would later urge his descendants to wage: "overcome 'em with yeses, undermine 'em with grins, agree 'em to death and destruction, let 'em swoller you till they vomit or bust wide open" (16). Sapphira is a white monstrosity, literally swollen to bursting—a calamity which, Cather's novel suggests, is an American legacy of having metaphorically cannibalized generations of slaves. Any analysis of the ways in which Cather's work is a critique of slavery, however, has to be complicated by the likelihood that Cather was also using an available American story of racial mixing to discuss possibilities for white women's sexual freedom in the context of white heterosexual patriarchy. In one very important way, Cather is not writing about slavery at all. Rather, she is using the rhetorical trope employed by sexologists—referencing Sapphira's monstrous, sadistic lesbianism—by comparing her to a mythic savage, an African cannibal with a remarkable anatomy, castrating jaws, and a peculiar taste for girls.

Seven

Conclusion

All four of the writers I discuss here reject conventions of white femininity by writing white women characters into contact with dark-skinned or working-class people or colonial settings. They do this as part of their critiques of imperialism, capitalism, or the sexual violence of slavery, and also because their worldviews are influenced by the comparative ethnographic mode of sexological writing of the turn of the century. Olive Schreiner defines a new, free, and equal womanhood for white woman as proximity and similarity to African figures; this similarity, however, relies on the stasis of Africans to expose the progress of white womanhood into modernity characterized by freedom. Schreiner's narrative of primitivism and the struggle for new gender identities provides, I argue, a model for the questions asked in the modernist fictions written by authors in the generation that followed Schreiner. Virginia Woolf uses references to colonized spaces and people as placeholders for lesbianism in her fiction. In Woolf's novel, lesbianism places Rhoda simultaneously into alliance with the colonized and with the colonizer. She is the character "amidst" as well as against the waves/warriors with assegais, and she is the snail/child/cobra left to die, pecked and festering, in the garden the other children explore. At the same time, however, Rhoda's lesbianism is also an imperialist fantasy, a dreamed voyage to "islands where the parrots chatter and the creepers . . . " (*The Waves* 19). Perhaps as a result of this ambivalence, Woolf leaves us, finally, with an agonized view of the lesbian as a Sapphic suicide victim and not an imperialist voyager. For Sylvia Townsend Warner, Sapphism is, similarly, a fantasy of escape from class and country, but also no escape. The heroine must take up the racial and the economic burden of her own imperialist past, since both the political process of doing so and the antiracist, pro-communist effect are necessary for sensual fulfillment. Warner's representation of lesbian possibility is, finally, much less agonized than Woolf's is: lesbian fulfillment is possible on the barricades, in the context of antiracist, anti-imperialist struggle for economic justice. Willa Cather presents the characters Jezebel and Sapphira as a pair to emphasize a shared savagery. She shows both as, at core, cannibals whose desire is for a girl's body; in this way she introduces homoerotics into her novel. Perhaps, in writing *Sapphira,* Cather shrugs off the once-empowering identity of the male "dang'ous nigger" of her childhood fantasy and takes upon her writing self an identity of old, savage Jezebel, an even more "dangerous" black woman figure who suggests to her—and whose oppression suggests to her—the possibility of white lesbian erotic freedom. Cather's representation of lesbian possibility, however, raises questions about the relationship between erotic fulfillment for white women and the subjugation of black women in the United States. In *Sapphira and the Slave Girl,* erotic fulfillment for Sapphira is utterly dependent on the subjugation of Nancy, Jezebel, and Till. Taken together, the four novels form a series of intertextual queries about Sapphism, class, and race.

It would be easy to stop with an admonishment to writers and artists who seek to represent lesbianism textually not to fall into Sapphic primitivism such as it is employed by Schreiner, Woolf, Warner, and Cather.[1] Sapphic primitivism is a strong legacy, after all, considering how often readers and writers, especially since the 1970s, have taken Olive Schreiner, Virginia Woolf, Sylvia Townsend Warner, Willa Cather, as well as Gertrude Stein, Radclyffe Hall, Djuna Barnes, among others whose works I might have discussed in this context, as literary and feminist foremothers. Despite this legacy, writers and readers need modes of lesbian representation that do not rely on the fetishization of individuals of color, members of the working class, or people from specific geographies. Such fetishizing, as Heather Findlay puts it, "allows us to circumvent the Real of racial disintegration" (472).

Pointing out racisms of the past, or of elsewhere, however, is one of those comforting things "well-meaning white people" often do without necessarily having any transformative effect on racist logic.[2] My larger concern has been to understand the multiple significances of the fact that "lesbian" and "homosexual" are constructs that developed in tandem with racialized and class-inflected identities. For political organizing, teaching, reading, and writing, we need to understand "black," "working class," and "lesbian," among other constructions, as intersecting and interdependent. And we need to use knowledge of this interdependence to develop coalitional politics built on a sense of mutuality rather than on inclusion. Political strategies based on inclusion begin to address some of the problems with single-issue organizations such as the Human Rights Campaign; but strategies based on inclusion also seem to lapse into assimilationist strategies that maintain supremacies based on race, sex, sexuality, and class. A politics of mutuality, on the other hand, would involve acting on the assumption that the logic behind heterosexist politics is often if not always racist and biased against the working class; it would involve acting on the assumption that the logic behind racist politics is often if not always heterosexist as well as sexist and biased against the working class. In this context, anti-heterosexist politics must address racism and class bias in order to be in any reliable way anti-heterosexist; antiracist politics must address questions of sexuality and class to be in any reliable way antiracist.

Theorists of race show that the only coherence "whiteness" has comes from inscribing "blackness" elsewhere. Similarly, normative heterosexuality gains coherence from being defined against homosexuality and other, often class-inflected, "perversions." Olive Schreiner, Virginia Woolf, Sylvia Townsend Warner, and Willa Cather began to understand this characteristic of boundary marking because of their interest in representing autonomous female sexuality or lesbianism textually, and because the sexological models they had for this kind of representation relied on a comparative ethnographic mode. To some degree, textually representing lesbianism meant to Woolf, Warner, and Cather disrupting the stability of the lines between human categories and figuring alliances between characters with different racial and class designations. This, in turn, potentially challenges the basis on which privileges accrue to middle-class "white" individuals—individuals who, in a given historical moment, are able to inscribe themselves into whiteness by excising blackness from their self or group definition. If Schreiner, Woolf, Warner, and Cather stopped at what I am calling Sapphic primitivism, they still leave a legacy contemporary writers and cultural critics can use to investigate the mutuality of constructions of race, class, and sexuality and to further disrupt the coherence of whiteness as well as heterosexuality.

Notes

One   Sapphic Primitivism, an Introduction

1. By civil-rights era I mean the last few hundred years of post-enlightenment agitation for legislative change meant to increase access to civil rights for groups of people organized in terms of identity. Familiar events in civil-rights era struggles include the Montgomery bus boycott of 1955–56, the Stonewall rebellion of 1969, and the publication of *Our Bodies, Ourselves* by the Boston Women's Health Book Collective in 1976, as well as earlier events such as the five Pan African Congresses held from 1919 to 1945, the Seneca Falls convention of 1848, and the founding of homophile organizations in Germany at the end of the nineteenth century. Civil-rights style political events continue to take place, but the widespread acceptance of deconstructionist theories of identity signals the end of an era dominated by identity politics.

2. The degree to which discursive theories of homosexuality are accepted suggests that the turn of the twentieth century is itself a transitional period between civil-rights era discourse, in which the homosexual is a naturalized identity category, and a twenty-first century understanding, still under construction, of sexual identities and behaviors. People working to newly imagine sexual identity categories since the late 1980s include Eve Sedgewick, Judith Butler, Gail Rubin, Michael Warner, Rosemary Hennessy, Lucy Bland, Jacqueline Zita, and many others. They build largely on the work of Michel Foucault.

3. Several critics have discussed New Woman fiction, including that of Olive Schreiner, as modernist and proto-modernist. See for instance Ann Heilmann's *New Woman Fiction*, Ann Ardis's *New Women, New Novels*, and Jane Eldridge Miller's *Rebel Women*.

4. During the early stages of its development, Woolf described *The Waves* as a "play-

poem," referring to what she imagined would be a new form: a mix of novel and play, poetry and prose (*Diary* 3: 128, 236).

5. There is, of course, debate about what these historical events are. See note 21.

6. See my discussion of Sapphic modernism as a genre in the text following.

7. See Deborah McDowell's introduction to Nella Larsen's *Quicksand and Passing*; Siobhan Somerville's *Queering the Color Line: Race and the Invention of Homosexuality in American Culture* on Pauline Hopkins's *Contending Forces* and *Winona;* Hazel Carby's *Reconstructing Womanhood: The Emergence of the Afro-American Woman Novelist* on Harriet Jacobs, Zora Neale Hurston, and Pauline Hopkins; and Karla Caplan's "The Erotics of Talk: 'That Oldest Human Longing' in *Their Eyes Were Watching God*" on Hurston.

8. Djuna Barnes's *Nightwood* is one obvious example, as are Paule Marshall's *The Chosen Place, The Timeless People*, Gertrude Stein's "Melanctha," and H.D.'s *Hermione*.

9. Scott, *Refiguring Modernism* xl. Scott discusses Virginia Woolf and Djuna Barnes specifically, but her remark is equally true for other writers of the era including Sylvia Townsend Warner and Willa Cather.

10. In *Queering the Color Line: Race and the Invention of Homosexuality in American Culture,* Siobhan Somerville writes that discourses of sexuality are "embedded within discourses of race and racialization, particularly bifurcated constructions of 'black' and 'white' bodies" (175).

11. Turn-of-the-century discourse about homosexuality is usually not about lesbians, but this does not exclude lesbian writers from making use of discourse primarily about men for their own purposes in efforts to represent or narratively explore lesbianism. Julie Abraham points out that "gay men appear in 'lesbian novels' throughout the pre-Stonewall decades of the twentieth century," often as guides to the gay underworld. That men are representative guides in lesbian novels, she argues, "reflects the extent to which gay men rather than lesbians served culturally as representative of homosexuality" (33). For the same reason that lesbian writers write about male homosexuality, as Abraham claims, I believe they use tropes from scientific discourse written primarily about male homosexuality in their explorations and representations of lesbianism.

12. Abraham 27. Gay Wachman complicates Scott's and Abraham's focus on the Hall trial as the beginning of a new era in lesbian writing in *Lesbian Empire: Radical Crosswriting in the Twenties*. Wachman discusses several highly public legal maneuvers in addition to the Hall trial, including the trials involving Oscar Wilde (1895) and Maud Allen (1918) as well as the Labouchere amendment of 1885, which criminalized acts of gross indecency between men. Wachman argues that publicity surrounding these events produced a discourse about a lesbian identity that, while negative, might have enabled women to begin to build contrary, subversive, sexual identities earlier than Scott and Abraham indicate.

13. In "'Remembering the Jungle': Josephine Baker and Modernist Parody," Wendy Martin argues that the idea of the primitive even predates "the description of the acorn-eating primeval man in Boethius's *Consolation of Philosophy* (535 A.C.E.)" (321).

14. For a discussion of the role of travel writings in the construction of the primitive, see Christopher Steiner's "Travel Engravings and the Construction of the Primitive." For a discussion of the overlap between the noble savage of the eighteenth century and modernist primitivism, see Vincent Crapanzano's "The Moment of Prestidigitation."

15. See Elazar Barkan and Ronald Bush's introduction to *Prehistories of the Future: The Primitivist Project and the Culture of Modernism*. Also see Annie Coombes's *Reinventing Africa: Museums, Material Culture, and Popular Imagination in Late Victorian and Edwardian England* for a discussion of British museum culture's response to imperialist encounters with the art of West Africa and the Benin bronzes in particular.

16. See, for instance, Chinua Achebe's "A Vision of Africa," Anne McClintock's *Imperial Leather: Race, Gender, and Sexuality in the Colonial Contest;* Edward Said's *Orientalism;* Marianna Torgovnick's *Gone Primitive: Savage Intellects, Modern Lives;* and David Theo Goldberg's *Racist Culture: Philosophy and the Politics of Meaning.*

17. Torgovnick 20. Torgovnick bases her analysis on works by Edgar Rice Burroughs, Joseph Conrad, Sigmund Freud, D. H. Lawrence, Bronislaw Malinowski, James Frazer, and Roger Fry.

18. Henry Louis Gates uses the phrase "mutually constituted" on the dust jacket of Sieglinde Lemke's *Primitivist Modernism: Black Culture and the Origins of Transatlantic Modernism.* Lemke discusses aesthetic collaborations between "white" and "black" cultures in early twentieth-century art and literature. See also Houston Baker's *Modernism and the Harlem Renaissance*, Michael North's *The Dialect of Modernism: Race, Language, and Twentieth-Century Literature,"* George Hutchinson's *The Harlem Renaissance in Black and White*, Shelley Fisher Fishkin's *Was Huck Black? Mark Twain and African American Voices*, and Paul Gilroy's *The Black Atlantic: Modernity and Double Consciousness.*

19. See Susan Gubar's "Sapphistries," Shari Benstock's *Women of the Left Bank: Paris, 1900–1940*, Jane Marcus's "Sapphistries: Narration as Lesbian Seduction in *A Room of One's Own*," Karla Jay's "The Outsider among the Expatriates: Djuna Barnes' Satire on the Ladies of the *Almanack*," Cassandra Laity's "H.D. and A. C. Swinburne: Decadence and Sapphic Modernism," Ruth Vanita's *Sappho and the Virgin Mary: Same-Sex Love and the English Literary Imagination*, Erin Carlston's *Thinking Fascism: Sapphic Modernism and Fascist Modernity*, and Yopie Prins's *Victorian Sappho.*

20. See also Michael Omi and Howard Winnant, *Racial Formation in the United States: From the 1960s to the 1980s;* David Theo Goldberg, *Racist Culture: Philosophy and the Politics of Meaning;* David Theo Goldberg, ed., *Anatomy of Racism;* Nancy Stepan, *The Idea of Race in Science: Great Britain, 1800–1960;* Ruth Frankenberg, *White Women, Race Matters: The Social Construction of Whiteness;* Elazar Barkan, *The Retreat of Scientific Racism: Changing Concepts of Race in Britain and the United States between the World Wars;* Dominick LaCapra, ed., *The Bounds of Race: Perspectives on Hegemony and Resistance;* Evelyn Brooks Higginbotham, "African-American Women's History and the Metalanguage of

Race"; bell hooks, *Black Looks: Race and Representation*; Henry Louis Gates Jr., ed., *"Race," Writing, and Difference.*

21. Beginning with Michel Foucault's *History of Sexuality*, various histories of homosexuality have elaborated this point. In addition to Foucault's work see Alan Bray, *Homosexuality in Renaissance England*; David Halperin, *One Hundred Years of Homosexuality*; Jeffrey Weeks, *Sex, Politics and Society: The Regulation of Sexuality since 1800*; Valerie Traub, "The Psychomorphology of the Clitoris"; George Chauncey, "From Sexual Inversion to Homosexuality: Medicine and the Changing Conceptualization of Female Deviance"; John D'Emilio, "Capitalism and Gay Identity"; and Martha Vicinus, "'They Wonder to Which Sex I Belong': The Historical Roots of the Modern Lesbian Identity." See also Judith Butler's *Gender Trouble*, Eve Kosofsky Sedgwick's *Epistemology of the Closet*, and Michael Warner's *Fear of a Queer Planet.*

22. Upper-class and aristocratic status has also been characterized as sexually deviant. For a discussion of this class-sex-race construct, see Michael Bacchus's "Not a Bedspread, But a Counterpane: Under the Covers with Gay Men and Aristocrats in Twentieth-Century British Literature."

23. Many indigenous people from around the world were shown as ethnographic exhibits in world's fairs and other public events in the eighteenth and nineteenth centuries.

24. About Saartjie Baartman, the legal case in which she was involved, and the treatment of her body in life and after death, see also Sander Gilman's *Difference and Pathology: Stereotypes of Sexuality, Race, and Madness*, 78–108, and Rosemary Wiss's "Lipreading: Remembering Saartjie Baartman."

25. Davis, *Women, Race, and Class* 182. Patricia Morton makes this comparison between Davis and Stember in *Disfigured Images: The Historical Assault on Afro-American Women.*

26. McClintock 22. See also Peter Fryer's *Staying Power: The History of Black People in Britain*, especially chapter 7, and Edward Said's *Orientalism.*

27. Obviously I am not talking about women as heterosexual sex objects, which is common, but rather about desirous female heterosexuality.

28. Gilman 83. Gilman calls the black figure "girl" and "child," but her age is ambiguous, which might be part of the way in which hypersexuality is constructed.

29. Gilman 83, 89. I would add to Gilman's discussion of how the sexuality marked is specifically lesbian by pointing out that the black girl in *The Servant* is leaning toward the white woman and touching her back, while the white woman is leaning away from the black girl and is poised to receive touch. To the degree that action upon passive women is what defines (always already masculine) desire, the black girl, by virtue of being an actor relative to a passive female, is a masculinized woman, which is evocative of lesbianism.

30. Williams 291. Emma Mae Martin is Clarence Thomas's sister, vilified as a "welfare queen" (Williams 290).

31. Human Rights Campaign is the largest national U.S. gay and lesbian political organization. HRC was sharply criticized for this endorsement of D'Amato over Congressman Chuck Schumer, the democratic candidate, an act which was

based on what a majority on the board perceived as D'Amato's improved voting record with regard to lesbian and gay issues. They responded to criticism for this endorsement of a New York candidate by agreeing to make their policy about endorsements include consultation with local organizations. This corrective satisfied some of their critics, but does not address problems with the single-issue focus that was behind the original vote. More information about these events is available at the PlanetOut website at http://www.planetout.com/pno/splash. html, among other places.

Two The Homosexual Primitivism of Modernism

1. See Lucy Bland and Laura Doan's collection *Sexology Uncensored: The Documents of Sexual Science* for evidence and discussion of the diversity among sexologists, as well as individual sexologist's changes in point of view over time.

2. Djuna Barnes's characterization of Robin Vote in *Nightwood* reflects this construction of the homosexual as atavistic.

3. Ellis also cites another sexologist, Magnus Hirschfeld, who says that intermediate sexual types were especially "widespread among the Egyptians" (9).

4. Sexologists write almost exclusively about men, sometimes referring to lesbianism as an afterthought as if to say that lesbianism doesn't exist much, or is comparable to male homosexuality, or is different to the degree that women are less sexual than men in general.

5. Traub 88. These narratives ultimately contribute to the erotic representations of Englishwomen via seventeenth-century writings by midwives. Valerie Traub writes that in *The Midwives Book* by Jane Sharp, "the first Englishwoman to write her own midwifery," Sharp explains that unnatural sex between women is frequent in India and Egypt and usually has to do with large clitorises such as she has never heard of in England (Traub 89).

6. The first German edition appeared in 1905, the first English translation in 1910 under the title *Three Contributions to the Sexual Theory*. Later English translations are entitled *Three Contributions to the Theory of Sex* and *Three Essays on the Theory of Sexuality*.

7. Freud writes, "The information contained in this first essay is derived from the well-known writings of Krafft-Ebing, Moll, Moebius, Havelock Ellis, Schrenk-Notzing, Lowenfeld, Eulenberg, Bloch, and Hirschfeld" (1n).

8. Freud 5. Freud makes this claim in the context of an argument that homosexuality is not degenerate.

9. Malinowski protests that his book is not meant to be titillating. In the preface, he assures readers that he is a scholar and not a pornographer: there is no indecent pleasure in his book, nothing "suggestive or alluring" (xxiii, xxiv) that will interest the "seeker after pornography" (xxiii) or "entice the unripe interest of the young" (xxiv). Readers, this preface assures, can position themselves as scientifically rather than erotically interested. Also, for Malinowski himself, any "value or interest" in the book comes only from his wife's "share in the common work" (xxviii). The reference to his wife asserts Malinowski's sexual normalcy

and morality, as the book itself defines the normal and the moral: egalitarian and heterosexual. His feigned indifference to the subject of his work also claims for himself the properly matter-of-fact approach to sexuality he will describe as evidence of the particular healthfulness of Trobrianders' attitudes about sex. But despite these protestations, the book is designed for his own and his readers' sexual pleasure in looking at and talking about Trobriand Islanders, their sexual habits, as well as their sensuous home. In the first few pages, he describes his approach along the beach toward the village. "Fertile" flat expanses are broken up by occasional "tabooed groves." Following his introduction and an approach of 276 pages describing family life, kinship and economic systems, marriage rites, gender relations, courtship, always suggesting and circling around sex, he gets to what he has promised from the beginning: a close look at the sexual behaviors of his subjects, detailing positions, acts, favorite places, and accompanying talk and games. As he turns his focus to sex, he writes: "Let us return once more to a Trobriand village and approach a group of young people playing in the moonlight, in festive mood and dress; let us try to see them as they see each other; follow up their attractions and repulsions. So far we have kept at a discreet distance from the intimate behavior, the motives and feelings of lovers. More especially we have never attempted to spy upon their passionate caresses. Now we must try to reconstruct the history of a personal intrigue, to understand the first impressions made by beauty and charm, and to follow the development of a passion to its end" (285).

10. Carpenter professes to exempt sodomy from praiseworthy homosexuality, finding it "gross" to the point of not being able to use the word (209). He cites Krafft-Ebing's case studies as proof that among the congenitally inverted "while bodily congress is desired, the special act with which they are vulgarly credited is in most cases repugnant to them" (209). Moreover, he claims, prohibitions and anxiety over such love are the cause of such vulgarity. Especially in schools, prohibitions pervert the purity of homogenic love and lead it away from exalted expression. But in "Self-Analysis for Havelock Ellis," he writes, "pederasty, either active or passive, might seem in place to me with one I loved very devotedly and who also loved me to that degree; but I think not otherwise" (291).

11. Woolf refers to empire exhibits several times in her works. See for instance *Jacob's Room,* 167, *The Waves,* 135–136, as well as "Thunder at Wembley."

12. Hart 4. In this context, it is interesting to note that during the trial involving *The Well of Loneliness,* which she attended, Virginia Woolf described Radclyffe Hall as "lemon yellow, tough, stringy, exacerbated" (*Diary* 3: 207).

Three   Olive Schreiner and the Late Victorian New Woman

1. Schreiner's parents, her German father and English mother, were missionaries who married in England and immediately afterward went to work for the London Missionary Society in what was then the Cape Colony. Schreiner always identified as English and later in her life as an English South African.

2. *The Story of an African Farm* was Schreiner's second novel, but the first that

she published. She wrote her first novel *Undine, African Farm,* and part of *From Man to Man, or Perhaps Only* while in her teens and twenties working as a governess in South Africa. *From Man to Man* and *Undine* were published posthumously by Schreiner's husband in 1927 and 1928, respectively. Her other major works incude *Dream Life and Real Life: A Little African Story* (1891); *Trooper Peter Halket of Mashonaland* (1897); *The South African Question, by an English South African* (1899, also printed as *An English South-African's View of the Situation: Words in Season* in 1899); *So Here Then Are Dreams* (1901, also printed as *Dreams* in 1891, 1910); *A Letter on the Jew* (1906); *Woman and Labor* (1911); and *Thoughts on South Africa* (1923). Editions of her letters have been edited and posthumously published by her husband, S. C. Cronwright-Schreiner; Richard Rive; and Yaffa Claire Draznin. See note 5 below.

3. Schreiner was living in England at the time. She arrived in England in 1881 and traveled there and in Europe until she went back to South Africa in 1889.

4. Carpenter speaks of meeting Schreiner in his autobiographical *My Days and Dreams.*

5. While Schreiner made sure that many of her letters were destroyed, several volumes of her correspondence have been published. Her husband edited one volume in 1924; Richard Rive edited another volume covering the years 1871–1899 in 1988. The letters between Schreiner and Havelock Ellis were edited by Yaffa Claire Draznin in 1992. The correspondence between Ellis and Schreiner, which begins in 1884 and continues until Schreiner's death in 1920, reveals that the two had a troubled romance early in their friendship.

6. See letters to Mary Saur, Mrs. Issie Smuts, and Schreiner's brother Will in Rive (275–276, 364, 366, 368).

7. Schreiner was hostile to the social approval of prostitution not to individual prostitutes, with whom she sought to be friendly and to discuss questions about sexual desire in men and women. See, for instance, letters to Karl Pearson in Rive (65, 69, 73, 83, 178–179). About marriage she was more indifferent. She advocated freely chosen monogamous relationships and didn't see any harm in conforming to social requirements that couples legally marry. See, for instance, letters to Edward Carpenter, Karl Pearson, Mary Roberts, and the Rev. J. T. Lloyd in Rive (96, 121–122, 145, 259).

8. Smith-Rosenberg 268. Several authors in addition to Bland and Smith-Rosenberg have discussed the relationship between the late Victorian New Woman and the lesbian in public discourse in England and in the United States. See, for instance, Jennifer Terry's *An American Obsession: Science, Medicine, and Homosexuality in Modern Society,* Esther Newton's "The Mythic Mannish Lesbian: Radclyffe Hall and the New Woman," and Ann Heilmann's *New Woman Fiction: Women Writing First-Wave Feminism.*

9. Brittain, "The Influence of Olive Schreiner" 125. See also Nadine Gordimer's "Review of *Olive Schreiner: A Biography* by Ruth First and Ann Scott." Gordimer writes that "through *Woman and Labour,* [Schreiner] is a founding member of women's liberation in Britain" (14). For more discussion about the effect of Schreiner's work on late-nineteenth- and early-twentieth-century feminists, see

also Alan Bishop's "'With suffering and through time': Olive Schreiner, Vera Brittain, and the Great War," Laurence Lerner's "Olive Schreiner and the Feminists," and Lucy Bland's *Banishing the Beast.*

10. Schreiner uses the term "race" variously to mean all of humanity and at other times to indicate specific groups such as English or Bantu or Boer.

11. Schreiner 28. She refers to the "first man" without specifying that she means European man, but her subsequent examples are from European contexts.

12. In her later work, including *Thoughts on South Africa,* Schreiner praises many parts of Southern African society, particularly Boer culture, in her efforts to ease Anglo-Boer tensions and avoid war. She praises the English racial love of freedom specifically to criticize Cecil Rhodes's capitalist expansionism, which she interprets as a trespass on the freedom of the Boers. Boer colonization is not a trespass, but rather a fair process by which one group fights against another for land on which to survive. In the earlier work *The Story of an African Farm,* however, Schreiner is disparaging of the cultures around her.

Four   Empire, Social Rot, and Sexual Fantasy in *The Waves*

1. The anti-imperialism of *The Waves* is not obvious to all readers. Prior to the publication of Jane Marcus's work on the novel, much criticism proceeded without mentioning Woolf's references to empire at all. See in the text a discussion of the way in which Marcus's work changed the direction of Woolf criticism.

2. In her biography *Virginia Woolf,* Hermione Lee calls life-writing a "perpetual preoccupation" of Woolf's "essays and diaries and fiction" (4).

3. *Les Vagues* is the title of Marguerite Yourcenar's translation of *The Waves* into French.

4. Juxtaposition is also vitally important in others of Woolf's works. Perhaps the most obvious example is in *Three Guineas,* where pictures of men in uniforms signaling military, juridical, and academic rank are juxtaposed with text about war. By this juxtaposition, Woolf implicates patriarchal hierarchies of all kinds with the tyranny of the fascism that is on the rise in 1930s Europe.

5. Woolf herself said that her chief goal was "to criticize the social system, and to show it at work, at its most intense" (*Diary* 2: 248). Kathy Phillips, in her book devoted to describing the anti-imperialist stance in Woolf's work, argues that Woolf uses juxtaposition of detail and imagery to "map social vistas," orient the reader's gaze toward links between empire, militarism, and gender relations, and to satirize those links (xxvii). By 1997, enough had been written about Woolf's anti-imperialism for Hermione Lee to presume, in her biography, that readers would understand all Woolf's work as politically engaged.

6. Woolf, *Mrs Dalloway* 47. Many critics have discussed the lesbian eroticism of Sally's kiss and the orgasmic description of a crocus in *Mrs. Dalloway.* See Gay Wachman's essay "Pink Icing and a Narrow Bed" and her book *Lesbian Empire: Radical Crosswriting in the Twenties* for comprehensive discussions of the ways in which Woolf explores lesbianism in *Mrs. Dalloway.*

7. Oxindine 173. See Wachman's *Lesbian Empire* for an analysis of the atmosphere

of repression between 1880 and World War I. Wachman emphasizes the importance of imperialist discourse and discusses several anti-homosexual trials, the most famous being those against Oscar Wilde and Radclyffe Hall, but also includes the lawsuit against the bookseller of Havelock Ellis's and J. A Symonds's *Sexual Inversion* (1897).

8. Woolf was never called to take the stand. See Woolf, *Diary* 3: 193, 206–207; and *Letters* 3: 520, 529–530, 555, 563. See also Jane Marcus's *Virginia Woolf and the Languages of Patriarchy*, 210n; and Hermione Lee's *Virginia Woolf*, 524–527.

9. For a full analysis of the ways in which Woolf responded to the trial in *A Room of One's Own* in particular, see Jane Marcus's *Virginia Woolf and the Languages of Patriarchy*, 163–187. See also Vera Brittain, *Radcliffe Hall,* for details about the trial.

10. Lee, *Virginia Woolf* 524. The more significant reason Woolf got away with writing the distinctly Sapphic novel *Orlando* while Radclyffe Hall's novel was banned is that *Orlando* is fantastic rather than realist fiction. See Jane Marcus's *Virginia Woolf and the Languages of Patriarchy*, 163–187.

11. See the section on degeneracy in chapter 2.

12. In Bernard's summing up, Woolf suggests that the birds and the children are the same.

13. Houses in *The Years* and *Orlando*, for instance.

14. A soliloquy of Rhoda's later in the novel also puts these "blue fingerprints"— shadows from leaves—in a place distant, dark, and also sexual. "Dark leaved bushes" and "their darkness" are characteristics of a distant place into which Rhoda constantly looks to "fill [her nights] fuller and fuller with dreams," and where she imagines she sees "a shape, white [perhaps herself] . . . moving, perhaps alive" against "their [the leaves'] darkness" (139). The dreams Rhoda mentions recur in the novel and in the holograph drafts are the more specifically sexual dreams about kissing Alice.

15. See Ruth Vanita's *Sappho and the Virgin Mary* for a discussion of the homoeroticism associated with medieval and Romantic uses of myths of Mary and Jesus, and ways in which Woolf's *The Waves* participates in this Romantic tradition.

16. Lee, *Virginia Woolf* 524. For further discussion of homoeroticism in Shakespeare's sonnets see Jonathan Goldberg's *Queering the Renaissance* and *Sodometries*, Gregory Bredbeck's *Sodomy and Interpretation*, Joseph Pequigney's *Such Is My Love*, Eve Sedgwick's *Between Men,* and Bruce Smith's *Homosexual Desire in Shakespeare's England.* For further discussion of Woolf's use of Shakespeare's sonnets in *The Waves,* see my essay "Supplanting Shakespeare's Rising Sons: A Perverse Reading through Woolf's *The Waves*."

17. J. Marcus, *Virginia Woolf and the Languages of the Patriarchy* 169. Using an example from *Jacob's Room*, Kathy Phillips argues, in *Virginia Woolf against Empire,* that Woolf's breaks and ellipses "do not testify merely to [modernist] sportive 'free play'" of signifiers; rather, "breaks and ellipses yield a coherent pattern of satire" (xiv).

18. Later in *The Waves* Rhoda also characterizes herself as one who lies and prevaricates in opposition to Jinny's sexual truthfulness about "dealing her looks adroitly here and there" (106).

19. The original kiss is on pages 11–13. The suggestion that Louis is masturbating is in his lines, "I hold a stalk in my hand. I am the stalk," and "My body is a stalk. I press the stalk. A drop oozes from the hole at the mouth and slowly, thickly, grows larger and larger."

20. Drowning in the mill-race for forbidden love is also the theme of Ibsen's play *Rosmersholm*.

21. Her face reflected in the mirror also has echoes of Rhoda's constant inability, through the novel, to see her own face. She insists that, unlike other girls, she has no face (43). This facelessness is one of the characteristics that Oxindine argues marks Rhoda as a lesbian in the final version of *The Waves*.

Five   Class, Race, and Lesbian Erotics in *Summer Will Show*

1. For other references to Warner's persistent neglect, see Clare Harman's "Sylvia Townsend Warner, 1893–1978: A Celebration," J. Lawrence Mitchell's "'The Secret Country of Her Mind,'" Eleanor Perenyi's "The Good Witch of the West," Robert Caserio's "Celibate Sisters-in-Revolution," Barbara Brothers's "Writing against the Grain," Janet Montefiore's "Listening to Minna," Arnold Rattenbury's "Literature, Lying, and the Sober Truth," Simon Watney's "Who Is Sylvia?" Jane Marcus's "Alibis and Legends: The Ethics of Elsewhereness, Gender, and Estrangement" and "Bluebeard's Daughters: Pretexts for Pre-Texts," Terry Castle's *The Apparitional Lesbian: Female Homosexuality and Modern Culture*, and Maroula Joannou's "Sylvia Townsend Warner in the 1930s."

2. Harman, *Sylvia Townsend Warner* 66, 71. *Lolly Willowes* was nominated for the Prix Femina, and *Mr. Fortune's Maggot* for the James Tait Black prize. Collections of poetry published during Warner's life include *The Espalier* (1925), *Time Importuned* (1928), *Opus 7* (1931), *Whether a Dove or Seagull* (1933), which is a joint collection with Valentine Ackland, *Boxwood* (1957), *King Duffus and Other Poems* (1968). Some of the collections are small and with small presses, such as the pamphlet *King Duffus and Other Poems*. But most are published by Viking or Chatto and Windus. The *New Yorker* magazine published over 140 stories and nine poems by Warner between 1936 and 1976, close to a record according to William Maxwell, one of Warner's editors at the magazine (Maxwell, "Introduction" xv, "Sylvia Townsend Warner and *The New Yorker*" 44). Volumes of stories published during her lifetime include *Some World Far from Ours* (1929), *Elinor Barley* (1930), *A Moral Ending and Other Stories* (1931), *The Salutation and Other Stories* (1932), *More Joy in Heaven* (1935), *The Cat's Cradle Book* (1940), *A Garland of Straw* (1943), *The Museum of Cheats* (1947), *Winter in the Air* (1955), *A Spirit Rises* (1962), *A Stranger with a Bag,* published in the United States as *Swans on an Autumn River* (1966), *The Innocent and the Guilty* (1971), and *Kingdoms of Elfin* (1977). Novels published during her lifetime include *Lolly Willowes* (1926), *Mr. Fortune's Maggot* (1927), *The True Heart* (1929), *Summer Will Show* (1936), *After the Death of Don Juan* (1938), *The Corner That Held Them* (1948), and *The Flint Anchor* (1954). Warner also translated Proust's *Contre Sainte-Beuve* (By way of Sainte-Beuve) (1958) and Jean-Rene Huguenin's *La Côte Sauvage* (A

place of shipwreck) (1962), wrote a biography of T. H. White (1967), contributed numerous articles to journals including *New Masses, Left Review,* The *Nation, Time and Tide, Life and Letters Today, Daily Worker, Left News,* The *Countryman, Our Time,* and The *Country Standard.* Posthumous publications of Warner's work include three more collections of poetry: *Arazel and Other Poems* (1978), *Twelve Poems* (1980), and *Collected Poems* (1982); three collections of stories: *Scenes of Childhood and Other Stories* (1981), *One Thing Leading to Another and Other Stories* (1984), and *Selected Stories of Sylvia Townsend Warner* (1988); *The Diaries of Sylvia Townsend Warner* (1994); *Letters* (1982); and *I'll Stand by You: Selected Letters of Sylvia Townsend Warner and Valentine Ackland* (1998).

3. Critics include Wendy Mulford, Barbara Brothers, Arnold Rattenbury, Jan Montefiore, Thomas Foster, Simon Watney, and Maroula Joannou.

4. These critics include Jane Marcus, Terry Castle, Thomas Foster, Gillian Spraggs, Robert Caserio, and Gay Wachman.

5. Critics include William Maxwell, Clare Harman, and Eleanor Perenyi.

6. Arnold Rattenbury writes, "Sylvia kept a deliberate distance from literary gangs, but was widely recognized for all that. How else could she have conducted those great round robin collections and exhortations during the Spanish Civil War? Why else would the royal society of arts invite her to lecture, or Penguin include her so early in their fiction list" ("Literature, Lying, and the Sober Truth" 234).

7. Joannou writes that "the revolutionary rhetoric of the Internationale made much of the insurrectionary potential of the peasantry but in the 1930s the Communist Party prided itself on deriving its support from workers in the large industrial cities. Sylvia's public opposition to rural squalor was a salutary reminder to many socialists that poverty and deprivation were not exclusively urban phenomena" (93).

8. Perenyi also addresses the diversity and quantity of Warner's production as factors contributing to her neglect.

9. See especially the later stories collected in *The Cat's Cradle Book* and *Kingdoms of Elfin* as well as *Lolly Willowes.*

10. See, for instance, Jane Marcus's essay "A Wilderness of One's Own: Feminist Fantasy Novels of the Twenties: Rebecca West and Sylvia Townsend Warner" and Thomas Foster's "'Dream Made Flesh': Sexual Difference and Narratives of Revolution in Sylvia Townsend Warner's *Summer Will Show.*"

11. Warner and Ackland lived together for thirty-eight years from 1930 until 1968 when Ackland died of breast cancer. They referred to January 12, 1931, as their wedding night and kept January 12 as an anniversary. See Warner, *Diaries* 337, 339. Warner delighted in characterizing the two as an "old married couple" and their pleasure in living together as "wedded bliss" or "wedded lives" or "a long happy marriage." See *Diaries* 337, 340, 350, 357, for instance. After Ackland died, Warner began to live in what she called her "widowed estate" and "widowhood." See, for instance, *Diaries* 332, 340, 345. See also Wendy Mulford's *This Narrow Place,* which describes their lives together; Valentine Ackland's posthumously

published *For Sylvia* (1986); and the collection of love letters between Warner and Ackland, *I'll Stand by You* (1998), which also includes narrative passages Warner wrote as she edited the letters for publication. Warner's delight in calling her relationship a marriage has to be contrasted with her hostility to patriarchal marriage as an institution. Husbands and wives in general who act out conventionally gendered domestic roles are lambasted in a letter to Nancy Cunard in which Warner describes her work arranging housing for evacuees from London during World War II. She writes, "Dorchester is crammed with evacuees. . . . I spend miserable mornings going from one billet to another, always hearing the same complaints, the same incessant preoccupations with pillow-cases and tea-cups. My heart is entirely with the Londoners, yet if their billets are to be even tolerable to them I have to placate their blasted hostesses; and anyway the hostesses are as much to be pitied, for they are all bred and born slaves . . . with noses never raised from the floor polish, and husbands who don't like to be put out" (Letter to Nancy Cunard 7/17/44). In another letter to Cunard, Warner rages about governmental privileges that accrue to women simply for having husbands and argues that the sexism that prompts this privilege must be resolved before other kinds of injustice can be addressed adequately: "Now I have a notice on my table telling me to attend at the Labour Exchange with a view to taking up employment of national importance—which means they will try to put me into a laundry. If I had taken to myself a husband, lived on him and made his life a misery (as undoubtedly I should have done, as no man has ever been able to bear me as a continuity) I should not be troubled with any of this. Being kept by a husband is of national importance enough. But to be feme sole [*sic*], and self supporting, that hands you over, no more claim to individual choice than a biscuit. This great civil war, Nancy, that will come and must come before the world can begin to grow up, will be fought out on this terrain of man and woman, and we must storm and hold Cape Turk before we talk of social justice" (*Letters* 84).

12. Many years later, when Miss Green's cottage is destroyed by a bomb, the tragedy is neither her loss of property nor the loss of a place nostalgic for her and Ackland. Rather, as Warner rails in a letter to Nancy Cunard and Morris Gilbert, the tragedy is that "the only decent cottage in that village, the only cottage kept in order, [is] gone, while the hovels belonging to the Weld estate, God damn it, are untouched in all their filth, scarcely a bug shaken out of them" (*Letters* 85).

13. Early reviewers and critics do not mention the novel's lesbian erotics. In a 1975 celebration of Sylvia Townsend Warner edited by Claire Harman, neither Warner's lesbianism nor the lesbianism of the novel is mentioned specifically, but Arnold Rattenbury says Sophia and Minna "meet and eventually live together" ("Plain Heart" 47), and J. Lawrence Mitchell writes that Sophia is "drawn to Minna" (52). Jane Marcus, Thomas Foster, Barbara Brothers, and Janet Montefiore also assume Sophia's lesbianism in essays that focus more specifically on the politics of the novel. Terry Castle is the first to take the lesbianism of the novel as a point of analysis. In an essay that borrows from Eve Sedgwick's

theory that homosocial relations between men are central to canonized English and American literature, Castle calls *Summer Will Show* "exemplary 'lesbian fiction'" and "paradigmatically 'lesbian'" because the novel "depicts a sexual relationship between two women" and because it "figures this relationship as a breakup of the supposedly 'canonical' male-female-male erotic triangle" (74). Castle admits that Warner "renders the scene of [Sophia and Minna's] coming together elliptically—with only a cry (and an oyster) to suggest the moment of consummation" but argues that "the meaning is clear" (79). Two critics have challenged Castle's claim that Minna and Sophia's relationship is sexual: Robert Caserio claims that Sophia and Minna are part of a literary tradition of chaste sisters; Sandy Petrey argues that the pair is ambiguously sexual at most, and signals more than anything else a characteristic ambiguity on Warner's part. But Castle's interpretation and her subsequent responses to Caserio and Petrey in the notes to the version of the essay published in *The Apparitional Lesbian* are persuasive and have set the standard for subsequent discussion of *Summer Will Show*, such as Foster's "Dream Made Flesh" and Julie Abraham's *Are Girls Necessary*.

14. Castle 83; Foster 545. Foster argues that Warner's narrative "can avoid more direct sexual references [about Sophia and Minna] in part because they are displaced onto an earlier scene between Sophia and the wife of a doctor, Mrs. Hervey" (545).

15. Warner often describes workingmen's hands, always "hard," especially capable politically, and often bearing a broken or blackened nail. This hand also appears in Cather's short story "Neighbor Rosicky" as a symbol of Rosicky's experience as an urban laborer and his wisdom about work and freedom.

16. This is perhaps a sexual wandering similar to Melanctha's wandering in Gertrude Stein's *Three Lives*.

17. Nearly all critics, including those who focus on the lesbianism as well as those who focus on the politics of the novel, have ignored the importance of the lime-kiln man and Caspar. Foster's "Dream Made Flesh" is an important exception. Foster discusses the lesbianism in *Summer Will Show* in terms of both the class politics of the novel and the conventions of modern narrative, including the "problematic relation between women's stories and Marxist traditions of historical analysis" (538). Foster credits Warner's disruption of the "boundary between domestic or sentimental fiction and the historical novel" with enabling "the narrativizing of other forms of social difference, including not only alternative sexualities but also race and class differences" (536). About the scene involving the lime-kiln man, Foster argues that Sophia's decision to go to Paris to seek impregnation by Frederick "represents an identification with the different class sexuality of 'other women'" (541). About Caspar, Foster argues that the subplot involving him "returns the story of the women's participation in revolutionary struggle to the women's relationship and its consequences" because it reveals "the conflicts between a lesbian who has chosen not to reproduce and the social forces that demand she assume the role of mother" (553). Foster also claims, importantly, that the subplot about Caspar "points to the existence of narratives

organized around other social antagonisms, between a member of an English colonial family and a West Indian mulatto, between a Jewish emigrant and a child indoctrinated with nationalist and anti-Semitic propaganda" (553–554).

18. In a few ways, including Warner's punning creation of Sophia as "husband," Sophia seems modeled on Valentine Ackland. Like Ackland, for instance, Sophia shoots and cuts down trees (52).

19. Warner is evoking and perhaps making fun of widespread eighteenth- and nineteenth-century acceptance of romantic friendship between women based on the assumption that such friendships were necessarily asexual. Sophia embraces conventional beliefs about the asexuality of romantic friendship when she thinks Mrs. Hervey might be in love with her and is at the same time unconscious of the erotic tension that readers can't fail to see.

20. Boarding school is for people of Mrs. Hervey's class. People of Sophia's class have governesses and tutors at home.

21. Even before they meet, Sophia becomes obsessed with Minna, though this could be interpreted as sexual fascination for Minna specifically as her husband's lover. When Frederick arrives at Blandamer to see his dying children, Sophia reflects that the "Jewess" has improved him. If he once left Sophia "cold and unamorous," he is transformed into a sensual figure. He is a "foreigner" (80) a "stranger" (82) who walks with a "freer gait, a liberated air" (81). His words *"ma fleur,"* spoken to Augusta as she is dying, echo in Sophia's ears after Frederick has gone, alternately "an enigma, a nettle-sting" and, most suggestively, "a caress" (83). Textures of Frederick's speech, "modelled on that Minna's Jewish contralto," "fascinate" and "elude" Sophia (84). His improved French accent is the result of Minna having "suppled his tongue" (85). Sophia can "smell Minna on him, as though he had brought bodily into the house the odour of his mistress," and can't "remember Frederick without snuffing Minna" (87). Sophia's obsession even includes dreams of Minna that are so disturbing she decides to give her thoughts about Mrs. Hervey "free rein, since it was better to be teased by Mrs. Hervey than by Minna" (88–89).

22. The reference to an "eiderdown" in this suggestive scene between Minna and Sophia is a private joke as well as further evidence for reading Minna and Sophia's relationship as sexual.

23. Whether or not Minna dies after Caspar stabs her is left ambiguous.

24. See Peter Fryer's *Staying Power: The History of Black People in England*, chapters 2, 3, 6, and 8, and James Walvin's *Making the Black Atlantic: Britain and the African Diaspora* for discussions of the slave trade and its abolition, sugar production, and English wealth.

25. Historians of slavery argue that the slave trade was abolished because it was no longer as profitable as wage labor and capitalism. See, for instance, Peter Fryer's *Staying Power*.

26. Sophia doesn't use this word, but Warner called herself and Ackland lesbians in her correspondence with Ackland. See Warner and Ackland, *I'll Stand by You* 111.

Six   Jezebel and Sapphira: Willa Cather's Monstrous Sapphists

This chapter was inspired by Lisa Marcus's analysis of *Sapphira and the Slave Girl* in "'The Pull of Race and Blood and Kindred': Willa Cather's Southern Inheritance."

1. Wilde used this phrase—a quote from a poem by his lover Lord Alfred Douglas—during his 1895 trial for gross indecency between males (Hogan and Hudson 576).

2. Cather wrote about Wilde's drama and poetry, also making reference to his trial, in 1894 and 1895. See Cather, *The Kingdom of Art* 387–393.

3. Cather's major publications include *April Twilights* (1903), *The Troll Garden* (1905), *Alexander's Bridge* (1912), *O Pioneers!* (1913), *The Song of the Lark* (1915), *My Ántonia* (1918), *Youth and the Bright Medusa* (1920), *One of Ours* (1922), *A Lost Lady* (1923), *The Professor's House* (1925), *My Mortal Enemy* (1926), *Death Comes for the Archbishop* (1927), *Shadows on the Rock* (1931), *Obscure Destinies* (1932), *Lucy Gayheart* (1935), *Sapphira and the Slave Girl* (1940), and *The Old Beauty and Others* (1948).

4. Cather's collection of essays *Not under Forty* is her response to some of those who attacked her nostalgia as a mark of political conservatism. With the title of the collection, she accepts the challenge of those who would denigrate her for preferring the old to the new artistically and socially. See Deborah Carlin's *Cather, Canon, and the Politics of Reading,* 13–17, for further discussion of this critique and Cather's response.

5. Biographies include those by Mildred Bennet (1951), E. K. Brown and Leon Edel (1953), Edith Lewis (1953), and Elizabeth Sergeant (1953).

6. The exception to the silence is Mildred Bennet's work on the board of the Willa Cather Pioneer Memorial and Education Foundation in Red Cloud, Nebraska, and on the Willa Cather Pioneer Newsletter. The later biographies include those by James Woodress (1970, 1987), Marion Marsh Brown and Ruth Crone (1971, 1980), Sharon O'Brien (1987), and Hermione Lee (1989).

7. Another instance of Cather's presence in popular journalism is Joan Acocella's 1995 article "Cather and the Academy," also published in the *New Yorker*. Acocella offers a sharp critique of "political readings" (70) of Cather's work, attacking feminist scholarship in particular. Acocella's book, *Willa Cather and the Politics of Criticism*, has also been very well received.

8. Carlin argues that there are four main academic reading communities of Cather scholars: "those concerned with art, style and form in Cather's fiction; those who attempt to place Cather historically and thematically in the 'main currents' of twentieth-century American literature; feminist critics; and lesbian feminist scholars" (8). Mildred Bennet's *The World of Willa Cather* (1951), James Woodress's *Willa Cather: A Literary Life* (1987), and Mary Ruth Ryder's *Willa Cather and Classical Myth* (1990) focus on the ways in which Cather's work is fundamentally about art and the role of the artist in society (Carlin 8). See also Joyce Macdonald's *The Stuff of Our Forebears*, David Stouck's *Willa Cather's Imagination*, and Marilyn Arnold's "The Allusive Cather." Other critics emphasize

Cather's engagement with political and social issues of her day, and/or with modernist literary concerns and aesthetics. These writers respond to critics such as Granville Hicks, who argues that Cather is antimodern, and more recent critics such as Hugh Kenner, who ignores her in his 1984 essay on modernism. See, for instance, Susan Rosowski's *The Voyage Perilous*, Phyllis Rose's "Modernism: The Case of Willa Cather," Jo Ann Middleton's *Willa Cather's Modernism: A Study of Style and Technique*, Guy Reynolds's *Willa Cather in Context: Progress, Race, Empire*, Hermione Lee's *Willa Cather: Double Lives*, Marilee Lindemann's *Willa Cather: Queering America*, Paul Petrie's "'Skulking Escapist' vs. 'Radical Editor,'" and Elizabeth Ammons's "Cather and the New Canon: 'The Old Beauty' and the Issue of Empire."

9. Lee, *Willa Cather* 256. Lee cites Phyllis Rose, here, who discusses the similarity between Cather and other modernists' interest in myth, heroism, and fractures with the past.

10. Notably, Carolyn Heilbrun's *Reinventing Womanhood*; Sandra Gilbert and Susan Gubar's *No Man's Land,* especially vol. 2, *Sexchanges*; Ellen Moers's *Literary Women*; Sharon O'Brien's "The Unity of Willa Cather's 'Two-Part Pastoral': Passion in *O Pioneers!*" and *Willa Cather: The Emerging Voice*; Susan Rosowski's "Willa Cather's Women" and *The Voyage Perilous*; Judith Fryer's *Felicitous Space*; Janice P. Stout's *Strategies of Reticence*; and Hermione Lee's *Willa Cather: Double Lives*.

11. For instance, Jane Rule's *Lesbian Images*, Sharon O'Brien's *Willa Cather: The Emerging Voice*, Timothy Dow Adams's "My Gay Antonia: The Politics of Willa Cather's Lesbianism," Catherine Stimpson's "Zero Degree Deviancy: The Lesbian Novel in English," Bonnie Zimmerman's "What Has Never Been: An Overview of Lesbian Feminist Literary Criticism," Joanna Russ's "To Write 'Like a Woman': Transformations of Identity in the Work of Willa Cather," Judith Fetterley's "*My Antonia*, Jim Burden and the Dilemma of the Lesbian Writer," John H. Flannigan's "Issues of Gender and Lesbian Love: Goblins in 'The Garden Lodge,'" and Deborah Lambert's "The Defeat of a Hero."

12. Joan Acocella, an exception, strongly objects.

13. As is well known, Cather, like Olive Schreiner, destroyed most of her letters in the later part of her life. Also, in her will she prohibited direct quotation from any surviving letters. Sharon O'Brien and Marilee Lindemann paraphrase in discussing the letters. (See O'Brien, *Willa Cather* 130–134, Lindemann 17–31, 146n.) Both Lindemann and O'Brien make it clear that "unnatural" is Cather's word to describe her relationship with Pound.

14. Butler, *Bodies That Matter* 143. Butler's essay deals with *My Antonia*, "Tommy the Unsentimental," and "Paul's Case."

15. See Minrose Gwin's *Black and White Women of the Old South: The Peculiar Sisterhood in American Literature* (1985), Katrina Irving's "Displacing Homosexuality: The Use of Ethnicity in Willa Cather's *My Antonia*" (1990), Carlin's *Cather, Canon, and the Politics of Reading* (1992), Lisa Marcus's "'The Pull of Race and Blood and Kindred': Willa Cather's Southern Inheritance" (2000), Walter Benn Michaels's *Our America: Nativism, Modernism, and Pluralism* (1995), Naomi

Morgenstern's "'Love Is Homo-sickness': Nostalgia and Lesbian Desire in *Sapphira and the Slave Girl* (1996) and Marilee Lindemann's *Willa Cather: Queering America* (1999).

16. Lindemann 169n, 134. Fetterley 43. Julie Abraham also discusses the limitations of masquerade models of lesbian representation in *Are Girls Necessary* (see 23–26).

17. Cather's representations of force participate in what Carlin calls "the heroic myth of national destiny" (7). For more discussion of Cather's works as they relate to national identity, see also Lindemann's *Willa Cather: Queering America*, Walter Benn Michaels's *Our America*, Joseph Urgo's *Willa Cather and the Myth of American Migration*, and Guy Reynolds's *Willa Cather in Context*.

18. See Maynard Fox's "Two Primitives" for a discussion of Tom Outland as primitive. Walter Benn Michaels also argues that the bond between the three men isolated on the Blue Mesa in this novel represent national purity (47–48).

19. Consistent with this idea that creative force is masculine, Lindemann points out that in Cather's 1925 preface to a collection of Sarah Orne Jewett's stories, Cather's use of the generic *he* "makes a linguistic 'man' out of Jewett" (93). Cather's discussion of Jewett's poetics "cross-dresses [Jewett] and cloaks her art of sympathy and suggestion in terms that define it as a masculine achievement" (93–94).

20. See Judith Butler's *Bodies That Matter*, for instance.

21. Lindemann argues that *Alexander's Bridge* can be compared to cautionary tales meant to show non-reproductive sexuality as a form of race suicide. With Rhoda's suicide, Woolf may also have been literalizing, as a form of critique, moral purity campaigners' cautions against homosexuality as race suicide.

22. Later in the novel, Thea's brothers also berate her for socializing with Mexicans (213–214).

23. See the earlier discussion of the critical response to Cather.

24. Lisa Marcus 101. Gay Wachman discusses English novelists who crosswrite female homoerotic desire through gay male narrators in *Lesbian Empire: Radical Crosswriting in the Twenties*.

25. See, for instance, Susan Rosowski, Sharon O'Brien, Hermione Lee, James Woodress, and Merrill Maguire Skaggs and Ann Romines's collection *Willa Cather's Southern Connections*. But it is also worth noting that until Toni Morrison wrote about *Sapphira* in 1990, it was one of Cather's least-discussed novels. See Deborah Carlin's *Cather, Canon, and the Politics of Reading*, 8–26, for a discussion of why Cather's later works in general have been much less frequently discussed than her earlier works. Joyce Macdonald discusses the ways in which Cather used the autobiographical content to make claims about the role of art and the artist in society.

26. Joyce Macdonald writes that "Willa Cather's versions of the pastoral are a product of her Southern sensibility and share common factors with the Southern literary tradition" (x). But Macdonald also discusses the ways in which Cather resists this tradition.

27. Many critics have also attempted to show that Cather's novel makes a critique

of slavery that is in conflict with her nostalgia for antebellum Virginia. Loretta Wasserman argues that Cather's novel is a critique of stereotypes of blacks in Margaret Mitchell's *Gone with the Wind*. Merrill Maguire Skaggs argues that *Sapphira* is exceptional among southern women's writing of the late 1930s for its dramatization of "the evils of slavery" (171). Joyce Macdonald argues that *Sapphira* is "a finely tuned study of the negative effects of the institution of slavery on the minds both of slaveholders and of those living within the system, as well as the corrosive impact on the moral, spiritual, and artistic sensibility" (89). Naomi Morgenstern takes a slightly different view; she discusses the ways in which the nostalgic affect of the plot and the brutality of the antebellum setting work together in the novel to position idealized mother-daughter bonding as an alternative to initiation into brutal heterosexuality.

28. That the sexologists entirely created the modern category lesbian is disputed. See the discussion of Valerie Traub's work in chapter 2, George Chauncey's "From Sexual Inversion to Homosexuality: Medicine and the Changing Conceptualization of Female Deviance," and Gay Wachman's *Lesbian Empire*.

29. Cather, *Kingdom of Art* 186. Cather wrote a regular Sunday column for the *Journal* for nearly seven years beginning in the winter of 1893–1894 (Slote 12–13).

30. Lindemann 22. Lindemann interprets Cather's choice of gift through Edward Said's concept of orientalism. Lindemann writes, "As a gift, the Rubaiyat is a safe choice in that gift editions of FitzGerald's translation were enormously popular at the turn of the century, but it is also a risky, risque invitation to revel in the Orientalist fantasy of the Orient as a space of 'sexual promise (and threat), untiring sensuality, unlimited desire, deep generative energies'" (Said qtd. in Lindemann 22).

31. Other critics have also noted that Cather makes Jezebel and Sapphira parallel. Hermione Lee argues that "the macabre detail [Jezebel wanting to eat a hand] reflects on Sapphira's likeness to Jezebel (she is a kind of cannibal herself) but also on the cannibalizing of a whole people" (*Willa Cather* 366). Deborah Carlin suggests that the two have a kind of equality of shared humanity (157). And Merrill Maguire Skaggs writes that Sapphira "understands" Jezebel's cannibalism (173).

32. Morgenstern argues that "Sapphira wants to rape Nancy if only by making use of [Martin as] a surrogate male body" (191).

33. See, for instance, David Stouck's *Willa Cather's Imagination*.

34. See note 31.

Seven Conclusion

1. In "Sexualities without Genders and Other Queer Utopias," Biddy Martin discusses contemporary examples of what might be called Sapphic primitivism. See also Jewelle Gomez's essay, "Across the Glittering Sea."

2. Naomi Wolf uses this phrase in her essay "The Racism of Well-Meaning White People."

Works Cited

Abelove, Henry, Michèle Anina Barale, and David M. Halperin, eds. *The Lesbian and Gay Studies Reader*. New York: Routledge, 1993.

Abraham, Julie. *Are Girls Necessary? Lesbian Writing and Modern Histories*. New York: Routledge, 1996.

Achebe, Chinua. "An Image of Africa." *Massachusetts Review* 18 (1877): 782–794.

Ackland, Valentine. *For Sylvia: An Honest Account*. New York: Norton, 1986.

Acocella, Joan. "Cather and the Academy." *New Yorker* 27 November 1995: 56–71.

——. *Willa Cather and the Politics of Criticism*. New York: Vintage, 2002.

Adams, Timothy Dow. "My Gay Antonia: The Politics of Willa Cather's Lesbianism." *Journal of Homosexuality* 12.3–4 (1986): 89–98.

Ammons, Elizabeth. "Cather and the New Canon: 'The Old Beauty' and the Issue of Empire." *Cather Studies*. Ed. Susan Rosowski. Vol. 3. Lincoln: U of Nebraska P, 1996. 256–265.

Ardis, Ann. *New Women, New Novels: Feminism and Early Modernism*. New Brunswick: Rutgers UP, 1990.

Arnold, Marilyn. "The Allusive Cather." *Cather Studies*. Ed. Susan Rosowski. Vol. 3. Lincoln: U of Nebraska P, 1996. 137–147.

Bacchus, Michael. "Not a Bedspread, But a Counterpane: Under the Covers with Gay Men and Aristocrats in Twentieth Century British Literature (Ronald Firbank, Nancy Mitford, P. G. Wodehouse, Evelyn Waugh)." Ph.D. diss., University of Southern California, 1997.

Baker, Houston A., Jr. *Modernism and the Harlem Renaissance*. Chicago: U of Chicago P, 1987.

Barkan, Elazar. *The Retreat of Scientific Racism: Changing Concepts of Race in Britain and the United States between the World Wars*. New York: Cambridge UP, 1992.

Barkan, Elazar, and Ronald Bush. *Prehistories of the Future: The Primitivist Project and the Culture of Modernism.* Stanford: Stanford UP, 1995.

Barnes, Djuna. *Ladies Almanack.* 1928. Reprint, New York: Harper, 1972.

———. *Nightwood.* 1937. Reprint, New York: New Directions, 1961.

Barthes, Roland. "The Third Meaning: Research Notes on Some Eisenstein Stills." *Image—Music—Text.* Trans. Stephen Heath. New York: Hill and Wang, 1977. 52–68.

Beeton, Ridley. "Olive Schreiner's Fiction Revisited." Smith and MacLennan 35–45.

Benstock, Shari. *Women of the Left Bank: Paris, 1900–1940.* Austin: U of Texas Press, 1986.

Berkman, Joyce Avreck. *The Healing Imagination of Olive Schreiner: Beyond South African Colonialism.* Amherst: U of Massachusetts P, 1989.

Bishop, Alan. "'With suffering and through time': Olive Schreiner, Vera Brittain, and the Great War." Smith and MacLennan 80–92.

Bland, Lucy. *Banishing the Beast: Sexuality and the Early Feminists.* New York: New Press, 1995.

Bland, Lucy, and Laura Doan, eds. *Sexology Uncensored: The Documents of Sexual Science.* Chicago: U of Chicago P, 1998.

Bray, Alan. *Homosexuality in Renaissance England.* London: Gay Men's P, 1982.

Bredbeck, Gregory W. *Sodomy and Interpretation: Marlowe to Milton.* Ithaca, N.Y.: Cornell UP, 1991.

Brittain, Vera. "The Influence of Olive Schreiner." *Until the Heart Changes: A Garland of Olive Schreiner.* Ed. Zelda Friedlander. [Cape Town]: Tafelberg-Uitgewers, 1967.

———. *Radclyffe Hall: A Case of Obscenity?* South Brunswick: A. S. Barnes, 1968.

Brothers, Barbara. "Writing against the Grain: Sylvia Townsend Warner and the Spanish Civil War." *Women's Writing in Exile.* Ed. Mary Lynn Broe and Angela Ingram. Chapel Hill: U of North Carolina P, 1989. 350–368.

Brown, Marion Marsh, and Ruth Crone. *Willa Cather: The Woman and Her Works:* New York: Scribner's, 1970.

Butler, Judith. *Bodies That Matter: On the Discursive Limits of "Sex."* New York: Routledge, 1993.

———. *Gender Trouble: Feminism and the Subversiveness of Identity.* New York: Routledge, 1990.

Carby, Hazel. "Policing the Black Woman's Body in an Urban Context." *Identities.* Ed. Kwame Anthony Appiah and Henry Louis Gates. Chicago: U of Chicago P, 1995. 115–132.

———. *Reconstructing Womanhood: The Emergence of the Afro-American Woman Novelist.* New York: Oxford UP, 1987.

Carey, Shaun. "A Sacrifice of Wild Ecstacy: Race and Sexuality in *Passing.*" Unpublished essay, 1994.

Carlin, Deborah. *Cather, Canon, and the Politics of Reading.* Amherst: U of Massachusetts P, 1992.

Carlston, Erin G. *Thinking Fascism: Sapphic Modernism and Fascist Modernity.* Stanford, Calif.: Stanford UP, 1998.

Carpenter, Edward. *The Intermediate Sex: A Study of Some Transitional Types of Men and Women.* 1908. Reprint, London: George Allen and Unwin, 1983.

———. *Intermediate Types among Primitive Folk.* 1914. Reprint, Greig and Fernbach 247–288.

———. "Self-Analysis for Havelock Ellis." Greig and Fernbach 289–291.

Caserio, Robert. "Celibate Sisters-in-Revolution: Towards Reading Sylvia Townsend Warner." *Engendering Men: The Question of Male Feminist Criticism.* Ed. Joseph A. Boone and Michael Codden. New York: Routledge, 1990.

Castle, Terry. *The Apparitional Lesbian: Female Homosexuality and Modern Culture.* New York: Columbia UP, 1993.

Cather, Willa. *Alexander's Bridge.* 1912. Reprint, Lincoln: U of Nebraska P, 1977.

———. *Death Comes for the Archbishop.* 1926. Reprint, New York: Knopf, 1946.

———. *The Kingdom of Art.* Ed. Bernice Slote. Lincoln: U of Nebraska P, 1977.

———. *The Lost Lady.* 1923. Reprint, New York: Random House, 1990.

———. *Lucy Gayheart.* 1935. Reprint, New York: Random House, 1995.

———. *My Ántonia.* 1918. Reprint, Lincoln: U of Nebraska P, 1997.

———. *My Mortal Enemy.* 1926. Reprint, New York: Random House, 1990.

———. *Not under Forty.* New York: Knopf, 1936.

———. *O Pioneers!* 1913. Reprint, New York: Quality Paperback, 1955.

———. *The Professor's House.* 1925. Reprint, New York: Random House, 1990.

———. *Sapphira and the Slave Girl.* 1940. Reprint, New York: Random House, 1975.

———. *The Song of the Lark.* 1915. Reprint, Boston: Houghton Mifflin, 1987.

Chauncey, George, Jr. "From Sexual Inversion to Homosexuality: Medicine and the Changing Conceptualization of Female Deviance." *Salmagundi* 58–59 (1982–83): 114–116.

Clayton, Cherry. "Dependence and Control in Olive Schreiner's Fiction." Smith and MacLennan 20–29.

Conrad, Joseph. *Heart of Darkness.* 1902. Reprint, New York: Norton, 1988.

Coombes, Annie. *Reinventing Africa: Museums, Material Culture, and Popular Imagination in Late Victorian and Edwardian England.* London: Yale UP, 1994.

Cory, Donald Webster. *Homosexuality: A Cross Cultural Approach.* New York: Julian, 1956.

Crapanzano, Vincent. "The Moment of Prestidigitation." Barkan and Bush 95–113.

Cunard, Nancy. Nancy Cunard Papers. Humanities Research Center, University of Texas at Austin.

D'Emilio, John. "Capitalism and Gay Identity." Abelove, Barale, and Halperin 467–476.

Davis, Angela Y. *Blues Legacies and Black Feminism: Gertrude "Ma" Rainey, Bessie Smith, and Billie Holiday.* New York: Pantheon Books, 1998.

———. *Women, Race, and Class.* New York: Vintage, 1983.

Draznin, Yaffa Claire, ed. *"My Other Self": The Letters of Olive Schreiner and Havelock Ellis, 1884–1920.* New York: Peter Lang, 1992.

Dunne, John Gregory. "The Humboldt Murders." *New Yorker* 13 January 1997: 45–62.

DuPlessis, Rachel Blau. "Woolfenstein." *Breaking the Sequence: Women's Experimental Fiction.* Ed. Ellen Friedman. Princeton: Princeton UP, 1989. 99–114.

Eliot, T. S. "Introduction." *Nightwood*. By Djuna Barnes. 1937. Reprint, New York: New Directions, 1961. xi–xvi.

Ellis, Havelock. *Studies in the Psychology of Sex*. Vol. 2: *Sexual Inversion*. 1897. Reprint, Philadelphia: F. A. Davis Company, 1904.

Ellison, Ralph. *The Invisible Man*. 1947. Reprint, New York: Random House, 1972.

Fetterley, Judith. "*My Antonia*, Jim Burden and the Dilemma of the Lesbian Writer." *Gender Studies: New Directions in Feminist Criticism*. Ed. Judith Spector. Bowling Green, Ohio: Bowling Green State U Popular P, 1986. 43–59.

Findlay, Heather. "'Freud's Fetishism' and the Lesbian Dildo Debates." *Feminist Theory and the Body: A Reader*. Ed. Janet Price and Margrit Shildrick. New York: Routledge, 1999. 466–476.

First, Ruth, and Ann Scott. *Olive Schreiner*. New York: Schocken Books, 1980.

Fishkin, Shelley Fisher. *Was Huck Black: Mark Twain and African American Voices*. Oxford: Oxford UP, 1993.

Flannigan, John H. "Issues of Gender and Lesbian Love: Goblins in 'The Garden Lodge.'" *Cather Studies*. Ed. Susan Rosowski. Vol. 2. Lincoln: U of Nebraska P, 1993. 23–40.

Foster, Thomas. "'Dream Made Flesh': Sexual Difference and Narratives of Revolution in Sylvia Townsend Warner's *Summer Will Show*." *Modern Fiction Studies* 41 (1995): 531–562.

Foucault, Michel. *The History of Sexuality*. Vol. 1: *An Introduction*. Trans. Robert Hurley. New York: Vintage, 1980.

Fox, Maynard. "Two Primitives: Huck Finn and Tom Outland." *Western American Literature* 1 (1996): 26–33.

Frankenberg, Ruth. *White Women, Race Matters: The Social Construction of Whiteness*. Minneapolis: U of Minnesota P, 1993.

Freud, Sigmund. *Three Essays on the Theory of Sexuality*. Trans. James Strachey. 1910. Reprint, N.p.: Basic Books, 1962.

Fryer, Judith. *Felicitous Space*. Chapel Hill: U of North Carolina P, 1986.

Fryer, Peter. *Staying Power: The History of Black People in Britain*. London: Pluto, 1984.

Gates, Henry Louis, Jr., ed. *"Race," Writing, and Difference*. Chicago: U of Chicago P, 1986.

Gibson, Margaret. "Clitoral Corruption: Body Metaphors and American Doctors' Constructions of Female Homosexuality, 1870–1900." *Science and Homosexualities*. Ed. Vernon A. Rosario. New York: Routledge, 1997. 108–132.

Gilbert, Sandra M., and Susan Gubar. *No Man's Land: The Place of the Woman Writer in the Twentieth Century*. 2 Vols. New Haven: Yale UP, 1989.

Gilman, Sander. *Difference and Pathology*. Ithaca, N.Y.: Cornell UP, 1985.

Gilroy, Paul. *The Black Atlantic: Modernity and Double Consciousness*. Cambridge, Mass.: Harvard UP, 1993.

Goldberg, David Theo, ed. *Anatomy of Racism*. Minneapolis: U of Minnesota P, 1990.

———. *Racist Culture: Philosophy and the Politics of Meaning*. Oxford: Blackwell, 1993.

Goldberg, Jonathan, ed. *Queering the Renaissance*. Durham: Duke UP, 1994.

―――. *Sodometries: Renaissance Texts, Modern Sexualities.* Stanford: Stanford UP, 1992.

Gomez, Jewelle. "Across the Glittering Sea." *Skin Deep: Black Women and White Women Write about Race.* Ed. Marita Golden and Susan Richards Shreve. New York: Anchor, 1995. 148–161.

Gordimer, Nadine. "Review of *Olive Schreiner: A Biography* by Ruth First and Ann Scott." Smith and MacLennan 14–19.

Greig, Noel, and David Fernbach, eds. *Edward Carpenter: Selected Writings.* Vol. 1: *Sex.* London: Gay Men's Press, 1984.

Gubar, Susan. *Racechanges: White Skin, Black Face in American Culture.* New York: Oxford UP, 1997.

―――. "Sapphistries." *Signs* 10 (1984): 43–62.

Gwin, Minrose C. *Black and White Women of the Old South: The Peculiar Sisterhood in American Literature.* Knoxville: U of Tennessee P, 1985.

Hackett, Robin. "Supplanting Shakespeare's Rising Sons: A Perverse Reading through Woolf's *The Waves.*" *Tulsa Studies in Women's Literature* 18 (1999): 263–280.

Hall, Radclyffe. *The Well of Loneliness.* 1928. Reprint, New York: Doubleday, 1990.

Halperin, David M. *One Hundred Years of Homosexuality.* New York: Routledge, 1989.

Harman, Claire. *Sylvia Townsend Warner: A Biography.* 1989. London: Minerva, 1991.

―――, ed. "Sylvia Townsend Warner, 1893–1978: A Celebration." *PN Review* 23 (1981): 30–61.

Hart, Lynda. *Fatal Women: Lesbian Sexuality and the Mark of Aggression.* Princeton: Princeton UP, 1994.

Heilbrun, Carolyn. *Reinventing Womanhood.* New York: W. W. Norton, 1978.

Heilmann, Ann. *New Woman Fiction: Women Writing First-Wave Feminism.* Houndmills, Basingstoke, Hampshire, and London: Macmillan Press, 2000.

Higginbotham, Evelyn Brooks. "African-American Women's History and the Metalanguage of Race." *Signs: Journal of Women in Culture and Society* 17 (1992): 251–274.

Hogan, Steve, and Lee Hudson. *Completely Queer: The Gay and Lesbian Encyclopedia.* New York: Henry Holt, 1998.

hooks, bell. *Black Looks: Race and Representation.* Boston: South End Press, 1992.

Hopkins, Pauline. *Contending Forces: A Romance Illustrative of Negro Life North and South.* 1900. The Schomburg Library of Nineteenth-Century Black Women Writers. Reprint, New York: Oxford UP, 1988.

Hovey, Jaime. "'Kissing a Negress in the Dark': Englishness as a Masquerade in Woolf's *Orlando.*" *PMLA* 112 (1997): 393–404.

Hurston, Zora Neale. *Their Eyes Were Watching God.* 1937. Reprint, Urbana: U of Illinois P, 1978.

Hutchinson, George. *The Harlem Renaissance in Black and White.* Cambridge: Belknap Press for Harvard UP, 1995.

Huyssen, Andreas. *After the Great Divide: Modernism, Mass Culture, Postmodernism.* Theories of Representation and Difference. Bloomington: Indiana UP, 1986.

Ibsen, Henrik. *Rosmersholm*. Trans. Rolf Fjelde. *The Complete Major Prose Plays*. New York: Farrar, 1978. 491–585.

Irving, Katrina. "Displacing Homosexuality: The Use of Ethnicity in Willa Cather's *My Antonia*." *Modern Fiction Studies* 36 (1990): 91–102.

Jacobs, Harriet A. *Incidents in the Life of a Slave Girl, Written by Herself*. 1861. Ed. Jean Fagan Yellin. Reprint, Cambridge, Mass: Harvard UP, 1987.

Jacobson, Dan. Introduction. *The Story of an African Farm*. By Olive Schreiner. London, New York: Penguin, 1971. 7–27.

Jay, Karla. "The Outsider among the Expatriates: Djuna Barnes' Satire on the Ladies of the *Almanack*." Jay and Glasgow 204–216.

Jay, Karla, and Joanne Glasgow, eds. *Lesbian Texts and Contexts: Radical Revisions*. New York: New York UP, 1990.

Joannou, Maroula. "Sylvia Townsend Warner in the 1930s." *A Weapon in the Struggle: A Cultural History of the Communist Party in Britain*. Ed. Andy Croft. London: Pluto, 1998. 89–105.

Kaplan, Carla. "The Erotics of Talk: 'That Oldest Human Longing' in *Their Eyes Were Watching God*." *American Literature: A Journal of Literary History, Criticism, and Bibliography* 67 (1995): 115–142.

Katz, Leon. Introduction. *Fernhurst, Q.E.D., and Other Early Writings*. By Gertrude Stein. London: Peter Owen, 1972. i–xxxiv.

Kenner, Hugh. "The Making of the Modernist Canon." *Canons*. Ed. Robert von Hallberg. Chicago: U of Chicago P, 1984. 363–375.

Krafft-Ebing, Dr. R. v. *Psychopathia Sexualis with Especial Reference to the Antipathic Sexual Instinct: A Medico-Forensic Study*. Trans. R. J. Rebman. 12th ed. New York: Physicans and Surgeons Book Co., 1926.

LaCapra, Dominick, ed. *The Bounds of Race: Perspectives on Hegemony and Resistance*. Ithaca, N.Y.: Cornell UP, 1991.

Laity, Cassandra. "H.D. and A. yC. Swinburne: Decadence and Sapphic Modernism." Jay and Glasgow 217–240.

Lambert, Deborah. "The Defeat of a Hero: Autonomy and Sexuality in *My Ántonia*." *American Literature* 53 (1982): 676–690.

Larsen, Nella. *Quicksand* and *Passing*. 1928 and 1929. Reprint, New Brunswick: Rutgers UP, 1986.

Lee, Hermione. *Virginia Woolf*. London: Chatto and Windus, 1996.

———. *Willa Cather: Double Lives*. New York: Pantheon, 1989.

Lemke, Sieglinde. *Primitivist Modernism: Black Culture and the Origins of Transatlantic Modernism*. W.E.B. Du Bois Institute 3. Oxford: Oxford UP, 1998.

Lerner, Laurence. "Olive Schreiner and the Feminists." Smith and MacLennan 67–79.

Lewis, Edith. *Willa Cather Living: A Personal Record*. New York: Knopf, 1953.

Lindemann, Marilee. *Willa Cather: Queering America*. Between Men—Between Women: Lesbian and Gay Studies. New York: Columbia UP, 1999.

Macdonald, Joyce. *The Stuff of Our Forebears: Willa Cather's Southern Heritage*. Tuscaloosa: U of Alabama P, 1998.

Malinowski, Bronislaw. *The Sexual Life of Savages in North-Western Melanesia: An Ethnographic Account of Courtship, Marriage, and Family Life among the Natives of the Trobriand Islands, British New Guinea*. New York: Halcyon, 1929.

Marcus, Jane. "Alibis and Legends: The Ethics of Elsewhereness, Gender, and Estrangement." *Women's Writing in Exile*. Ed. Mary Lynn Broe and Angela Ingram. Chapel Hill: U of North Carolina P, 1989. 269–294.

———. *Art and Anger: Reading Like a Woman*. Columbus: Ohio State UP, 1988.

———. "Bluebeard's Daughters: Pretexts for Pretexts." *Feminist Critical Negotiations*. Ed. Alice Parker and Elizabeth Meese. Amsterdam: John Benjamins, 1992. 19–32.

———. "Britannia Rules *The Waves*." *Decolonizing Tradition: New Views of Twentieth-Century "British" Literary Canon*. Ed. Karen P. Lawrence. Urbana: U of Illinois P, 1992. 136–162.

———. "Laughing at Leviticus: *Nightwood* as Woman's Circus Epic." *Tradition and the Talents of Women*. Ed. Florence Howe. Urbana: U of Illinois P, 1991. 211–247.

———. "Sylvia Townsend Warner." Scott, *The Gender of Modernism* 531–538.

———. *Virginia Woolf and the Languages of the Patriarchy*. Bloomington: Indiana UP, 1987.

———. "A Wilderness of One's Own: Feminist Fantasy Novels of the Twenties: Rebecca West and Sylvia Townsend Warner." *Women Writers and the City*. Ed. Susan Squire. Knoxville: U of Tennessee P, 1984. 134–160.

Marcus, Lisa. "'The Pull of Race and Blood and Kindred': Willa Cather's Southern Inheritance." Romines 98–119.

Martin, Biddy. "Sexualities without Genders and Other Queer Utopias." *Coming Out of Feminism*. Ed. Mandy Merck, Naomi Segal, and Elizabeth Wright. Malden, Mass.: Blackwell P, 1998. 11–35.

Martin, Wendy. "'Remembering the Jungle': Josephine Baker and Modernist Parody." Barkan and Bush 310–325.

Maxwell, William. Introduction. *Letters*. By Sylvia Townsend Warner. Ed. William Maxwell. London: Chatto, 1982. 7–20.

———. "Sylvia Townsend Warner and *The New Yorker*." Harman, "A Celebration" 44–45.

McClintock, Anne. *Imperial Leather: Race, Gender, and Sexuality in the Colonial Contest*. New York: Routledge, 1995.

McDowell, Deborah E. Introduction. *Quicksand and Passing*. By Nella Larsen. New Brunswick, N.J.: Rutgers UP, 1993. ix–xxxv.

McGee, Patrick. "The Politics of Modernist Form; Or, Who Rules *The Waves*?" *Modern Fiction Studies* 38 (1992): 631–650.

Michaels, Walter Benn. *Our America: Nativism, Modernism, and Pluralism*. Durham, N.C.: Duke UP, 1995.

Middleton, Jo Ann. *Willa Cather's Modernism: A Study of Style and Technique*. Rutherford, N.J.: Fairleigh Dickinson UP, 1990.

Miller, Jane Eldridge. *Rebel Women: Feminism, Modernism, and the Edwardian Novel*. London: Virago, 1994.

Mitchell, J. Lawrence. "'The Secret Country of Her Mind'—Aspects of the Novels of Sylvia Townsend Warner." Harman, "A Celebration" 52–56.

Moers, Ellen. *Literary Women*. Garden City, N.Y.: Doubleday, 1976.

Montefiore, Janet. "Listening to Minna: Sylvia Townsend Warner and Historical Realism." *Men and Women Writers of the 1930s: The Dangerous Flood of History*. London: Routledge, 1996. 168–177.

Morgenstern, Naomi E. "'Love Is Homo-sickness': Nostalgia and Lesbian Desire in *Sapphira and the Slave Girl*." *Novel* (winter 1996): 184–205.

Morrison, Toni. *Playing in the Dark: Whiteness and the Literary Imagination*. New York: Vintage, 1993.

Morton, Patricia. *Disfigured Images: The Historical Assault on Afro-American Women*. New York: Greenwood, 1991.

Mulford, Wendy. Introduction. *After the Death of Don Juan*. By Sylvia Townsend Warner. London: Virago, 1989.

——. *This Narrow Place: Sylvia Townsend Warner and Valentine Ackland: Life, Letters, and Politics, 1930–1951*. London: Pandora, 1988.

Murphy, John, ed. *Critical Essays on Willa Cather*. Boston: G.K. Hall, 1983.

Newton, Esther. "The Mythic Mannish Lesbian: Radclyffe Hall and the New Woman." *Hidden from History: Reclaiming the Gay and Lesbian Past*. Ed. Martin Duberman, Martha Vicinus, and George Chauncey Jr. New York: Penguin, 1990. 281–293.

North, Michael. *The Dialect of Modernism: Race, Language, and Twentieth-Century Literature*. New York: Oxford UP, 1994.

Nye, Robert. "Savage Crowds, Modernism, and Modern Politics." Barkan and Bush 42–55.

O'Brien, Sharon. "'The Thing Not Named': Willa Cather as a Lesbian Writer." *Signs* 9 (1984): 576–559.

——. "The Unity of Willa Cather's 'Two-Part Pastoral': Passion in *O Pioneers!*" *Studies in American Fiction* 6 (1978): 157–170.

——. *Willa Cather: The Emerging Voice*. New York: Oxford UP, 1987.

Omi, Michael, and Howard Winnant. *Racial Formation in the United States: From the 1960s to the 1980s*. New York: Routledge, 1986.

Oxindine, Annette. "Sapphist Semiotics in Woolf's *The Waves*: Untelling and Retelling What Cannot Be Told." *Virginia Woolf: Themes and Variations. Selected Papers from the Second Annual Conference on Virginia Woolf*. Ed. Vara Neverow-Turk and Mark Hussey. New York: Pace UP, 1993. 171–181.

Pequigney, Joseph. *Such Is My Love: A Study of Shakespeare's Sonnets*. Chicago: U of Chicago P, 1985.

Perenyi, Eleanor. "The Good Witch of the West." *New York Review of Books*, 18 July 1985: 27–29.

Petrey, Sandy. "Ideology, *Écriture*, 1848: Sylvia Townsend Warner Unwrites Flaubert." *Recherches Sémiotiques/Semiotic Inquiry* 11 (1990): 159–180.

Petrie, Paul. "'Skulking Escapist' vs. 'Radical Editor': Willa Cather, the Left, and *Sapphira and the Slave Girl*." *Southern Quarterly* 34.2 (1996): 27–37.

Phillips, Kathy. *Virginia Woolf against Empire*. Knoxville: U of Tennessee P, 1994.

Prins, Yopie. *Victorian Sappho*. Princeton: Princeton UP, 1999.

Rattenbury, Arnold. "Literature, Lying, and Sober Truth: Attitudes to the Work of

Patrick Hamilton and Sylvia Townsend Warner." *Writing and Radicalism*. Ed. John Lucas. London: Longman, 1996. 201–244.

———. "Plain Heart, Light Tether." Harman, "A Celebration" 46–48.

Reynolds, Guy. *Willa Cather in Context: Progress, Race, Empire*. New York: St. Martin's P, 1996.

Rive, Richard. *Olive Schreiner Letters*. Vol. 1: *1871–1899*. Oxford, U.K.: Oxford UP, 1988.

Robson, Ruthann. *Lesbian (Out)law: Survival under the Rule of Law*. Ithaca, N.Y.: Firebrand Books, 1992.

Romines, Ann, ed. *Willa Cather's Southern Connections: New Essays on Cather and the South*. Charlottesville and London: UP of Virginia, 2000.

Rose, Phyllis. "Modernism: The Case of Willa Cather." *Modernism Reconsidered*. Ed. Robert Kiely and John Hildebidle. Cambridge, Mass.: Harvard UP, 1983. 123–145.

———. *Writing of Women: Essays in a Renaissance*. Middleton, Conn.: Wesleyan UP, 1986.

Rosowski, Susan J. *The Voyage Perilous: Willa Cather's Romanticism*. Lincoln: U of Nebraska P, 1986.

———. "Willa Cather's American Gothic: *Sapphira and the Slave Girl*." *Great Plains Quarterly* 4 (1984): 220–230.

———. "Willa Cather's Women." *Studies in American Fiction* 9 (1981): 261–275.

Rubin, William, ed. *"Primitivism in Twentieth-Century Art: Affinity of the Tribal and the Modern."* 2 vols. New York: Museum of Modern Art, 1984.

Rule, Jane. *Lesbian Images*. Trumansburg, N.Y.: Crossings P, 1982.

Russ, Joanna. "To Write 'Like a Woman': Transformations of Identity in the Work of Willa Cather." *Journal of Homosexuality* 12.3–4 (1986): 77–87.

Ryder, Mary Ruth. *Willa Cather and Classical Myth: The Search for a New Parnassus*. Studies in American Literature 11. Lewiston, N.Y.: Edwin Mellen P, 1990.

Said, Edward. *Orientalism*. New York: Random House, 1979.

Sanjek, Roger. "The Enduring Inequalities of Race." *Race*. Ed. Steven Gregory and Roger Sanjek. New Brunswick, N.J.: Rutgers UP, 1994. 1–17.

Schreiner, Olive. *From Man to Man, or Perhaps Only . . .* New York and London: Harper, 1927.

———. *The Letters of Olive Schreiner, 1876–1920*. 1924. Ed. S. C. Cronwright-Schreiner. Pioneers of the Woman's Movement. Reprint, Westport, Conn.: Hyperion, 1976.

———. *Letters*. Ed. Richard Rive. Vol. 1: *1871–99*. Oxford, U.K.: Oxford UP, 1988.

———. *So Here Then Are Dreams*. East Aurora: Andrew Andrews, Honest Roycrofter, 1901.

———. *The South African Question, by an English South African*. Chicago: Charles H. Sergel Co., 1899.

———. *The Story of an African Farm*. 1883. Reprint, London: Penguin, 1995.

———. *Thoughts on South Africa*. 1923. Forward by Richard Rive. Africana Reprint Library vol. 10. Reprint, Johannesburg: Africana Book Society, 1976.

———. *Trooper Peter Halket of Mashonaland.* Boston: Roberts Brothers, 1897.

———. *Undine.* 1928. Reprint, New York: Johnson Reprint Corporation, 1972.

———. *Woman and Labor.* New York: Frederick A. Stokes, 1911.

Scott, Bonnie Kime. Introduction. *The Gender of Modernism: A Critical Anthology.* Ed. Bonnie Kime Scott. Bloomington: Indiana UP, 1990. 1–18.

———. *Refiguring Modernism.* Vol 1: *The Women of 1928.* Bloomington: Indiana UP, 1995.

Sedgwick, Eve Kosofsky. *Between Men: English Literature and Male Homosocial Thought.* New York: Columbia UP, 1985.

———. *Epistemology of the Closet.* Berkeley, U of California P, 1990.

Shakespeare, William. "Sonnet VII." *The Complete Works of Shakespeare.* Ed. Hardin Craig. Chicago: Scott, 1961.

Skaggs, Merrill Maguire. *After the World Broke in Two: the Later Novels of Willa Cather.* Charlottesville and London: UP of Virginia, 1990.

Slote, Bernice. "First Principles: Writer in Nebraska." *The Kingdom of Art.* By Willa Cather. Ed. Bernice Slote. Lincoln: U of Nebraska P, 1977.

Smith, Bruce. *Homosexual Desire in Shakespeare's England: A Cultural Poetics.* Chicago: U of Chicago P, 1991.

Smith, Malvern Van Wyk, and Don MacLennan, eds. *Olive Schreiner and After: Essays on Southern African Literature in Honour of Guy Butler.* Cape Town: David Philip, 1983.

Smith-Rosenberg, Carroll. "Discourses of Sexuality and Subjectivity: The New Woman, 1870–1936." *Hidden from History: Reclaiming the Gay and Lesbian Past.* Ed. Martin Duberman, Martha Vicinus, and George Chauncey Jr. New York: Penguin, 1990. 264–280.

Somerville, Siobhan B. Introduction. Bland and Doan 201–203.

———. *Queering the Color Line: Race and the Invention of Homosexuality in American Culture.* Series Q. Durham: Duke UP, 2000.

Spraggs, Gillian. "Exiled to Home: The Poetry of Sylvia Townsend Warner and Valentine Ackland." *Lesbian and Gay Writing.* Philadelphia: Temple UP, 1990. 109–125.

Stein, Gertrude. *Fernhurst, Q.E.D., and Other Early Writings.* London: Peter Owen. 1972.

———. *Three Lives.* 1909. Reprint, New York: Vintage, 1936.

Steiner, Christopher. "Travel Engravings and the Construction of the Primitive." Barkan and Bush 202–225.

Stember, Charles Herbert. *Sexual Racism: The Emotional Barrier to an Integrated Society.* New York: Elsevier, 1976.

Stepan, Nancy. *The Idea of Race in Science: Great Britain, 1800–1960.* Hamden, Conn.: Archon Books, 1982.

Stimpson, Catherine. "Zero Degree Deviancy: The Lesbian Novel in English." *Feminisms: An Anthology of Literary Theory and Criticism.* Ed. Robyn R. Warhol and Diane Price Herndl. New Brunswick: Rutgers UP, 1991. 301–315.

Stouck, David. *Willa Cather's Imagination.* Lincoln: U of Nebraska P, 1975.

Stout, Janice P. *Strategies of Reticence: Silence and Meaning in the Works of Jane*

Austen, Willa Cather, Katherine Anne Porter, and Joan Didion. Charlottesville: UP of Virginia, 1990.

Symonds, John Addington. *Sexual Inversion: A Classic Study of Homosexuality.* 1928. Reprint, New York: Bell, 1984.

Terry, Jennifer. *An American Obsession: Science, Medicine, and Homosexuality in Modern Society.* Chicago: U of Chicago P, 1999.

Torgovnick, Marianna. *Gone Primitive: Savage Intellects, Modern Lives.* Chicago: U of Chicago P, 1990.

Traub, Valerie. "The Psychomorphology of the Clitoris." *GLQ: A Journal of Lesbian and Gay Studies* 2 (1995): 81–113.

Urgo, Joseph R. *Willa Cather and the Myth of American Migration.* Urbana: U of Illinois P, 1995.

Vanita, Ruth. *Sappho and the Virgin Mary: Same-Sex Love and the English Literary Imagination.* New York: Columbia UP, 1996.

Vicinus, Martha. "'They Wonder to Which Sex I Belong': The Historical Roots of the Modern Lesbian Identity." Abelove, Barale, and Halperin 432–452.

Wachman, Gay. "Lady into Fox, Fox into Lady: Rewriting Lesbian Stereotypes in *Summer Will Show.*" *Critical Survey* 10 (1998): 105–113.

———. *Lesbian Empire: Radical Crosswriting in the Twenties.* New Brunswick, N.J.: Rutgers UP, 2001.

———. "Pink Icing and a Narrow Bed: *Mrs. Dalloway* and Lesbian History." *Virginia Woolf and the Arts: Selected Papers for the Sixth Annual Conference on Virginia Woolf.* Ed. Diane F. Gillespie and Leslie K. Hankins. New York: Pace UP, 1997. 344–350.

Walvin, James. *Making the Black Atlantic: Britain and the African Diaspora.* London and New York: Cassell, 2000.

Warner, Michael, ed. *Fear of a Queer Planet: Queer Politics and Social Theory.* Minneapolis: U of Minnesota P, 1993.

Warner, Sylvia Townsend. *After the Death of Don Juan.* 1938. Reprint, London: Virago, 1989.

———. "Behind the Firing Line: Some Experiences in a Munition Factory by a Lady Worker." *Blackwood's Edinburgh Magazine* 199 (1916): 200.

———. "Catalonia in Civil War." *New Masses* 21.9 (1936): 3–4.

———. *The Diaries of Sylvia Townsend Warner.* Ed. Claire Harman. London: Chatto, 1994.

———. *The Flint Anchor.* New York: Viking, 1954.

———. "The Foregone Conclusion." *Selected Stories of Sylvia Townsend Warner.* New York: Viking, 1988.

———. "In Conversation." "Sylvia Townsend Warner: A Celebration." Harman, "A Celebration" 35–38.

———. Letter to Nancy Cunard, 17 July 1944. Nancy Cunard Papers. Humanities Research Center, University of Texas at Austin.

———. *Letters.* Ed. William Maxwell. London: Chatto, 1982.

———. *Lolly Willowes; or, The Loving Huntsman.* 1926. Reprint, London: Chatto, 1975.

————. *Mr. Fortune's Maggot.* 1927. *Four in Hand: A Quartet of Novels.* New York: Norton, 1986. 135–263.

————. "Review and Comment by Dorothy Parker and Sylvia Townsend Warner." *New Masses* 32.1 (1939): 21–22.

————. *Scenes of Childhood.* Ed. Susanna Pinney and William Maxwell. New York: Viking, 1982.

————. *Summer Will Show.* 1936. Reprint, London: Virago, 1987.

————. *The True Heart.* New York. Viking, 1929.

————. "The Way by Which I Have Come." *The Countryman* July (1939): 473–486.

Warner, Sylvia Townsend, and Valentine Ackland. *I'll Stand by You: Selected Letters of Sylvia Townsend Warner and Valentine Ackland.* Ed. Susanna Pinney. London: Pimlico, 1998.

Wasserman, Loretta. "*Sapphira and the Slave Girl*: Willa Cather vs. Margaret Mitchell." *Willa Cather Pioneer Memorial Newsletter* 38.1 (1994): 1+.

Watney, Simon. "Who Is Sylvia? Townsend Warner: Love's Labours Lost." *Village Voice* 23 (January 1990): 54+.

Weeks, Jeffrey. *Coming Out: Homosexual Politics in Britain, from the Nineteenth Century to the Present.* London: Quartet Books, 1977.

————. *Sex, Politics, and Society: The Regulation of Sexuality since 1800.* London: Longman, 1981.

Williams, Patricia J. "American Kabuki." *Birth of a Nation'hood: Gaze, Script, and Spectacle in the O. J. Simpson Case.* Ed. Toni Morrison and Claudia Brodsky Lacour. New York: Pantheon, 1997. 273–292.

Wiss, Rosemary. "Lipreading: Remembering Saartjie Baartman." *Australian Journal of Anthropology* 5.1–2 (1994): 11–40.

Wolf, Naomi. "The Racism of Well-Meaning White People." *Skin Deep: Black Women and White Women Write about Race.* Ed. Marita Golden and Susan Richards Shreve. New York: Anchor, 1995. 37–46.

Woodress, James. *Willa Cather: A Literary Life.* Lincoln: U of Nebraska P, 1987.

Woolf, Virginia. *A Change of Perspective: The Letters of Virginia Woolf.* Vol. 3: *1923–1928.* Ed. Nigel Nicholson and Joanne Trautmann. London: Hogarth P, 1977.

————. *The Diary of Virginia Woolf.* Ed. Anne Olivier Bell and Andrew McNeillie. 5 vols. London: Hogarth, 1977–1984.

————.*The Essays of Virginia Woolf.* Vol. 3: *1919–1924.* Ed. Andrew McNeillie. San Diego: Harcourt, 1988.

————. *The Letters of Virginia Woolf.* Vol. 1: *1888–1912.* Ed. Nigel Nicholson and Joanne Trautman. New York: Harcourt, 1975.

————. *Mrs. Dalloway.* 1925. Reprint, San Diego: Harcourt, 1985.

————. "Olive Schreiner." 1925. *Women and Writing.* Ed. Michèle Barrett. San Diego: Harcourt, 1979. 180–183.

————. *Orlando: A Biography.* 1928. Reprint, New York: New American Library, 1960.

————. *A Room of One's Own.* 1929. Reprint, New York: Harcourt, 1957.

————. *Three Guineas.* San Diego: Harcourt, 1938.

————. *The Waves.* 1931. Reprint, San Diego: Harcourt, 1959.

————. *The Waves: The Two Holograph Drafts.* Transcribed and edited by J. W. Graham. Toronto: U of Toronto P, 1976.

Yourcenar, Marguerite. *Les Vagues.* Paris: Librairie Plon, 1969.

Zimmerman, Bonnie. "What Has Never Been: An Overview of Lesbian Feminist Literary Criticism." *Feminisms: An Anthology of Literary Theory and Criticism.* Ed. Robyn R. Warhol and Diane Price Herndl. New Brunswick: Rutgers UP, 1991. 117–137.

Index

Abraham, Julie, 8, 65, 119, 152n11, 163n13, 167n16
Achebe, Chinua, 153n16
Ackland, Valentine, 86, 87, 88, 94, 95, 111, 120, 160n2, 161–162n11, 164n18, 164n26
Acocella, Joan, 165n7, 166n12
Adams, Timothy Dow, 166n11
Allen, Maud, 152n12
Ammons, Elizabeth, 166n8
anachronistic space, 43–44, 46, 48, 49, 50, 93
Anglo-Boer war, 40, 46, 158n12
antiracism, 3, 4, 7, 9, 12, 19, 95, 149–150
Ardis, Ann, 151n3
Arnold, Marilyn, 165n8
Austen, Jane, 86

Baartman, Saartjie, 16, 154n24
Bacchus, Michael, 154n22
Baker, Houston A. Jr., 153n18
Barkan, Elazar, 10, 11, 153n15, 153n20
Barnes, Djuna, 148, 152n19, 155n2
Barthes, Roland, 60
Beauvoir, Simone de, 2
Beeton, Ridley, 54

Behn, Aphra, 10
Benin bronzes, 10, 35, 153n15
Bennet, Mildred, 165n6
Benstock, Shari, 12–13, 153n19
Berkman, Joyce Avreck, 40
Bhabha, Homi K., 12
Bishop, Alan, 158n9
Bland, Lucy, 35, 41, 151n, 155n1, 157n8, 158n9
Boston Women's Health Book Collective, 151n1
Bray, Alan, 154n21
Bredbeck, Gregory W., 159n16
Brittain, Vera, 43, 66, 157n9
Brothers, Barbara, 160n1, 161n3, 162n13
Brown, Marion Marsh, 165n6
Burroughs, Edgar Rice, 153n17
Burton, Richard. *See* Sotadic Zone
Bush, Ronald, 10, 11, 153n15
Butler, Judith, 125, 127, 151n2, 154n21, 166n14, 167n20

Carby, Hazel, 6, 17, 152n7
Carlin, Deborah, 125, 165n4, 165n8, 166n15, 167n25, 168n31

About the Author

Robin Hackett received her Ph.D. in English with a certificate in women's studies at the City University of New York and is an assistant professor of English at the University of New Hampshire.